Determining How Much to Make

Whether you are hosting a simple cocktail party or a more elaborate appetizers-as-a-meal party, you need to know how much to make. The following table can help.

Party Type	Number of Guests	Number of Appetizers	Amount to Make
The Cocktail Party	Featuring 6 guests for 1 hour	3 or 4 choices	Each guest will eat 2 or 3 pieces/servings of each
The Cocktail Party	Featuring 12 guests for 1 hour	4 or 5 choices	Each guest will eat 2 or 3 pieces/servings of each
The Cocktail Party	Featuring 6 guests for 2 hours	4 or 5 choices	Each guest will eat 3 or 4 pieces/servings of each
The Cocktail Party	Featuring 12 guests for 2 hours	5 or 6 choices	Each guest will eat 3 or 4 pieces/servings of each
The Appetizer Party	Featuring 12 guests for 3 hours	6 or 8 choices	Each guest will eat 2 or 3 of each
The Appetizer Party	Featuring 24 guests for 3 hours	8 or 10 choices	Each guest will eat 2 or 3 of each
The Sit-Down Appetizer Party	—	—	If the recipe is one large item, such as a stuffed artichoke, then serve one per person. If it is something you can weigh, like smoked salmon, figure on $1/8$ to $1/4$ pound per person, depending on how filling the remaining meal is.

Stocking Your Pantry

What follows are two lists. The first is a list of basic ingredients you can use to make a wide variety of appetizers. The second list adds some items that, while not necessarily common pantry ingredients, will help you on your way to being more completely prepared.

The Basic Appetizer Pantry

- Table salt and kosher salt
- Fresh-ground black pepper
- Spray pan-coating, such as PAM
- Vegetable oil
- Light olive oil
- Extra-virgin olive oil
- Red wine vinegar
- Balsamic vinegar
- Soy sauce
- All-purpose flour
- Cans of beans: cannellini and garbanzo (also known as chickpeas)
- Jars of roasted peppers
- Crackers
- Heads of garlic
- Onions
- Popcorn
- Loaf of bread
- High-quality corn chips
- High-quality potato chips
- Nonfood essentials: plastic wrap, aluminum foil, and paper towels

The Extended Pantry

- Sun-dried tomatoes
- Cider vinegar
- White wine vinegar
- Tahini
- Extra bottle of lemon juice
- Fish sauce (nam pla)
- Hoisin sauce
- Potatoes

Setting Up Your Home Bar

Here are the bare-bones items you need for a home bar to serve a party of 12:

- Two bottles of red wine
- Two bottles of white wine
- 24 bottles of beer (maybe 6 of them a "lite" version)
- One bottle of vodka or gin
- One bottle of scotch or bourbon
- One bottle of dry vermouth
- ½ gallon of orange juice
- One bottle of club soda and/or tonic water
- Wedges of lemons and limes

Here are the basic bar tools you need:

- Corkscrew
- Bottle cap opener
- Ice bucket with ice
- Ice scoop or tongs
- Cocktail shaker
- Jigger/measuring cup
- Strainer
- Long spoon for stirring
- Small cutting board
- Sharp knife

Appetizers FOR DUMMIES®

by Dede Wilson, CCP

Wiley Publishing, Inc.

Appetizers For Dummies®

Published by
Wiley Publishing, Inc.
909 Third Avenue
New York, NY 10022
www.wiley.com

Copyright © 2002 by Wiley Publishing, Inc., Indianapolis, Indiana

Published simultaneously in Canada

For general information on our other products and services or to obtain technical support, please contact our Customer Care Department within the U.S. at 800-762-2974, outside the U.S. at 317-572-3993, or fax 317-572-4002.

Wiley also publishes its books in a variety of electronic formats. Some content that appears in print may not be available in electronic books.

Library of Congress Control Number: 2002108097

ISBN: 07645-5439-5

Manufactured in the United States of America

10 9 8 7 6 5 4 3 2 1

1B/RZ/QY/QS/IN

🦅Wiley Publishing, Inc. is a trademark of Wiley Publishing, Inc.

About the Author

Dede Wilson, CCP (Certified Culinary Professional), is a self-taught chef who loves making appetizers and organizing parties. She has worked professionally for more than 17 years as a restaurant chef, bakery owner, caterer, recipe developer, radio talk-show host, and frequent television guest. Dede is also a frequent contributor to *Bon Appétit* magazine and a contributing editor to *Pastry Art and Design* magazine. She is the food and entertainment expert for CanDoWoman.com. Dede has written three other cookbooks, including *The Wedding Cake Book* (Wiley, 1997), which was nominated for an IACP Julia Child Cookbook Award. She also authored *Christmas Cooking For Dummies*.

Dedication

To my departed Mom, Barbara Rusitzky Acosta, hummus aficionado and all-around great cook. She always encouraged my experimenting in the kitchen.

Author's Acknowledgments

As always, a big thanks to Maureen and Eric Lasher, my agents, who have become good friends. You two are a joy to work with, and your voices and encouragement always put a smile on my face.

Thanks to the Dummies crew who helped shape the book: to Linda Ingroia, senior editor, for entrusting the world of appetizers to me, and to Pam Mourouzis, acquisitions editor, for guiding the book to completion. Thanks to Tim Gallan, senior project editor, and Tina Sims, senior copy editor, for such good queries and good humor. And I cannot overlook Lindsay MacGregor and April Fazio in publicity, who are always there to help me get the word out.

Several people function as my support team: my Dad, Moses Acosta, who calls every day to chat about food; Mary McNamara, best friend, superb cook, and recipe tester; Juanita Plimpton, another best friend and my physical therapist (our walks) and psychotherapist (our talks); David Caputo and Positronic Design for Web and tech support; Harry Wilson, great Dad and computer guru; and, of course, David Kilroy, my partner; and the kids, Ravenna, Freeman, and Forrester.

Publisher's Acknowledgments

We're proud of this book; please send us your comments through our Dummies online registration form located at www.dummies.com/register/.

Some of the people who helped bring this book to market include the following:

Acquisitions, Editorial, and Media Development

Senior Project Editor: Tim Gallan

Acquisitions Editors: Linda Ingroia, Pam Mourouzis

Senior Copy Editor: Tina Sims

Recipe Tester and Technical Reviewer: Emily Nolan

Nutritional Analyst: Patty Santelli

Editorial Manager: Christine Meloy Beck

Editorial Assistant: Melissa Bennett

Photography Art Director: Edwin Kuo

Photographer: David Bishop

Food Stylist: Brett Kurzweil

Prop Stylist: Randi Barritt

Illustrator: Liz Kurtzman

Production

Project Coordinator: Dale White

Layout and Graphics: Joyce Haughey, Brent Savage, Jacque Schneider, Betty Schulte, Erin Zeltner

Proofreaders: Charles Spencer, TECHBOOKS Production Services

Indexer: TECHBOOKS Production Services

Publishing and Editorial for Consumer Dummies

> **Diane Graves Steele,** Vice President and Publisher, Consumer Dummies
>
> **Joyce Pepple,** Acquisitions Director, Consumer Dummies
>
> **Kristin A. Cocks,** Product Development Director, Consumer Dummies
>
> **Michael Spring,** Vice President and Publisher, Travel
>
> **Brice Gosnell,** Publishing Director, Travel
>
> **Suzanne Jannetta,** Editorial Director, Travel

Publishing for Technology Dummies

> **Andy Cummings,** Vice President and Publisher

Composition Services

> **Gerry Fahey,** Vice President of Production Services
>
> **Debbie Stailey,** Director of Composition Services

Contents at a Glance

Cartoons at a Glance

By Rich Tennant

page 223

page 47

page 5

page 111

page 197

Cartoon Information:
Fax: 978-546-7747
E-Mail: richtennant@the5thwave.com
World Wide Web: www.the5thwave.com

Recipes at a Glance

Dips

Fish, Seafood

Formal, Plated Appetizers

Salads

Snacks: Nuts, Chips, Popcorn

Asian, Indian Appetizers

French Appetizers

Greek Appetizers

Italian Appetizers

Mexican, Latin American, Southwestern Appetizers

Scandinavian Appetizers

Spanish Appetizers

Table of Contents

Introduction

A whole book about appetizers? Absolutely! The little nibbles or substantial offerings that you set out before the main course are very important. Remember, just as Mom always said, first impressions count. What you offer guests or family to eat before the meal sets the tone and creates a mood. Many cooks design a menu around the main meal (or even dessert), but they don't think about the appetizer until the last minute or leave it out entirely. Big mistake. Appetizers can be quick, easy, and inexpensive to make. Or they can be extravagant and the highlight of a meal.

Whether your approach is fast or fancy, appetizers can add tremendously to your meal. *Appetizers For Dummies* helps you decide what appetizers to make and when and how to make them — with the least muss and fuss possible.

How to Use This Book

Whether you want general ideas about designing appetizer menus or need helpful lists of convenient ingredients, it's all here. So are almost 100 recipe ideas, ranging from an Italian-inspired antipasto to a classic shrimp cocktail. Read the book through to gather ideas, or look up an old favorite like onion dip, and get cooking. I organized the book so that you can use it in the way that best suits your lifestyle.

How This Book Is Organized

Appetizers For Dummies is divided into five parts, which I describe in the following sections. Each part is made up of multiple chapters that cover everything from basics, such as what to keep in the pantry for impromptu events, to a recipe for a fresh-as-a-garden salsa. You can also find menus that cover a variety of situations, such as what to feed the dozens of guests arriving for an open house or what to serve that is low in fat but big on flavor. I also include chapters on flavored nuts and nibbles, classics such as stuffed mushrooms, dips and dippers, bread-based appetizers, hot hors d'oeuvres, international favorites, plated appetizers, and dishes to serve when you want to pull out all the stops.

Part I: Appetizer Basics

The opening chapter of this part defines appetizers and explains that they're flexible and can be made on a tight budget. You also find out that appetizers can be quick and easy to make and can serve as a way to introduce yourself to an exotic cuisine. Chapter 2 discusses popular situations when appetizers are most welcomed, including at cocktail parties, parties where appetizers make up a whole meal, and formal meals where appetizers can take the form of a plated first course. This chapter also provides a primer on drinks to serve with your dishes. Chapter 3 has helpful lists of pantry ingredients and how to use those ingredients to make appetizers almost instantly, without recipes. Chapter 4 gives you some ready-to-go menus for such occasions as a classic American spread, an open house cocktail party, or a party featuring an array of Asian flavors.

Part II: Easy Pleasers: Simple Recipes You Should Know

This part starts with a chapter on very easy recipes for munchies that you can eat by the handful, such as spiced nuts and flavored popcorn. You also can find recipes for such traditional favorites as deviled eggs, stuffed mushrooms, and crab cakes. The chapter on dips and dippers may just prove to be the most popular in the book. After all, what's a party without at least one dip?

Part III: Special Touches: Recipes to Impress

If you want to go beyond the basics and expand your culinary horizon, this part is for you. The chapter on appetizers made from various forms of bread covers everything from preparing tea sandwiches and canapés to making a serving bowl out of bread. This same chapter also includes recipes for quesadillas (the Mexican answer to grilled cheese) and instructions for working with puff pastry and phyllo dough and for making miniature tartlets, muffins, and biscuits. Another chapter contains recipes for chicken wings, potato skins, and a host of other hot favorites. The last chapter in this part takes you on a trip around the world through French, Greek, Italian, Indian, Mexican/Latin American, Scandinavian, Asian, and Spanish recipes.

Part IV: Formal and Fabulous: Starters for Sit-Down Dinners and Special Occasions

Sometimes a little lavishness is called for, so this part is the place to turn. Here's where to find ten delicious and beautiful plated recipes, such as artichokes with vinaigrette and a warm goat cheese salad. If you really want to go all out, you can also find out everything you need to know about serving smoked salmon, caviar, and foie gras.

Part V: The Part of Tens

Check out this part to discover some great planning tips for your appetizer parties. I also give you some mail-order sources and Web sites if you're looking for special ingredients or kitchen tools.

Icons Used in This Book

Assorted icons are sprinkled throughout the book along the left-hand margin of the pages. They are there to call your attention to a fact that will help you make the most out of the projects and recipes.

When you see this icon, I include some information to help you make the most of a recipe.

Occasionally a technique or idea has been presented earlier in the book but bears repeating. The Remember icon brings this previously mentioned tip front and center to help you get the most out of a recipe or cooking tip.

I don't use this icon often, but when I do, it conveys important information about cooking or food safety that you should look out for.

This icon lets you know that I'm including an additional ingredient or a twist on the basic technique that can elevate the basic recipe into something above the ordinary.

Sometimes you like the recipe or technique, but you still want a simpler way to do it. This icon gives you the information you need to pare it down.

A Few Guidelines Before You Begin

Here are some tips to follow to ensure success when following the recipes in this book:

✔ Always read a recipe through, from beginning to end, to make sure that you have all the ingredients or necessary equipment and understand the directions.

✔ Use kosher salt for seasoning recipes except where specified.

✔ Pepper always means freshly ground black pepper unless specified otherwise, so keep a pepper mill filled with black peppercorns handy.

✔ All herbs and spices are dried unless specified otherwise.

✔ All eggs are large.

✔ All milk is whole.

✔ All temperatures are Fahrenheit.

Where to Go from Here

Do you think that dry onion soup mix makes the best onion dip? I challenge you to a taste test. Just turn to Chapter 7, where you'll find my recipe for The Best Onion Dip. This recipe and many others are just waiting for you. Read on and enjoy these easy recipes for appetizers that everyone is sure to love.

Part I
Appetizer Basics

The 5th Wave   By Rich Tennant

"The guests are getting hungry. You'd better push over another garbage dumpster."

In this part . . .

If you're new to the world of appetizers, this part is definitely the place to start. And even if you have years of experience in making appetizers, you may want to refer to this part as a refresher course or to pick up a tip you haven't heard before. This part gives you compelling reasons for making appetizers as well as definitions of exactly what an appetizer is. You also find lists of ingredients to keep in your pantry and refrigerator, advice on kitchen tools to make appetizer preparation easier, suggestions on attractive presentations of appetizers, tips on planning menus, and actual party menus.

Chapter 1

Who Needs Appetizers? You Do!

In This Chapter

▶ Discovering the appeal of appetizers

▶ Letting your creative side show

▶ Mastering appetizer terminology

You probably know that an appetizer is traditionally what you eat at the beginning of a meal. It acts as a small, flavorful enticement to prime you for the main course. These days, though, you don't need to be so strict in your interpretation. Sure, you can serve wonderful temptations at the beginning of a meal (and I offer a number of these recipes for you to try), but why limit yourself? You can eat them for snacks, you can have them before dinner, you can even have them *for* dinner. They're just that versatile.

But first and foremost, appetizers and hors d'oeuvres are particularly good for entertaining. They are what make a party, a party! The appearance of appetizers signals that it's party time. You don't have to be a chef or break the bank to prepare appetizers, nor do you need to spend weeks planning and cooking. The key to serving great appetizers is finding out what basic foods complement one another and then being creative when preparing and presenting them (so enjoy experimenting!). When you serve a variety of creatively presented appetizers, you'll please everybody because your menu is bound to include one or two dishes — or more — that your guests will enjoy.

I hope this book inspires you to entertain — even if you never have before — and to use my recipes as an excuse to turn your home into Party Central.

Why Appetizers Kick Butt

Appetizers rule! The prep and cooking times are short, the ingredients are mostly simple to find, and it is easy to make a few different recipes at once to have an assortment to offer. Need more reasons? Read on.

You can have appetizers any time

People's eating patterns vary greatly these days, and the traditional habit of three square meals a day is no longer the norm. Some people eat five smaller meals a day, and others graze all day long or eat only two larger meals. Appetizers can figure into all of these scenarios. They also can stand as small meals all by themselves. There's no end to the ways that appetizers can fit into your eating habits. The Artichokes with Vinaigrette in Chapter 11 make a lovely luncheon dish. You can add some roast chicken from the deli to the Caesar Salad with Garlic Croutons in Chapter 11 and have a light dinner on the table in no time flat. A container of homemade hummus (see Chapter 7) can stay in the refrigerator all week long, providing you with a healthy snack whenever you need it.

Never went to cooking school?
That's okay!

Please believe me when I tell you that most appetizers are very easy to make. You don't need a culinary degree to make these recipes. In fact, even if you have never cooked before, these recipes are so carefully written and tested that I guarantee excellent results. As with any cookbook, you should read the recipe through first. Make sure that you understand what ingredients you need and then follow the recipe word for word. The recipe is your map to success. If, after making it the first time, you decide that you want to add more salt or cook it a bit more, be my guest. But by following the recipe verbatim the first time, you can taste the recipe as it was originally envisioned. Still wondering if this is for real? Turn to Chapter 10 and make the Herbed Goat Cheeses. After much thought and deliberation, I have declared this recipe to be absolutely foolproof and the easiest one in the book. If you feel like you're on shaky ground in the kitchen, start with this one. There is no cooking involved and it will take you 10 minutes or less!

Before you can put your own twist on a recipe, you must understand what that recipe was originally supposed to taste and look like. After you have made a recipe and are thoroughly familiar with the instructions and ingredients, you can then begin to add your own flourishes. Maybe you love garlic and want to add some to a recipe that initially didn't call for any. Or maybe cayenne is your thing — if so, sprinkle it on. This is how new recipes are born — go play! And write down your new recipe so that you can refer to it again next time.

Prep times are short

Some folks don't like to cook because they think that they'll be chained to the stove for hours at a time. Yes, some classic dishes, such as roast turkey, do take a long time to cook, and they're worth the wait. Luckily for you, however, none of the recipes in this book have a preparation time longer than 30 minutes or a cooking time longer than 1.25 hours. In fact, you can prepare most of my recipes in 10 minutes or less. If you are short on time but still want a big return on flavor and impact of presentation, these appetizers are the way to go. If you don't believe me, just turn to Chapter 8 and try the Basic Crostini, which you can prep in 1 minute!

Small food means a small budget

By definition and in comparison to main dishes, appetizers are either small in size or are served in small quantities, often both. Because you need only small amounts of ingredients, the dent in your budget will be small. So, if you're having friends over for cards or it's your turn to host the favorite TV show night, you can please a crowd with Hot-n-Spicy Pecans, Super Nachos, and Potato Skins for only pennies.

Even if the occasion calls for more sophisticated foods, you can afford to buy the best-quality ingredients. For instance, if you make the Seared Tuna with Wasabi Cream (see Chapter 11), you need only 1 pound of tuna for 6 people. In contrast, if you serve tuna to the same group for a main course, you'll shell out at least four times as much. So take advantage of appetizers' diminutive scale.

Or choose to splurge

Sometimes you want to pull out all the stops. Offering good-quality caviar, even in a small amount, can be an experience never to be forgotten. Or, if caviar is a bit too over the top, a nice side of smoked salmon is an elegant option. These aren't everyday food items, but for a special occasion such as a birthday party or intimate dinner for two, either of these would fit the bill. See Chapter 12 for more information on these more upscale recipe ideas.

Appetizers please the whole crowd

If I haven't convinced you by now to head for the kitchen and stir up some appetizers, maybe this final reason will help nudge you in that direction: An assortment of appetizers offers something for everyone. Cooks always face the challenge of trying to please everyone's palate. When you set out an array of appetizers, however, you offer an abundance of different ingredients and tastes. As a result, all your guests are likely to find something they like. For that reason, hosting an all-appetizer party is a great way to entertain. In fact, if you've never hosted a party before, an appetizer party is a great way to start. Simply prepare a vegetarian dish, such as Stuffed Grape Leaves; a hearty meat appetizer, such as Empanadas; Thai Spring Rolls, which are a lower-fat option; and maybe some rich indulgences like Cheese Fondue or baked brie.

And the Answer Is . . .

So the answer to the question "Who needs appetizers?" is simple. *You* need them because they can be made to suit your budget and occasion; they're quick, easy, and fun to make; they can substitute for a meal; and you can find recipes to please even the pickiest eaters. Enjoy!

Chapter 2

Serving Appetizers and Drinks

● ●

In This Chapter

▶ Considering what types of appetizers to serve

▶ Calculating how much food to make

▶ Planning your beverage service

● ●

*Y*ou can serve appetizers in a variety of forms and at a variety of occasions. They can appear as a small tray of finger foods that are passed
with cocktails before a sit-down dinner. They can appear as a formal plated
first course that awaits your guests when they come to the table. Appetizers
can even take the place of a meal at a party where several different dishes are
served.

And, to go along with appetizers, you need a refreshing drink. While this book
is primarily about what to eat, I have included a section at the end of this
chapter about drinks and setting up a bar in your own home. Don't panic, you
don't have to stock up like the corner bar; I will just help you be ready to
serve your guests appropriately and in style.

Knowing Where, When, and How to Serve Appetizers

Appetizers for breakfast? Well, maybe not, but you can serve appetizers
pretty much any other time of day. A selection of "apps," as we say in the
food world, can function as a lunch, a late afternoon snack, or as a prelude to
a formal dinner. You can serve them casually while standing around the
kitchen, al fresco on the deck, or tote them along on a picnic. Arrange them
on a platter, pile them in a basket, or serve them from a chafing dish. In other
words, appetizers are about as versatile as you can get.

The following sections present some scenarios for you to consider.

The cocktail party: Little bites

When you think about where appetizers can be served, the cocktail party is the perfect, classic example. The idea of a cocktail party is that you invite a group of people over for drinks and some light nibbles. This party is usually informal and relaxed. Even though this is called a cocktail party, you can choose to make your appetizers — not the cocktails — the focus of your food and beverage selection. By focusing on the food, you also help reduce the chances of upset stomachs and intoxication.

I think of cocktail party foods as "little bites" because food at such functions should be easy to eat. A one- or two-bite serving size is the way to go. You, your spouse, your kids, or, in a more formal situation, hired servers can circulate among your guests, offering these bite-size appetizers on platters. Or you may prefer to place the appetizers on platters on the coffee table, side tables, or a dining room table and let guests help themselves. Regardless of which way you decide to serve your appetizers, make sure that guests can pick up the food with their fingers; remember that they're milling about with a drink in one hand. Provide napkins, but your guests shouldn't need utensils or a plate.

Plates: Paper, china, or none at all?

If you're serving a plated appetizer at a formal dinner, a china plate is required. But at cocktail or appetizer parties, you have options about whether to use china or paper plates.

At some cocktail parties, the offerings are light enough that you don't need plates, only napkins. Use your common sense; if you're serving herbed olives and cheese and crackers, napkins may be enough. But if you add chicken wings to the mix, plates make the eating experience much more pleasant.

In terms of size, small plates, about 6 or 7 inches in diameter, are perfect for your guests to take the plate back to their seat or with them as they walk about. You can use china plates or paper. If you want to use china plates but don't have enough plates to serve the 20 people coming to your party, you can rent them. If you go the paper route, make sure that the plates are stiff enough to prevent any mishaps. You would think that the paper plate manufacturers would have thought of this, but believe me, some paper plates on the market are guaranteed to let, even encourage, food to slip off onto your lap and carpet. Those manufacturers must be working with the carpet cleaners. I usually don't recommend using regular paper plates. Some coated paper plates and plastic plates are more rigid and more serviceable. Styrofoam plates are another option, but some people don't consider them ecologically correct.

Count on needing about one and a half times as many plates as the number of guests. You need to figure on this amount because some people take a plate, fill it up, put the plate down, and then need another plate when they return for more food. Some people don't use plates at all, so this amount usually works out.

The appetizer party

The appetizer party is an extra-large version of the cocktail party. Simply put, this party is one where you offer a large selection of appetizers, even enough to make a meal. This kind of party also usually involves a larger group of people, usually 10 or more — even a lot more. I have catered weddings for 100 people where we served this kind of meal. The appetizer party is great fun to organize and cook for because you can either do a theme, such as an Italian antipasto party, or just make all the foods you have wanted to try, such as a little sushi, Indian-inspired samosas, exotic cheeses, or even calamari. Because this kind of party is all about a great selection of dishes, you need to offer plates and napkins. If at least half of your guests have a place to sit, with or without a table nearby, you can even consider offering an item that requires a fork. But don't serve anything that requires a fork and knife. Balancing a plate on your knees while sawing away with a knife is just too difficult.

Serve food that requires forks and knives only if all guests have a place to sit and a table in front of them.

The sit-down appetizer party

The sit-down appetizer party is the most formal appetizer event of them all. Envision stuffed artichokes, individual salmon mousse, or a warmed goat cheese salad. This kind of appetizer is just what it sounds like. You and your guests sit down at the table when you bite into these foods. Having an appetizer set at each place setting is a very welcoming site. They are formal appetizers in that only the most formal meals have this additional first course. Chapter 11 gives you a nice selection of formal appetizers from which to choose.

At a formal appetizer party, you can have the appetizer already set at the table when guests take their seat. You can set the appetizer on a plate that is set directly on the table, or you can set it on a plate that is then set on top of a larger plate. This larger plate, which is underneath, is sometimes called a charger or a service plate and is only used at the most formal of dinners. This plate remains on the table during this first appetizer course and possibly even for a second course, which at a formal party may be a fish course. Then the plate is removed before the main dish comes out. But I digress.

The advantage of the sit-down appetizer party is that you can arrange the food on plates in the kitchen, usually ahead of time. As a result, you don't have to worry about last-minute logistics, especially if the appetizers must be served cold or at room temperature.

Appetizers that travel

In this day and age of less formal parties, you may find that you need to tote an appetizer to a potluck event. When guests offer to bring something to a party, the host often suggests an appetizer. (No, I don't mean a can of aerosol cheese.) Here are a few things to consider when deciding whether an appetizer is a good traveler:

- ✔ Stick with foods that won't slide around and that can be safely nestled on a platter and covered with plastic wrap or aluminum foil. Tea sandwiches and canapés work well.

- ✔ If you can, have the appetizer on the plate on which it will be served. You want a stealth approach — easy in, easy out. Your host will appreciate your thoughtfulness.

- ✔ Bring only room-temperature appetizers. The host may be using her oven or stove, and her refrigerator may be full.

- ✔ Consider bringing dry, easy-to-eat, and easy-to-carry items, such as flavored nuts, seeds, or popcorn.

- ✔ Dips and dippers travel well. If you're traveling far, you can place both components in airtight plastic containers. These ensure that you don't need to worry about spills in your car or in the cab.

    Plastic containers are available that are less expensive than the ones you may be familiar with. They're considered disposable, even though you can use them multiple times. These are perfect for bringing to a party because they're relatively inexpensive so you don't have to worry about retrieving them at the end of the party.

- ✔ Consider taking advantage of ready-made items. I can't think of a host who would be disappointed if you brought a side of delicious smoked salmon. Don't forget to bring some dark bread and perhaps some sweet butter to go along with it. (See Chapter 12 for a full treatise on serving smoked salmon.) Also bring a serving platter for the salmon, unless the hostess has offered to provide one.

- ✔ A platter of cheeses and/or pâtés already set up on a cheese board or platter is a great idea. As an accompaniment, bring crackers already in a basket, too.

    If you're good friends with the host and her approach to entertaining is casual, then you can probably ask whether she has a platter that you can use for your cheeses. Use your judgment as to whether such a request is appropriate. You don't want to put yourself or the host in an uncomfortable position.

- ✔ Bring a finished dish. In other words, don't expect your host to have parsley or mustard or whatever it is that you may need to put the finishing touches on your appetizer.

Determining How Much to Make

Whether you're hosting a simple cocktail party before going out for dinner or a more elaborate appetizers-as-a-meal party, you need to know how much food to make. And different kinds of parties require different amounts of food. The number of guests also determines how much food to make. Table 2-1 gives you some guidance.

Table 2-1	How Much to Make for Appetizer Parties		
Party Type	*Number of Guests and Length of Party*	*Number of Appetizers*	*Amount to Make*
Cocktail party	6 guests for 1 hour	3 or 4 choices	2 or 3 pieces/servings of each item per guest
Cocktail party	12 guests for 1 hour	4 or 5 choices	2 or 3 pieces/servings of each item per guest
Cocktail party	6 guests for 2 hours	4 or 5 choices	3 or 4 pieces/servings of each item per guest
Cocktail party	12 guests for 2 hours	5 or 6 choices	3 or 4 pieces/servings of each item per guest
Appetizer party	12 guests for 3 hours	6 or 8 choices	2 or 3 of each item per guest
Appetizer party	24 guests for 3 hours	8 or 10 choices	2 or 3 of each item per guest
Sit-down appetizer party			If the recipe is one large item, such as a stuffed artichoke, then serve 1 per person. If it is something you can weigh, like smoked salmon, figure on 1/8 to 1/4-pound per person, depending on how filling the remaining meal is.

You know your friends better than I do. If they're all model-thin, weight-watching types, they may eat less or eat only lower-fat offerings. If the party is for a horde of hungry men, then you'll need much more food. Look, I know that the above statement may sound somewhat sexist, but I can think of only one or two women who can outdo my male friends in terms of volume of food consumed, and I bet your circle of friends is similar. But as I said, you know them best, so use your judgment.

If you're serving shrimp, all bets are off. I've seen people make absolute pigs of themselves — yes, me included — when confronted with a bowl of shrimp. Individuals usually eat as many as they can until the shrimp are all gone. I'm not kidding. If someone said, "Dede, have as many shrimp as you like," I'd be in front of the buffet table in a flash, stuffing my face, as delicately as I could, of course. My suggestion is to pass shrimp hors d'oeuvres to control portion size. No one likes to take too many items off a tray. Or serve it as a single-serving Shrimp Cocktail. (You can find that recipe in Chapter 6.) Both of these are great ways to control the serving per person.

Would You Care for a Drink?

Most people initially think of foods when they're planning menus, but the appropriate beverage can make all the difference. I feel very strongly that you should always make your guests feel comfortable. I mean, that's why you invited them over in the first place, right? With this in mind, I believe that proper etiquette requires you to provide an alcoholic drink, such as wine or beer, as well as some nonalcoholic choices. And no, water, sparkling or otherwise, is not enough, although you should have that, too. You also may want to consider offering a juice, such as orange or cranberry. Not everyone — me included — likes carbonation, so a sparkling water alone won't suffice.

If you invite folks over for cocktails, then offering mixed drinks is the order of the day. See the section "Setting up a mixed-drinks bar," later in this chapter.

If you don't have a liquor store that you regularly visit, ask around. Word-of-mouth can help you find a reputable wine merchant. If you enjoyed a bottle at a friend's house, ask the friend where he bought it. You also can find some great deals and helpful information on Web sites (see Chapter 14). Sometimes the shipping is free or a flat rate, and the wine is delivered to your door.

Putting the cocktails into the cocktail party

Have you ever been invited to a cocktail party and been offered wine but no mixed drinks? Some say this should not be called a cocktail party. A cocktail is a mixed drink; however, the term "cocktail party" has been used and abused to describe parties without these mixed libations. What am I saying here? Well, you could go along with the trend to call any stand-up-and-eat-appetizers-and-drink-wine party a cocktail party, but realize that you may incur the wrath of some guests who expect mixed drinks. It's up to you. One gracious way to get out of this is to invite people over for appetizers, using that term instead of cocktails. Then the drink selection is up to you.

Ordering wines through the mail isn't legal in every state. The merchant should be able to let you know whether the state in which you live permits this type of transaction.

When shopping for beer, search out local breweries; they're cropping up all over the place. They usually have a variety of interesting brews, with the advantage of usually being made to the demanding standards of the independent brewmaster. If no breweries are nearby, ask your liquor store owner for some suggestions. The store may carry a few regional brands.

Some states allow liquor sales on Sundays, and some don't. Know your local laws so that you won't be caught short. And if you find a wine or beer that you like, buy extra and have it on hand for unexpected guests.

When you invite friends over, whether it's for a couple of easy hors d'oeuvres or for a big appetizer spread, beverages should be part of the offerings. If you want to make your guests feel at home, you need to provide both food and drinks.

Setting up a mixed-drinks bar

I'm not suggesting that you become a full-fledged bartender, but if you're serving mixed drinks, you need at least a bit of an introduction to the art of mixology. This section gives you an outline for a complete bar. If you and/or your guests are not as ambitious, see the section titled "The minimalist's guide to the home bar."

For an easy-to-read and understandable bartending guide, check out *Bartending For Dummies* by Ray Foley (Wiley). If you want to know how to make the perfect martini or even obscure drinks with names like A-Bomb, Cocomotion, and Malibu Suntan, this book can tell you how.

Stocking your bar with hard alcohol

Here are the essential types of hard alcohol that you should keep in your bar:

- Bourbon
- Gin
- Rum
- Scotch
- Tequila
- Vermouth (both sweet and dry varieties)
- Vodka
- Whiskey

If you add a bottle of brandy or cognac and a cordial or two, such as Kahlua or Grand Marnier, you'll be prepared for almost any reasonable request.

Most standard-size bottles of alcohol are 750 milliliters. Buy this size. You don't need the larger bottles unless you know that your guests love vodka, for instance. In that case, you need either more bottles or larger (1.5 liter) bottles.

A 750-milliliter bottle gives you twenty-five 1-ounce servings.

Figuring out how much alcohol to buy

For a party of up to a dozen guests, consider one 750-milliliter bottle of each type of hard alcohol, two bottles of each wine (see the section "Selecting the wine and beer"), and two six-packs of beer. You'll have liquor left over, but it keeps for quite a while. For example, if you keep the cap on a bottle of bourbon and store it out of direct sunlight in a cool, dry place, it should be good for at least six months. The same advice applies to other hard liquors, such as vodka or gin. Most cordials and any cream-based liqueurs do not need to be refrigerated after opening, and they can keep for up to a couple of years. Some, however, will have expiration dates and specific storage instructions, so follow them if they are included.

Deciding what brands to buy

Just as a rose is not just a rose, gin is not just gin. On one end of the spectrum, you have bargain brands. These low-end brands are usually domestic and have a pretty generic flavor. This is a case where you get what you pay for. At the other end of the spectrum are the top-shelf brands, which will cost you much more, possibly 30 percent more.

So which should you buy? A 30 percent increase in expense for every bottle of liquor in your bar will cost you a pretty penny, or two or three. The decision is really up to you and your wallet. My best advice is to buy the best you can afford. If you love Scotch yourself, buy a great Scotch.

Selecting the wine and beer

Some guests may not like hard liquor, so you need to offer beer and wine as beverage options. Consider having the following on hand:

- Red wine
- White wine
- Domestic and/or imported beer
- Light beer
- Maybe even a bottle of champagne, which I discuss in the next section.

Wine and beer tastings

Wine and beer tastings are a festive way to organize a party. Ask the professionals at your local liquor store to suggest a variety of red wines or lagers for your guests to taste. Or offer your favorite white wine, a red wine, lighter beer (not lite beer!) and dark beer and taste them with your appetizers to see what food you like with each beverage. It's all about experimentation. You might like red wine with your cheese; a guest might like beer. Variety is where it's at.

Bubbling over about champagne

Champagne is usually reserved for special occasions, but why wait for a birthday or a raise? I always look for any excuse to drink champagne. Consider popping the cork when you have finally potty trained your puppy or because the sunset is beautiful. And don't forget that champagne will enliven many of your appetizers.

To properly be called champagne, the beverage must be made in the Champagne region of France, where it is made according to "method champenoise." However, many domestic American, as well as Spanish and Italian, sparkling wines rate quite high with professional tasters, and they will with you, too. Look for *brut* champagne (pronounced "broot"), which is the least sweet version and what I prefer with hors d'oeuvres. Here are all the types of champagne:

- Brut (the driest champagne that you're likely to find)
- Extra-dry
- Sec (dry)
- Demi-sec (partially dry)
- Doux (sweet)

You may want to try the drier styles with savory foods and the last two sweeter styles with desserts.

If you're serving a couple glasses of champagne — say, only for you and a special someone — consider buying what is called a *split,* which is a quarter bottle, or a half bottle. They're available from some very good champagne purveyors. If you need to serve 100 people, buy a *nebuchadnezzar.* That's a bottle that equals 20 standard 750-milliliter bottles! If you go this route, invite me. I've never seen one uncorked!

Adding nonalcoholic beverages to your bar

Your home bar set-up needs some nonalcoholic drinks. Colas, sodas, and sparkling waters come in 2-liter bottles and individual cans and bottles. Still water and juices are packaged by the quart, half gallon, and gallon. Keep the following nonalcoholic drinks in your home bar:

- Club soda
- Cola
- Cranberry juice
- Diet soda
- Ginger ale
- Grapefruit juice
- Orange juice
- Sparkling water
- Still water (or bottled, if your tap water isn't great)
- Tomato juice
- Tonic water

Consider buying small bottles of carbonated beverages, which come in six-packs. This way, if you use only a little bit of club soda during the evening, you'll lose only what's left in that small bottle, because it will go flat after a while. The other, unopened bottles, which you can store indefinitely, will still be ready for your next party.

In addition to the beverages, you need the following ingredients to help jazz up your drinks:

- Angostura bitters
- Lemon and lime wedges
- Lemon zest (called lemon twists at bars)
- Olives
- Salt and pepper
- Sour mix
- Superfine sugar (also called bar sugar because it dissolves quickly in drinks and is used by bartenders)
- Tabasco

If your party includes up to a dozen people, count on needing two 2-liter bottles of each fizzy beverage and a quart each of the juices. As far as still water is concerned, you can never have enough.

Icing down the beverages

You can't serve beverages unless you have a supply of ice. You need it to chill down juices and soft drinks and to add to on-the-rocks drinks and cocktails. You also need ice to chill down bottles of beer, wine, and champagne.

To be sure that you have enough ice for all of your guests, figure on 1 pound of ice per person in most situations. To be specific, if your drinks are already chilled, you need about ½ pound of ice person. If you need to ice drinks down, such as in an ice bucket for champagne, as well as provide ice for individual drinks, you're more likely to need the 1 pound amount.

If you have an automatic ice maker in your freezer, start bagging ice in resealable plastic bags and stockpile it for a few days before the party. This advice works for smaller parties requiring lesser amounts of ice. If you don't have an ice maker and you're having a larger party, don't bother making ice in those individual ice trays. Instead, buy bagged ice right before the party so you don't have to worry about having a place to store it.

One benefit of buying ice is that it's usually made with spring water so the ice will be very high quality. Read the bag to see what you're getting. Also, when shopping for ice, search for bags that have loose, clear cubes. Avoid the bags of cloudy ice cubes that have melded into large, lumpy masses. This happens when the ice hasn't been stored properly and has melted and rechilled, perhaps several times. You're paying for it, so be discerning.

Barware

You can mix drinks like a pro if you have the help of a few tools of the trade. Here are the basics:

- Corkscrew
- Bottle cap opener
- Ice bucket
- Ice scoop or tongs

- Cocktail shaker
- Jigger/measuring cup
- Strainer
- Long spoon for stirring
- Small cutting board
- Sharp knife

Consider purchasing a gadget that's a combined corkscrew and bottle opener. Such a tool means one less item to clutter up your kitchen accessory drawer.

Choosing glassware

If you feel compelled to have the perfect glass for every type of drink, you could go nuts collecting them all. But you don't have to own every shape and style of glass on the market. Figure 2-1 shows the only glasses you'll ever need for entertaining.

These glasses suit a variety of beverages. Use the rocks glass for any on-the-rocks drinks. Use the highball glasses for beer, soda, juices, and some mixed drinks. The all-purpose wine glass works for white or red wine. The cocktail glass is suitable for martinis, manhattans, and some other drinks. The cordial and brandy snifter are particular to those drinks only. The flute is designed for straight champagne and champagne drinks.

Sure, you can serve all your beverages in those jelly jars that you've been collecting for years. But beverage glasses come in different shapes to maximize the enjoyment of different drinks. For instance, champagne flutes are tall because the farther the bubbles have to travel, the longer the effervescence lasts.

The minimalist's guide to the home bar

I know, I know, gathering up all the booze and tools discussed in the previous sections is a lot of work. But if you're throwing a big engagement party or celebrating your parent's 50th wedding anniversary, you may want to be completely prepared. For many other parties, a pared-down list will probably suffice.

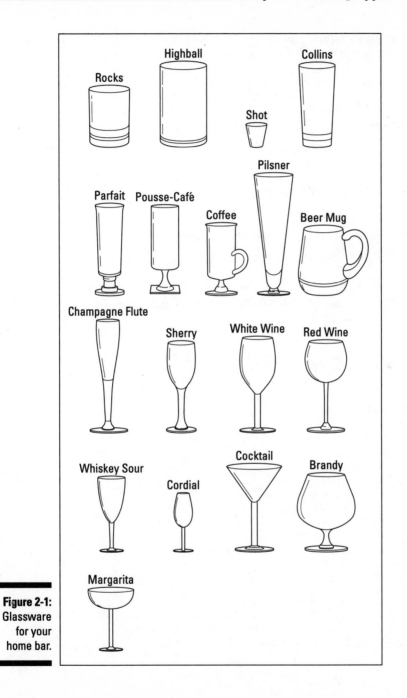

Figure 2-1:
Glassware
for your
home bar.

So how do you whittle down that list? For a party of 12, here are the bare-bones beverage essentials:

- ✔ 2 bottles of red wine
- ✔ 2 bottles of white wine
- ✔ 24 bottles of beer (including maybe 6 lite beers)
- ✔ 1 bottle of vodka or gin
- ✔ 1 bottle of scotch or bourbon
- ✔ 1 bottle of dry vermouth
- ✔ ½ gallon orange juice
- ✔ 1 bottle of club soda and/or tonic water
- ✔ Wedges of lemons and limes

If you refer to a guide such as *Bartending For Dummies* by Ray Foley (Wiley), you can find many drinks to make using the ingredients that I suggest for this minimalist home bar.

Chapter 3

Organizing Your Kitchen So That You're Always Ready for a Party

....

In This Chapter

▶ Stocking your pantry and refrigerator

▶ Acquiring the right tools and equipment

▶ Planning the presentation

....

*I*f you're the kind of person who panics when friends drop by unexpectedly because stale, store-brand potato chips and dried-out baby carrots are all you can offer them, this chapter is for you. I give you advice about what ingredients and equipment you need in your kitchen so that you can make appetizers on a moment's notice, even without recipes. Plenty of occasions that arise at a moment's notice deserve a little party; now you'll be ready.

With key items on hand, finished appetizers are always at your fingertips. Add to that a few serving pieces, even things you have around the house, like large dinner plates, and you can make these yummy recipes look as good as they taste.

Build a Better Bite: Creating Your Own Appetizers without Recipes

The key to being organized and effective in the kitchen is having the ingredients you need at hand in the pantry and the refrigerator. Some items may be obvious to you, like butter, or basic herbs and spices, but I am here to take the guesswork out of the situation. In the following sections are easy-to-follow lists that will guide you through the supermarket.

Don't be put off by the amount of pantry items I suggest. You can add a few items each time you shop to make it easy on your wallet.

Stocking your pantry

In the old days, a pantry meant a small room or closet off the kitchen where dry goods and kitchen utensils were stored. Today, most homes don't have pantries like our great-grandmothers had, so we use kitchen cabinets to store items such as canned, boxed, and bottled goods that don't need to be refrigerated.

Basic ingredients for your appetizer pantry

You really need these items in your pantry because they can help you whip up a wide assortment of appetizers:

- All-purpose flour
- Balsamic vinegar
- Beans such as cannellini and garbanzo (also known as chickpeas)
- Black pepper, freshly ground
- Bread (preferably close-grained white or wheat from a brand such as Pepperidge Farm)
- Corn chips (look for a high-quality unsalted or lightly salted brand)
- Crackers: I like a neutral tasting cracker like "Carr's Table Water Crackers," which show off your cheeses in style.
- Garlic
- Lemon juice (even if you have an opened bottle in your refrigerator, keep an extra bottle in the pantry)
- Nonstick vegetable spray, such as PAM
- Olive oil, both the light and extra-virgin varieties
- Onions
- Popcorn
- Potato chips (preferably the extra-thick, gourmet-type chips)
- Red wine vinegar
- Roasted peppers (in jars)
- Salt, both regular table salt and kosher salt
- Soy sauce
- Vegetable oil

The extended pantry

The following items aren't absolutely necessary, but they can give you more options when you're preparing your appetizer menu. Pick up these items if they catch your fancy:

- Cider vinegar
- Fish sauce (nam pla)
- Hoisin sauce
- Potatoes
- Sun-dried tomatoes
- Tahini: a Middle Eastern sesame paste with the texture of peanut butter; it's what makes hummus hummus!
- White wine vinegar

Adding herbs and spices to your kitchen provisions

Every kitchen should have a complement of herbs and spices that are ready at a moment's notice to enhance your food. You can't call your kitchen a kitchen if you don't have these basic herbs and spices on hand:

- Basil
- Bay leaves
- Black peppercorns in a pepper mill
- Cayenne
- Chili powder
- Cinnamon
- Cloves
- Curry powder
- Dill
- Nutmeg
- Oregano
- Paprika
- Rosemary
- Sage

✔ Tarragon

✔ Thyme

The following herbs and spices aren't essential, but they're nice to have, especially if you like to experiment in the kitchen:

✔ Coriander

✔ Cumin

✔ Dry mustard

✔ Herbes de Provence

✔ Marjoram

✔ White peppercorns (don't use the same pepper mill you use for the black peppercorns)

Keeping ingredients in cold storage

Some frequently used appetizer ingredients need to be stored in the refrigerator. You can store some of these items in the pantry when unopened, but you need to keep them in the refrigerator after you open them:

✔ Cheese, including the following:

- Grated Parmesan cheese (freeze in airtight containers for long-term storage)
- Cheddar or Swiss cheese in bulk

✔ Dijon mustard

✔ Mayonnaise

✔ Hot sauce such as Tabasco

✔ Large eggs

✔ Lemon juice

✔ Nuts (including whole nuts, such as almonds, and pecan or walnut halves)

✔ Oil-cured olives (in glass jars)

✔ Oil-cured sun-dried tomatoes

✔ Salsa, both mild and spicy

✔ Unsalted butter

✔ Whole milk

If you have extra room in the fridge, you may want to keep these items, too:

- ✔ Cream cheese (Choose the full-fat variety or the lower-fat Neufchâtel. Don't use the fat-free variety, which has a terrible, plastic-like texture and hardly any flavor.)
- ✔ Chutney, such as mango or cranberry
- ✔ Fancy mustards, such as tarragon, black pepper, or champagne
- ✔ Heavy cream
- ✔ Lemons
- ✔ Prepared pesto
- ✔ Sour cream (full-fat, lowfat, or nonfat)

Stashing things in the freezer

You can keep many items in your freezer for longer-term storage. If you have the space, consider keeping extra quantities of the following ingredients on hand in your freezer:

- ✔ Butter
- ✔ Grated cheese, such as Parmesan or cheddar
- ✔ Ice for drinks
- ✔ Nuts
- ✔ Prepared pie crusts (If you really want to use ready-made, try Pillsbury brand. Two crusts come in every box. You just unfold them and place them in a pie plate when you're ready to use them.)

Tools and Equipment for Making Appetizers

I assume that you have a stove and refrigerator and maybe even a microwave, blender, and food processor. Other tools and equipment, however, can help you make appetizers that are not only pleasing to look at but also enjoyable to make. Believe me, the right tools make it easier to work with your raw ingredients. Sure, you can peel a potato with a knife, but using a good vegetable peeler is quicker and easier and reduces the chance that you'll get nicked.

Peelers, knives, measuring cups, and more

In the kitchen, the little things are often what make your life easier. For example, when you're spreading something on bread, a butter knife works fine, but if you have a tiny offset spatula, the job will go more quickly and more smoothly. The items in the following list are fairly inexpensive, so if you want to expand your kitchen tool collection, they would be great additions. All of them have multiple uses. You can use them for all kinds of cooking and baking, not just for the recipes in this book, so they're a good investment.

✔ Baking sheets (typically about 12 x 15 inches with a lip on one side)

✔ Cheese plane (see Figure 3-1): It allows you to slice pieces of firm and hard cheeses, such as cheddar or Parmigiano-Reggiano, very thinly

✔ Cookie cutter, preferably a round one about 2 inches in diameter

✔ Cutting board

✔ Glass pie plate

✔ Jelly roll pan (15 x 10 inches)

✔ Knives:

- 4- to 5-inch paring knife

- 8- to 10-inch chef's knife

- Serrated knife

✔ Loaf pan (9 x 5 inches)

✔ Measuring cups for dry ingredients

✔ Measuring cups for liquid ingredients

✔ Measuring spoons

✔ Mixing bowls (in a nonreactive material such as glass or stainless steel)

✔ Pastry brush

✔ Scale (Look for a digital model. You could use a spring-loaded scale, which has a platform over a base with a dial that spins around when weight is applied, but this type isn't very accurate.)

✔ Spatulas (see Figure 3-2):

- Metal pancake turner (often referred to as a regular spatula)

- Rubber spatula

- Small offset spatula

- Small, straight-edged icing spatula

✔ Spoons:

    • Slotted spoon

    • Wooden spoon

✔ Vegetable peeler

✔ Whisk

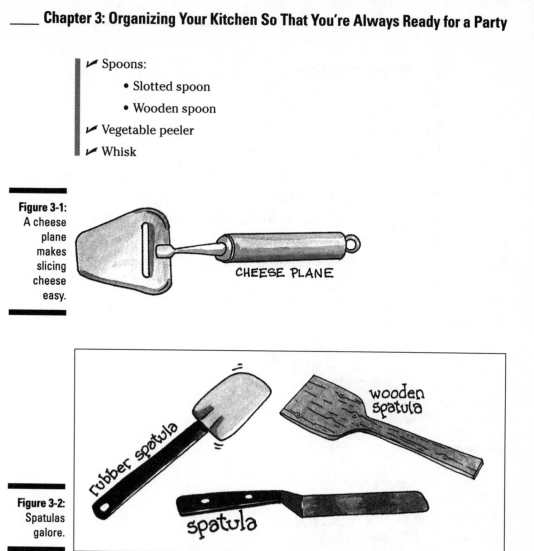

Figure 3-1: A cheese plane makes slicing cheese easy.

CHEESE PLANE

Figure 3-2: Spatulas galore.

rubber spatula

wooden spatula

spatula

In addition, don't forget to keep a supply of plastic wrap, aluminum foil, parchment paper, wax paper, and paper towels on hand.

More extras if you want to get fancy

The following list expands upon the former one. These tools and equipment do a job that can't be duplicated by something else. In other words, if you want to make mini muffins, you need the mini muffin pan.

- Bamboo skewers
- Chafing dish
- Citrus reamer (see Figure 3-3)
- Custard cups
- Fondue pot
- Mandoline (see Figure 3-4)
- Miniature muffin tins (1½ inches in diameter)
- Pastry bag (16-inch length) and a #30 tip and coupler
- Rolling pin
- Tartlet tins (2¼ inches in diameter)
- Warmer

Figure 3-3:
Use a citrus reamer to extract lemon, lime, and orange juice.

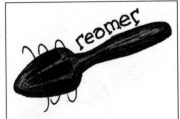

Figure 3-4:
A mandoline is a useful but expensive tool.

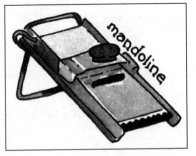

The microwave oven

A microwave oven can help you with a variety of tasks when you're making appetizers. It can melt butter, soften ingredients to room temperature, defrost a forgotten ingredient in no time, and, possibly most important of all, make the quickest plate of nachos you have ever eaten. (See Chapter 9 for the Super Nachos recipe.) It can heat hors d'oeuvres right on the serving platters.

Deep-fat fryers

A few recipes in this book, such as the potato chips (Chapter 7) and the Japanese-inspired tempura (Chapter 10), employ a deep-fat frying technique. For deep-fat frying, you can use a heavy, deep pot made of cast iron or enamel-coated iron, or you can use a deep-fat fryer. The advantage of the former equipment is that it's inexpensive, but you do need to buy a thermometer, which won't set you back much either. A deep-fat fryer, on the other hand, is an all-in-one unit, but it does have a limited purpose. If you're trying to decide whether to buy a deep-fat fryer, consider your budget as well as how often you like to fry food.

Whether you are using a pot or a fryer, always make sure you have plenty of oil. You will see in the recipes that require a deep-fry technique that the ingredient listing says "Oil for deep-frying." That's because it is very difficult to determine exactly how much oil you will need. Many recipes say that you need a 3-inch depth of oil in your pot. Well, if your pot is wider than my pot, you'll need more oil to meet the depth requirement. Best case scenario is to have plenty of oil on hand. My suggestion is to buy a gallon of oil when you are shopping for your deep-fry recipe ingredients and use a pot that is as tall as it is wide, or close too it. (You will notice that deep-fat fryers have a similar dimension.) If you only have wide pots, buy more oil!

To keep deep-fat fried foods as light and crisp as possible, follow these tips:

- ✔ Always use enough oil. The foods should have plenty of room to move around. Never crowd the pot.

- ✔ Make sure that the oil is hot enough. (Check individual recipes for the correct temperature.)

- ✔ Make sure that the oil comes back up to the correct temperature with subsequent batches.

- ✔ Oil is combustible, so don't let it get so hot that it begins to smoke. If it does begin smoking, immediately cover with a lid and turn off the heat source.

- ✔ As you fry batches of food, skim out any bits of food or batter floating in the oil. Keep the oil clean and clear.

- ✔ Always drain your fried foods on paper towels to absorb any excess oil.

- ✔ All deep-fat fried foods are best if eaten soon after frying.

- ✔ If you really want to deep-fat fry something and don't have a fryer or a thermometer, try this: Fill a heavy bottomed pot with at least 3 inches of oil and heat over high heat. Drop a 1-inch cube of bread into the hot oil and fry for 1 minute. If the bread turns a light golden brown in that 1-minute time period, the oil is approximately 365 degrees.

Serving Appetizers: It's All in the Presentation

Let the show begin! Presenting food attractively is like putting on a little show. Think about the analogy. When you go to a play, costumed performers and attractive sets contribute to the visual appeal. The same thing applies to your food — it always looks better when it's dressed up and presented against an attractive background. Guests will be sure to notice when you take the time to hollow out a delicious dark bread as a container for a white dip (see Figure 3-5) instead of serving white dip in a white bowl.

Figure 3-5:
A bread bowl makes a nice impression.

Platters, baskets, and serving dishes

Once you make your recipes, you need to find an attractive way to serve them. Even if you're only serving a party of four, you need to put those hors d'oeuvres on something. And if you're hosting a larger party, the logistics of serving get a bit more complicated. You don't need fine crystal or silver, you do need a few assorted serving pieces for entertaining, regardless of the size of your party. You can buy any of these new, but you can also search through flea markets and tag sales for bargains. Discount stores, such as T.J. Maxx, often have good bargains on serving pieces, too.

When deciding which platters and plates to use, consider the color. For example, if you're serving smoked salmon, don't put it on an orange plate — the colors are so similar that the salmon is no longer highlighted. Platters with very busy patterns may look pretty, but when you put food on them, the pattern either disappears or distracts from the food. All sorts of solid colors usually work well. Just be sure that your dishes complement rather than match the food.

✔ **Large dinner plates:** They don't even have to match. Shop at flea markets and pick up an assortment of plates. If you tend to like modern, clean lines, then look for plates that fit your scheme. I like to mix it up and find uses for flowery plates as well as contemporary designs.

- ✔ **Flat platters:** Look for a variety of shapes, such as rectangles and squares, in addition to round and oval. These platters should be completely flat or at least have a large flat area in the center. Some have very small flat areas and a very large rim, which really isn't practical when you're serving food.

- ✔ **Trays:** All sorts of trays come in handy when entertaining. You can put food right on them or use them to ferry glasses and plates to and from the kitchen. You can find some decorative plastic and metal trays on the market that are pretty inexpensive.

- ✔ **Baskets:** Large and small baskets can hold foods such as crackers, sliced French bread, and chips. Line the basket with a colorful oversized napkin or a pretty linen kitchen towel (both clean, of course). Remember that basket filled with fruit that someone gave you? Put it to use!

- ✔ **Crates:** I occasionally receive gifts that are packaged in crates, and some of them make handy serving pieces.

- ✔ **Ice bucket:** This item comes in handy whether you're just using it to hold ice for drinks or to ice down a bottle of champagne or wine.

Think height

To create a dynamic presentation for your appetizers, vary the height of your serving pieces. Use both flat platters and serving dishes that are attached on pedestals. Another way to create height on a table is by placing sturdy items, like wooden boxes of various sizes, underneath the tablecloth so that some serving pieces can be elevated. To do this, place a tablecloth on the table and then arrange your wooden boxes. Take another large tablecloth of the same color and drape it over the boxes, tucking and creating decorative folds here and there. Then place your platters on top of the risers. Two- or three-tiered plate racks, usually made of heavy-duty wire or wrought iron, also can add height and make good use of your serving space. These racks are available in styles that hold round, oval, or square plates. Just make sure to have the corresponding plates to match because the racks don't always come with matching plates.

Think theme

Try to match your serving dishes to the theme of your appetizers. For example, if you're serving an Asian-inspired appetizer, consider serving it on a bamboo tray or a red or black lacquered tray. Tapas, the appetizers of Spain, look great on Mediterranean inspired pottery.

When is a bowl not a bowl?

A bowl is not a bowl when it is a hollowed-out loaf of bread, cabbage, or red pepper, just to name a few alternative items.

You probably have things around your house that would make serving "bowls" even if they're actually designed for other purposes or for decoration only. You could put a bowl in a basket, so that it looks like the basket is the actual vessel. You could hollow out a winter squash for dip, or use a vase for breadsticks. You may have ideas that haven't even occurred to me. You also can purchase unusual items that can function as bowls. You never know where you might find such pieces, so when you're trying to add to your collection of serving bowls, don't overlook such places as craft shops, home and garden centers, and those stores where everything is $1. Just be sure that the item is considered safe for serving food. Some pieces carry a warning that they're not designed to hold foods or beverages.

Some ceramic glazes contain lead and are not food safe. What do you do if you buy something at a flea market and want to know if it is safe to use? For a few dollars at a hardware store, you can buy an easy-to-use kit that will tell you whether there is a high lead content in your dish. It's like a marker that you swipe over the dish, and if it turns a certain color, you will know whether lead is present.

Dressing up the appetizer on the platter

You can place appetizers directly on platters, of course, but by adding simple, inexpensive garnishes as a base for your appetizers, you can turn your presentation into something really special. Here are some ideas:

- ✔ Place purple and green flowering kale leaves on a platter before you arrange your appetizers, particularly crudité.

- ✔ Spread a layer of dried beans on a rimmed tray to act as a base for bite-sized appetizers. This idea may sound weird, but dried beans come in beautiful colors, they're dry, they won't stick to food, and they look cool. Trust me.

- ✔ You can also use rice or even very coarse salt as a base for little appetizers. This is a caterers' trick that I've seen done at very fancy parties, so go for it.

- ✔ Visit a florist's shop and ask for suggestions about leaves that are suitable as a decorative base for food on platters. Lemon balm leaves and rose leaves, both of which are great, will probably be their recommendations. Wash and dry the leaves and lay them flat on a tray under cheeses or other hors d'oeuvres.

- ✔ Use paper leaves that are specifically designed to be placed under cheeses and appetizers. You can find these at specialty food stores.

- ✔ Depending on where you live, banana leaves make a nice base and can sometimes be found in stores that feature Asian foods.

Chapter 4

Putting It Together: Menus

. . . .

. . . .

*W*hen you put together a party, whether it's for 4 or 24 (or more!), organization is the key. By planning a menu ahead of time, you can generate shopping lists and develop a timeline for preparing your food. Adequate planning and organization are by far the best ways to guarantee the success of your shindig.

Designing a menu isn't hard to do. It can be as simple as writing down a few of your favorite appetizers. Your menu items don't have to be related in any way. In other words, they don't have to all be French or low-fat, for instance, unless you want your party to have a certain theme. To help you plan your party fare, in this chapter I give you some guidelines for developing menus yourself as well as some actual menu suggestions that you can use.

Designing a Menu

Menu design doesn't have to be complicated, but there is an art to it. Some consultants and chefs make big bucks deciding what recipes should be offered on a menu. Your undertaking will be smaller, but no less important — yet it can still be easy! Sound confusing? Take a look at this list of things to consider when planning your menu:

✔ What kind of party are you having? Is it a formal event where tuxedos and evening gowns are required? Or is it a casual midweek get-together? A more upscale soiree may call for smoked salmon, while a relaxed come-as-you-are affair may dictate fare as simple as cheese, crackers, veggies, and dip. In other words, the more formal the party, the more formal the food.

✔ Consider including a selection of flavors and textures: something spicy, something creamy and soothing, maybe something crunchy. And make sure that you don't serve only salty items. Mix it up.

✔ Always have at least one appetizer that's bound to be familiar to almost everyone, such as an onion dip. Then get as creative as you want with the rest of the food. This approach guarantees that even the nonadventurous types will like something and that everyone will be happy.

✔ Include at least one dish that you are familiar with preparing and enjoy eating. Doing so will give you peace of mind and ensure at least one successful dish.

✔ Take advantage of recipes that can be partially or completely made ahead of time. Look for this information within the recipes. Be sure that you have only a few last-minute items to tend to — ideally one recipe. That way, you can enjoy the party, too.

✔ Think about the shape and color of food. A saying in the retail food business, "Eye appeal is buy appeal," can apply to your home entertaining as well. In other words, if the food looks good, people will buy it or, in the case of your party, try it. So the initial enticement is made through the presentation, making it important that you think about varied shapes and textures when designing your menu. For example, a dip in a round bowl surrounded by veggies contrasts nicely with small squares of bread topped with a creamy salmon mousse. If everything you offer sits on little crackers, you're not providing any visual variety. Or if all the food is beige, your serving table won't look appetizing.

✔ The seasons may suggest some items. Anything with asparagus is perfect for spring. A cheese ball just says winter holidays to some families. Also, if you buy produce that is in season, it not only tastes better but also is less expensive.

✔ Consider the calories in your menu. Include raw veggies so that anyone dieting or on high-fat diet restrictions can still nibble along with everybody else.

Great Menu Ideas

You can use the menus in this section as shown or as a jumping-off point for your own imagination. One advantage of these already completed menus is that I include a step-by-step list of how best to approach the preparation of your dishes as well as information on how to increase or decrease a recipe to suit the number of guests you are entertaining.

Each menu contains three parts:

✔ A list of the recipes that each menu includes and where to find them in this book

✔ A step-by-step guide to making the meal in the most efficient way

✔ Notes about how to tailor the menu to your party's size

Quick-to-make appetizers (menu for 8)

This menu is perfect when you want to entertain but don't have a lot of time to dedicate to preparation. These aren't make-ahead recipes; they are recipes that you can put together quickly right before you need them. This menu works partly because while one item is cooking, you can work on the component of another dish. I help you maximize your time. This entire menu can be made within the hour right before your party.

Menu

Parmesan-Garlic Popcorn (Chapter 5)

Hummus with pita triangles and baby carrots (Chapter 7)

Pesto Sun-Dried Tomato Baguette (Chapter 8)

Side of smoked salmon with dark bread and sweet butter (described in Chapter 12)

Countdown to mealtime

1. **Make the hummus and place in a serving bowl. (The flavor improves as it stands.) Set the bowl on a platter and arrange baby carrots on the platter.**

2. **Make the popcorn and place in a serving bowl. It doesn't have to stay warm.**

3. **Arrange the salmon on a platter and place sweet butter in a serving dish.**

4. **Make the pesto baguette.**

5. **Right before serving, slice the pesto baguette and arrange on a platter. Slice black bread and place alongside the salmon. Slice the pita bread and place alongside the carrots and hummus.**

Scaling up or down

The popcorn can be scaled down and up.

The hummus can easily be halved or doubled.

The size of the pesto baguette is dictated by the size of the bread. Some bakeries sell half loaves, in which case you can halve the recipe. Or just cut a baguette in half and use the other half for another recipe. Doubling, tripling, and so on is easy. Just buy more baguettes and ingredients to stuff them with.

You can scale the salmon on black bread up or down as you like.

The open house cocktail party (menu for 24)

Menu

Crudités (Chapter 6) and The Best Onion Dip (Chapter 7)

Hot 'n' Spicy Pecans (Chapter 5)

Stuffed Mushrooms (Chapter 6)

Shrimp Cocktail with Two Sauces (Chapter 6)

Cheese and Pâté Platter (serving cheeses is described in Chapter 2 and pâtés are described in Chapter 12)

Pesto Sun-Dried Tomato Palmiers (Chapter 8)

Buttermilk Biscuits with Turkey and Cranberry Chutney (Chapter 8)

Glazed Chicken Wings (Chapter 9)

Marinated Olives (Chapter 10)

Vietnamese Spring Rolls (Chapter 10)

Countdown to mealtime

1. Make the palmiers up to 2 weeks ahead and freeze them. Defrost them in the refrigerator the night before your party.

2. Make the olives, pecans, and cranberry chutney up to a week ahead.

3. Make the onion dip a few days ahead.

4. One day ahead, make the two sauces for the shrimp cocktail, the peanut sauce for the spring rolls, the mushrooms, and the chicken wings. Just heat them up right before serving. You can also prepare the crudités the day before.

5. The day of the party, steam the shrimp, set out the cheeses and pâté, and make the biscuits and spring rolls.

6. Shortly before serving, slice the French bread, assemble the biscuits, cook the mushrooms and palmiers, and heat up the chicken wings.

Scaling up or down

You can easily scale all these recipes up or down. I do want to point out, how-ever, that although the spring rolls are easy to make, they do take some time and concentration, and I don't think it's worth going through the trouble to make fewer of them than the recipe suggests. In other words, if you're going to assemble all the ingredients, you may as well make the full amount. It is possible to halve the recipe, though, so proceed as you like.

Also, the cheese and pâté platter is made up of cheeses and pâtés that you buy, ready to go. So if you need to add some items, consider starting here because it doesn't require any more cooking time for you. Arranging five types of cheese on a platter is really just as easy as putting out three types.

Appetizer party for $5 a person (menu for 10)

Sometimes you want to put on a big spread but must stick to a budget. I present to you an appetizer party that can even serve as a light meal.

Menu

Crudités (Chapter 6) and Blue Cheese Dip (Chapter 7)

Ginger-Orange Walnuts (Chapter 5)

Garlic Mussels on the Half-Shell (Chapter 9)

Indonesian-Inspired Chicken Saté (Chapter 10)

Root Veggie Chips (Chapter 7)

Tomato-Basil Crostini (Chapter 8)

Countdown to mealtime

1. **Make the walnuts up to 2 weeks ahead.**

2. **Make the dip up to 2 days ahead. You can also make the saté sauce and garlic butter for the mussels 2 days ahead.**

3. **Assemble the chicken saté and marinate overnight. You can prepare the crudités a day ahead as well.**

4. **The day of the party, assemble the crudité platter, make the crostini and the veggie chips, and cook the mussels and saté.**

Scaling up or down

You can scale all these recipes up or down. I want to point out that the deep-fat frying of the veggie chips does take a while because you have to do it in small batches — unless you have an industrial-size fryer worthy of McDonald's in your kitchen.

Spring and summer appetizers (menu for 6)

The warmer months steer us towards lighter food with fresh, vibrant colors. The asparagus included in this menu is even considered a harbinger of spring. Basil and tomatoes are both at their peak in late summer, but all these ingredients do overlap and make for a tasty assortment for an outdoor get-together.

Menu
Crab Cakes (Chapter 6)

Asparagus with Garlic Potato Dip (steam the asparagus until crisp yet tender and turn to Chapter 7 for the dip)

Tomato-Basil Crostini (Chapter 8)

Countdown to mealtime
1. **Make the dip and make and form the crab cakes a day ahead. Cook the asparagus a day ahead, too.**
2. **The day of the party, cook the crab cakes, assemble the asparagus and dip platter, and make the crostini.**

Scaling up or down
You can scale all these recipes up or down as you like.

Fall and winter appetizers (menu for 4)

I love cooking in the fall and winter and concentrating on warm and hearty foods. Pumpkins are omnipresent in autumn, and fresh pumpkin seeds, roasted and seasoned, make a tasty nibble. Cheese fondue is a perfect party food. Depending on the amounts you make, you can use this menu for appetizers or expand the quantities and make it a meal.

Menu
Crudités (Chapter 6) and bread

Spicy Tex-Mex Pumpkin Seeds (Chapter 5)

Cheese Fondue (Chapter 7)

Countdown to mealtime

1. **Make the pumpkin seeds up to one week ahead.**

2. **Prepare the crudités the day before the party.**

3. **As close to serving time as possible, make the fondue and slice the French bread.**

Scaling up or down

These can all be scaled up or down. For the fondue, keep in mind that you need a pot large enough to keep it warm if you increase the recipe, so plan ahead.

Lowfat, high-flavor fare (menu for 8)

Many people want to lower their fat intake, but the days of liquid diets are largely over, thank goodness. Now, dieters concentrate on solid foods that are lower in fat, but big on flavor. As you can see, these recipes use herbs and spices and unusual ingredients and textures to play up what is delicious and satisfying. None of your guests will miss the fat.

Menu

Herbed Popcorn (Chapter 5)

Marinated Olives (Chapter 10)

Vietnamese Spring Rolls (Chapter 10)

Tapenade with French bread and crudités (Chapter 7 for the dip, Chapter 6 for the crudité)

Countdown to mealtime

1. **Make the olives and tapenade 1 week ahead.**

2. **Prepare the crudités the day before.**

3. **Make the popcorn and the spring rolls the day of the party. Slice the bread as close to serving time as possible.**

Scaling up or down

You can scale all these recipes up or down. As I mention earlier in this chapter, I think it is worth making the whole batch of spring rolls and not halving it.

Regional American appetizers (menu for 8)

Some appetizers have been part of the American landscape for decades — and with good reason. They are simple and delicious and show good old American ingenuity when it comes to a combination of ingredients and taste. This menu is perfect for a family get-together.

Menu

Crudités and The Best Onion Dip (Chapter 6 for the crudité and Chapter 7 for the dip)

Deviled Eggs (Chapter 6)

Crab Cakes (Chapter 6)

Cheddar, Port, and Blue Cheese Ball (Chapter 6)

Countdown to mealtime

1. **Make the cheese ball up to 4 days ahead.**

2. **Make the onion dip up to 3 days ahead.**

3. **Prepare the crab cakes and the crudités the day before.**

4. **The day of the party, cook the crab cakes and make the deviled eggs.**

Scaling up or down

You can scale all these recipes up or down.

Italian antipasto (menu for 8)

Antipasto literally means "before the meal." My assortment of Italian appetizers works well before an Italian-inspired meal, or even an old-fashioned barbecue. These dishes are highly flavored and work well to pique the appetite — and they taste like you're eating in an Italian grandmother's kitchen.

Menu

Prosciutto (described in Chapter 10)

Marinated Mozzarella Balls (Chapter 10)

Fried Calamari (Chapter 10)

Roasted Vegetables Array (Chapter 10)

Countdown to mealtime

1. Make the mozzarella balls 2 days ahead.

2. Roast the veggies a day ahead.

3. Set out the prosciutto, slice some bread, and make the calamari as close to serving time as possible.

Scaling up or down

You can easily scale all these recipes up or down. The calamari, like all fried foods, will just be limited by the size of your deep-fat fryer or the pot you are frying in.

French charcuterie (menu for 6)

Strictly speaking, *charcuterie* is the word used to describe pork products in French. Pâtés immediately come to mind, but here I expand the idea to include some other starters that work well before a variety of meals.

Menu

Crudités (Chapter 6)

Cheese and Pâté (serving cheeses is described in Chapter 2 and pâté in Chapter 12)

Tapenade (Chapter 7)

Herbed Goat Cheese (Chapter 10)

Countdown to mealtime

1. Make the tapenade up to 1 week ahead.

2. Prepare the crudités up to a day ahead.

3. Make the goat cheese up to 6 hours ahead.

4. Shortly before serving, set out the cheeses and pâtés and slice the French bread, if using.

Scaling up or down

Scale all the recipes up or down as you like.

Asian flavors (menu for 6)

There is so much variety to Asian cooking, from the lemongrass found in Thai food, to the subtleties of Japanese food, to the great variety within Chinese cuisine. Here I suggest a focus on the Japanese dish tempura. It consists of a light, lacy batter covering all kinds of veggies and some shrimp. Served with a dipping sauce, it makes a great conversation starter. The Vietnamese Spring Rolls are a nice cold addition. Add some sake and beer for a complete experience.

Menu

Tempura, Veggies, and Shrimp (Chapter 10)

Vietnamese Spring Rolls (Chapter 10)

Countdown to mealtime

1. Make the sauce for the spring rolls 3 days ahead.

2. You can make the spring rolls as close to serving as possible. If you make them 2 hours ahead, you can focus your last-minute attention on the tempura. You also can prepare the veggies and shrimp for tempura a couple hours ahead.

3. Make the tempura as close to serving time as possible.

Scaling up or down

You can scale both of these recipes up or down. But, at least the first time you make them, you'll find it easier to make only the suggested amounts.

Part II
Easy Pleasers: Simple Recipes You Should Know

The 5th Wave   By Rich Tennant

@RICHTENNANT

"Do I like arugula? I _love_ arugula!! Some of the best beaches in the world are there."

In this part . . .

*T*his part begins with a chapter on easy-to-make flavored nuts and popcorn and other snacks that are easy to pop in your mouth. You also can find recipes for appetizers that have become classics over the years. They include such things as crudités (raw and steamed veggies) and deviled eggs. This part ends with a large chapter on dips and dippers. There, you find new versions of old favorites, including recipes for onion dip and blue cheese dip, and even a recipe for homemade potato chips.

Chapter 5

Cheese, Nuts, Popcorn, and Nibbles

In This Chapter

▶ Discovering cheese
▶ Sampling flavored nuts
▶ Experimenting with popcorn
▶ Noshing on assorted nibbles

Sometimes you don't want a sophisticated, grown-up appetizer, like a dainty open-faced sandwich. What you really want is to be able to grab handfuls of nuts or popcorn and just chow down, with total disregard for portion size or calorie content. These types of foods are sometimes referred to as bar foods because, as you may have guessed, they're often served in bars.

This chapter is all about that kind of food. From cheese to flavored nuts to seasoned popcorn and beyond, consider making at least one of these easy recipes for your next party, whether it's a casual get-together or a more sophisticated soiree. The recipes are also perfect munchies for serving your family when they're gathered around the TV to watch the latest video. Don't forget to supply their favorite beverages.

Beyond Cheese and Crackers

For decades, the definition of an appetizer was a plate of supermarket cheese and saltine crackers or a relish dish of raw celery, carrot sticks, and canned black olives. This minimal offering was probably served before dinner, most likely a special Sunday supper or before a meal including guests. As the saying goes, we've come a long way, baby! Today's appetizers can take the form of colorful vegetables with a protein-rich dip before a weekday meal — a great way to get your kids to eat healthy foods, by the way — to an elegant plated appetizer of Roasted Vegetable Terrine (see Chapter 11) prepared for honored guests. Or consider a party made up of nothing but appetizers with enough choices to please everyone.

Even though serving cheese with crackers is easy and maybe a little pedestrian, I don't want to give you the idea that there's anything wrong with cheese, or crackers, for that matter. *Au contraire.* Even supermarkets carry a varied selection of cheeses that goes far beyond American slices and basic orange-colored cheddar. So if cheese and crackers have always been your family's way of starting a meal, so be it. You may not want to change tradition, but I give suggestions in case you want to branch out. In fact, even when you serve appetizers such as smoked salmon or deviled eggs, you may still want to include some cheese, which is fairly universally liked. So here's a mini primer on what may be the most popular appetizer ingredient — cheese.

Cows, sheep, and goats, oh my!

Maybe you haven't given it much thought, but most of the cheese you eat is derived from cow's milk. But there is so much more to the world of cheese, including cheeses made from the milk of sheep and goats.

If a cheese is goat- or sheep-based, it will probably be labeled as such. If the label says nothing specific, assume that it's from cow's milk.

Moo to you

Here are some delicious cow's milk cheeses to look for:

- **Cheddars, both foreign and domestic:** Cheddars are traditionally made from cow, but there are exceptions.
- **Swiss-type cheeses:** This category includes Gruyère and Emmentaler.
- **Some Gouda cheeses:** Check the labels. Gouda can come from sheep's or goat's milk, too.
- **Many blue cheeses:** Some blue cheese can be made with sheep's or goat's milk.
- **Blue/Danish blue:** This hard, crumbly blue cheese is often used in salads.
- **Brie:** Usually a cow's milk cheese and oh so creamy! The rind is edible, by the way, so don't just peel it off.
- **Triple crèmes:** These cheeses, which are very high in fat but very yummy, include varieties such as St. Andre and Explorateur.

Baa baa

Sheep cheeses may sound exotic, but I bet many of you have had Pecorino Romano cheese. It, along with Parmesan, is a classic cheese used to top spaghetti. A friend of mine calls this type of cheese "shaker cheese" because you often find these blended in containers ready to shake on your pasta. Sheep cheeses are often described as having a nutty taste. Here is a short list of sheep cheeses to try:

- **Manchego:** Spanish cheese with character.
- **Pecorino Romano:** Hard in texture, strong in flavor.
- **Roquefort** (blue cheese): One of France's finest — made from ewe's milk!
- **Sheep's milk feta:** A classic Greek cheese.

Getting your goat

If your first experience with goat cheese was with a very mature, strong-smelling, and strong-tasting goat cheese, I can understand if you were turned off. Those kinds of cheeses can be an acquired taste. I happen to love them (consider giving them a second chance), but many mild easy-to-eat goat cheeses are available that aren't so "goaty." If you don't like that word, use one of the descriptive terms that professional cheese tasters do. They often describe goat cheese as having a "complex flavor and acidic bite or musty snap." How's that for cocktail conversation? Here are some goat cheeses to try:

- **Banon:** A medium strength French goat cheese from Provence.
- **Bucheron:** Crumbly with a mild to medium goat flavor.
- **Montrachet:** Particularly mild; a good starter goat cheese.
- **Valencay:** Soft and creamy with a mild taste.

If you're watching your fat intake, know that goat cheese is usually the lowest in fat, cow's milk is in the middle, and sheep cheeses are the richest in fat.

Including variety on your cheese tray

There are a few ways to offer cheese beyond cubes with toothpicks. There are literally hundreds of cheeses and they come in a variety of shapes, sizes, textures, flavors, and origins, not to mention that they are also made from various milks — either cow, goat or sheep. As you can imagine, given these factors, there are many ways to go about presenting a cheese array. Here are a few ideas to get you started:

- Offer at least one of each of the following types of cheese: hard, semi-soft, and soft.
- Set out two or three goat cheeses to compare them. Or three sheep cheeses. Or a goat, a sheep, and a cow (not the animal, the cheese).
- Include cheeses from different countries and group them accordingly, such as French, Italian, or domestic American.

✔ Don't forget a nice blue cheese, either domestic or imported.

✔ Serve a selection of triple crème cheese, with its rich 75 percent butterfat content! Remember, you can eat anything in moderation!

One of the biggest mistakes that people make when offering cheese is to serve it too cold. All cheeses, except very fresh cheeses, such as the Italian sour cream-like mascarpone, should be served at room temperature. This assures that their texture and flavor are at their best. For soft cheeses such as brie, the insides should be downright runny.

Measuring cheese

Now I know that you know that cheese is not just cheese. There are cheddar and Swiss cheeses, which are completely different in terms of taste and texture, and then there are Parmesan and mozzarella cheeses, which are also unique.

So it should come as no surprise that, when you grate various cheeses, you end up with different volumes and weights. For instance, you may need 1 cup of shredded cheese, which 3 ounces of cheddar might give you, but you need 4 ounces of mozzarella to yield the same amount. The size of the holes on your grater makes a difference, too. I find that the finer the shred, the lighter the yield will be. So what do you do? Well, I try to take out the guesswork by giving you both weights and volumes. Try to match them up as indicated in the recipes.

The Nutty World of Nuts

When shopping for nuts, you'll find that you have plenty of decisions to make. You can choose from the more popular types, such as almonds, peanuts, pecans, and walnuts, or from the less common types, such as cashews or macadamias. Depending on the variety you select, you also may have to decide whether you want the nuts shelled or in the shell. In addition, you often can choose whether you want whole or halved or pieces; slices or slivers; salted or preseasoned or plain. Sometimes you may have a choice between reasonably priced bulk nuts or expensive, prepackaged bags.

Here's my first helpful suggestion when it comes to nuts: Buy in bulk. You'll find that doing so is more economical than buying nuts already in cans or bags. Natural foods stores and well-stocked supermarkets often sell nuts in bulk by the pound. If you don't have that option, at least comparison shop. The larger bags found in the supermarket are probably less expensive than tiny cans in the long run, and you can freeze what you don't need right away.

TIP

Going nuts over hors d'oeuvres

Here are a few nut appetizers that are quick to make, delicious, and perfectly bite-sized:

- Sandwich a bit of blue cheese between toasted walnut halves and serve within 2 hours. (The nuts get soggy after that.)

- Combine mild goat cheese (such as Montrachet) and cream cheese to make a very soft spread. Add a bit of milk or cream if the spread is too stiff. Add grapes and stir to coat the grapes with the slightly sticky cheese mixture. Then one by one, roll the coated grapes in a bowl of toasted, chopped pecans or walnuts. Serve with toothpicks.

- Slice crisp red apples, with the skin on, into ¼-inch-thick slices. Dip in lemon water, dry, and top with a slice of sharp cheddar cheese and a toasted walnut or pecan half.

- If your party guests include children, here's a kid-friendly hors d'oeuvre: Fill 2- to 3-inch lengths of celery with cream cheese and top with raisins and chopped peanuts or walnuts. (With raisins they're called Ants on a Log.)

All nuts have volatile oils, which can eventually go rancid. When you buy nuts in bulk, give them a good sniff. They should smell fresh and nutty and should have no musty odor. A musty odor means that the nuts are stale and beyond their prime "snackability." For long-term storage, place nuts in resealable plastic bags or airtight plastic containers and freeze for up to 6 months. If using plastic bags, press out all the air. If using containers, fill them up so that there is little air space. Eliminating as much air space as possible helps minimize freezer burn.

Nuts in the shell: Very Ap-peeling

All nuts come in a shell, but they have varying degrees of hardness. Peanut shells, for instance, are very easily peeled away from the nut, while a pecan can be extracted from the shell only by using a nutcracker — or a hammer!

I love having a big bowl of nuts in the shell, either one kind or a mixture, with a nutcracker nearby. I find something extremely satisfying about the slow pace of cracking the nuts, one by one, and popping them in my mouth. In addition, the contrasting shapes and colors of the shells of walnuts, pecans, peanuts, and almonds combine to make an attractive centerpiece on a coffee table.

If serving nuts in the shell, don't forget the nutcracker as well as an empty bowl for the discarded shells.

Even if you enjoy cooking from scratch, I would never expect you to go so far as to shell your own nuts for a recipe. If a dish calls for only ½ cup of chopped walnuts, having to shell them first may discourage you from even making the recipe in the first place. So, for recipes, buy nuts that are already shelled.

Three nuts, three techniques, endless variations

The following recipes demonstrate the versatility of nuts. In one recipe, you toss the nuts with the flavorings and then bake them in the oven. In another recipe, you toss the nuts with egg whites and spices and bake them. In the last recipe, you sauté the nuts in butter, sugar, and spices until toasted. I hope to inspire you to create some of your own recipes, using an approach that tickles your fancy. So toss some nuts with oil or egg whites, bake them or sauté them, season them or sweeten them.

Although some of these techniques are mix and match, don't try to sauté a nut mixture that has been coated in egg whites. You'll end up with nuts that taste like they're coated with an egg-white omelet.

Dijon-Parmesan Almonds

These whole almonds are enhanced with Dijon mustard and Parmesan cheese with a hint of rosemary. These flavorful snacks are easy to make.

Preparation time: *5 minutes*

Cooking time: *20 minutes*

Yield: *4 cups*

4 tablespoons Dijon mustard	*¼ teaspoon black pepper*
2 tablespoons unsalted butter, melted	*¼ teaspoon salt*
1 teaspoon rosemary, crumbled between fingertips	*4 cups whole almonds, skin on*
	1 cup grated Parmesan cheese

1 Preheat the oven to 300 degrees. Line a jelly roll pan with parchment paper or aluminum foil; set aside.

2 Stir together the mustard, butter, rosemary, salt, and pepper in a medium mixing bowl. Add the almonds and stir to coat. Sprinkle the Parmesan cheese over the mixture and toss the almonds to coat them thoroughly with the cheese.

3 Spread the almonds in a single layer on the prepared baking sheet and bake for 10 minutes. Stir the nuts and bake for 10 minutes more. The almonds should be dry and lightly tinged with color, but not browned. Place the pan on a rack to cool completely. Store the almonds in an airtight container at room temperature for up to 2 weeks.

Tip: *I love the plastic bags with the zipper closures. They're more expensive than regular plastic bags, but much less expensive than plastic containers. These nuts are a perfect item to store in these bags, which are good for firm and/or dry items. Just make sure that you press out all the air before closing the bag.*

Per serving: Calories 251 (From Fat 195); Fat 22g (Saturated 4g); Cholesterol 9mg; Sodium 248mg; Carbohydrate 8g (Dietary Fiber 4g); Protein 10g.

Ginger-Orange Walnuts

These walnut halves are on the sweet side and are positively addictive. You can substitute an equal amount of pecan halves for variety.

Preparation time: *5 minutes*

Cooking time: *30 minutes*

Yield: *4 cups*

½ cup sugar	2 teaspoons ginger
½ teaspoon salt	2 egg whites
2 tablespoons grated orange zest	4 cups walnut halves

1 Preheat the oven to 300 degrees. Line a jelly roll pan with parchment paper or aluminum foil; set aside.

2 Stir together the sugar, salt, orange zest, and ginger in a small bowl; set aside.

3 Whip the egg whites in a separate medium bowl until foamy. Add the walnuts and toss to coat. Sprinkle the dry mixture from Step 2 over the nuts and toss to coat.

4 Spread the walnuts in a single layer on the prepared baking sheet and bake for 15 minutes. Stir the nuts — they'll be sticky — and bake for 15 minutes more. The walnuts should be dry and lightly tinged with color, but not browned. Place the pan on a rack to cool completely. Store the walnuts in an airtight container for up to 2 weeks.

Per serving: Calories 191 (From Fat 147); Fat 16g (Saturated 2g); Cholesterol 0mg; Sodium 80mg; Carbohydrate 10g (Dietary Fiber 2g); Protein 4g.

Hot 'n' Spicy Pecans

This recipe features pecan halves tossed and baked with sugar as well as cayenne. These are as hot as they are sweet, which makes for maximum snackability; they will appeal to hot and sweet lovers alike.

Preparation time: *5 minutes*

Cooking time: *10 minutes*

Yield: *2 cups*

2 tablespoons unsalted butter	*½ teaspoon salt*
2 cups pecan halves	*½ teaspoon curry powder*
3 tablespoons sugar	*¼ to ½ teaspoon cayenne*
3 tablespoons firmly packed light brown sugar	*¼ teaspoon black pepper*

1 Line jelly roll pan with parchment paper or aluminum foil; set aside.

2 Melt the butter in a heavy skillet. Add the pecans, toss to coat, and cook over medium heat for about 1 minute, stirring occasionally.

3 Meanwhile, combine the sugar, brown sugar, salt, curry, cayenne, and black pepper in a small bowl. Sprinkle the mixture over the nuts in the skillet, stirring well. Continue to cook until the sugars melt and caramelize, about 8 minutes. The mixture will start out grainy from the sugars and then turn shiny when it melts. Don't raise the heat, or the nuts and sugar will burn.

4 Spread the nuts in a single layer on the prepared pan. If the nuts lump together, break them apart by using two forks. Let them cool completely. Store the nuts in an airtight container at room temperature for up to 1 week.

Tip: *Those of you who like spicy dishes may find that this recipe isn't spicy enough to earn the moniker "hot 'n' spicy." Feel free to add the larger amount of cayenne if you're looking for some more zing. You'll also end up with a spicier recipe if you use fresh cayenne. When I tried this recipe with cayenne that had been sitting in my kitchen cabinet for a while, the pecans lacked bite. When I retested the recipe with new cayenne, the flavor went through the roof!*

Per serving: *Calories 250 (From Fat 201); Fat 22g (Saturated 4g); Cholesterol 8mg; Sodium 147mg; Carbohydrate 14g (Dietary Fiber 3g); Protein 3g.*

TIP

Easy flavored nuts

You can easily turn your favorite nut into a special treat to suit your taste. Simply take shelled, raw nuts and toss them in a heavy sauté pan, such as a cast-iron skillet, along with some butter, oil, or olive oil. Sprinkle with herbs or spices to your liking and toss and cook them for a few minutes, until the nuts become coated and lightly browned. Turn the nuts out onto a foil- or parchment-lined pan in a single layer until cooled. Pack in airtight containers. Here are some suggestions:

✔ Toss cashews with butter, curry powder, and cumin.

✔ Combine pecans with oil and chili powder.

✔ Toss walnuts in butter and season with salt and rosemary.

✔ Toast macadamia nuts, coat them with butter, add salt, and combine with flaked coconut. For great color and a chewy texture, add dried bits of mango.

✔ Combine mixed nuts with oil, soy sauce, garlic powder, and ginger.

✔ Combine mixed nuts with butter, a little sugar, and pumpkin pie spice. Cook until the sugar melts and coats the nuts.

I don't include amounts in the above recipes, so just use your judgment and start out conservatively. You can always add a little more salt or spice if you want to kick up the flavor a notch.

Pop Goes the Popcorn

When it comes to popping corn, you're probably used to eating either yellow or white corn, both of which are available in the supermarket in kernel form. I suggest that you buy yellow or white kernels in bulk bags or bottles in their raw state. Steer clear of microwave popcorns and other prepared packets because even the "lite" versions are overly salty and fat laden and they have a chemical taste. The popped corn that comes in a bag ready to eat is bad, too, except for some of the cheese popcorns, which can be delicious. Freshly popped corn is the way to go.

Popping corn: The kernels' not-so-secret recipes

There are two basic ways to pop corn. You can fix it the old-fashioned way, using oil in a pot on top of the stove. Or you can pop those kernels in a fat-free manner in an air popper.

Oil popping

Do you remember Jiffy-Pop? This is the popcorn that comes in an aluminum pie plate, which is covered with aluminum foil. It has a wire handle and when you place over a burner, the popcorn begins to pop and the aluminum foil on top expands many, many times its size. It looks cool, is easy to make, and was very possibly your childhood introduction to popping corn. The stovetop method below was possibly your next lesson in corn popping and the one I use often. To pop corn on the stove, you simply put a little oil in a pot, turn the heat to high, add the kernels, and — *voilà* — you have popcorn! But you can vary the flavor by using different cooking oils. For example, I sampled corn popped in flavorful olive oil a few years ago at a conference of culinary professionals. It tasted so good that it was like eating popcorn for the first time. The olive oil's rich flavor came shining through and transformed a fairly plain snack into a gourmet experience.

If you want to experiment with your popping oil, use a light olive oil first to see whether you like the taste. Then, if you do like it, graduate to an extra-virgin olive oil for the heartiest taste of all. You can try all sorts of flavored oils, too. Try a garlic, hot chili, or herb-flavored oil, such as basil oil.

Air popping

If you own an air-popper, you simply add corn kernels to the machine, and the hot air eventually pops the kernels. You place a bowl under the spout to catch the popped kernels. This method gives you fat-free popcorn, which is very low in calories and perfect for low-fat and low-calorie dieters. You can season it like any other popcorn. Follow the manufacturer's instructions for your particular popper.

Microwave popping

Microwave popcorn, consisting of premade packets of seasoned popcorn, is another option, but every type I've tried has been overly salty or chemical tasting. Gadgets on the market can help you make popcorn from scratch in the microwave, however. Microwave poppers are covered plastic containers with vents. You simply add the kernels and press a few buttons. Follow the manufacturer's instructions for your microwave oven.

Using an oil mister to season popped corn

After your corn is popped, you can eat it plain, but where's the fun in that? Melted butter is the classic topping, but for health and taste reasons, I urge you to try olive oil. To effectively apply olive oil to corn, you need an *oil mister,* which produces a fine mist of oil to spray on whatever you like, including popcorn! You can find them at almost any kitchenware store.

Herbed Popcorn

You can easily adapt this recipe to suite your own taste. I prefer to make it with herbes de Provence for a French touch, but feel free to experiment with your favorite herb or herb blend.

Preparation time: *5 minutes*

Cooking time: *5 minutes*

Yield: *14 cups*

¼ cup plus 2 tablespoons olive oil or vegetable oil (you can replace the 2 tablespoons oil with oil from an oil mister)

⅔ cup popcorn kernels

2 teaspoons herbes de Provence

¼ to ½ teaspoon salt

1 Place ¼ cup of the oil in a 3-quart pot. Add the popcorn kernels and place a lid on the pot, leaving it slightly askew so that the steam can escape. Place over high heat.

2 After about 1 minute, the popcorn will begin to pop. Place the lid on tightly and shake the pot gently back and forth until all the kernels are popped.

3 Pour the popped corn into a large serving bowl. Toss with the remaining 2 tablespoons oil or mist lightly or heavily (your choice) with the mister. In a small mixing bowl, combine the herbes de Provence and salt and stir to blend. Gradually sprinkle the dry mixture over the popcorn and toss until evenly coated. You can serve it immediately or hold it at room temperature for up to 3 hours.

Tip: *I suggest a range of salt for the recipes in this chapter because I prefer my popcorn less salty than the average person. If you are used to eating movie theatre popcorn or otherwise commercially prepared popcorn and like the way it tastes, then you'll probably want the larger portion of salt. Start with the lesser amount and adjust from there. You can always add more salt, but if you start with too much, there's no going back!*

Vary It! *Break out of the mold! Instead of the herbs in this recipe, try basil with some garlic salt, or toss with melted butter rather than oil and add dill or tarragon.*

Per serving: *Calories 87 (From Fat 56); Fat 6g (Saturated 1g); Cholesterol 0mg; Sodium 42mg; Carbohydrate 7g (Dietary Fiber 2g); Protein 1g.*

Parmesan-Garlic Popcorn

You like Parmesan cheese? You like garlic? Then this snack is for you. This boldly flavored popcorn is perfect to accompany an icy cold glass of beer while watching the game.

Preparation time: *5 minutes*

Cooking time: *5 minutes*

Yield: *14 cups*

¼ cup plus 2 tablespoons olive oil
or vegetable oil (you can replace
the 2 tablespoons oil with oil from
a mister)

⅔ cup popcorn kernels

1½ teaspoons garlic powder

¼ to ½ teaspoon salt

6 tablespoons grated Parmesan cheese

1 Place ¼ cup oil in a 3-quart pot. Add the popcorn kernels and place a lid on the pot, leaving it slightly askew so that the steam can escape. Place over high heat.

2 After about 1 minute, the popcorn will begin to pop. Place the lid on tightly and shake the pot gently back and forth until all the kernels are popped.

3 Pour the popped corn into a large serving bowl. Toss with the remaining 2 tablespoons oil or mist lightly or heavily (your choice) with the mister. In a small mixing bowl, combine the garlic powder and salt and stir to blend. Gradually sprinkle the dry mixture over the popcorn, tossing until evenly coated. Sprinkle the Parmesan cheese over all and toss again. You can serve it immediately or hold it at room temperature for up to 3 hours.

Tip: Garlic powder is not the same as garlic salt. Garlic powder is pure garlic in a finely powdered form. Look for it with the other herbs and spices. If you can find only garlic salt, start with ½ teaspoon and do not add the additional salt. Taste and keep adding more garlic salt, if necessary, to achieve the desired taste.

Per serving: Calories 100 (From Fat 64); Fat 7g (Saturated 1g); Cholesterol 2mg; Sodium 92mg; Carbohydrate 7g (Dietary Fiber 1g); Protein 2g.

Nibbles and Bits

In addition to nuts and popcorn, you may want to try serving some foods that you can eat by the handful. Pumpkin seeds are delicious, and I provide you with a recipe for toasting and seasoning them. The recipe uses purchased pumpkin seeds, sometimes called pepitas, which are small, green, and oval shaped. I also include a recipe for crispy, fried plantain chips. You can eat these as is or serve them with dip.

Spicy Tex-Mex Pumpkin Seeds

This recipe uses purchased, raw pumpkin seeds, which are the tender insides of the whole pumpkin seed.

Preparation time: *5 minutes*

Cooking time: *10 minutes*

Yield: *3 cups*

3 cups raw pumpkin seeds, without outer shell	1½ teaspoons oregano
2 teaspoons oil	1 teaspoon Tabasco
2 teaspoons Worcestershire sauce	½ teaspoon salt
1½ teaspoons chili powder	

1 Preheat the oven to 350 degrees. Have a jelly roll pan ready.

2 Place the pumpkin seeds in a bowl. Add the oil and toss to coat. Add the Worcestershire sauce, chili powder, oregano, Tabasco, and salt and toss thoroughly. Spread out in an even layer on the pan.

3 Bake for 5 minutes, stir the seeds, and bake for 5 minutes more, until they just start to lightly brown. Cool the pan on a wire rack until the seeds are at room temperature. Store up to 1 week at room temperature in an airtight container.

Tip: After the first 5 minutes of baking, you may hear some seeds popping in the oven. This reaction is normal. The seeds aren't exploding. Some of them just expand and become really crunchy.

Per serving: *Calories 80 (From Fat 35); Fat 4g (Saturated 1g); Cholesterol 0mg; Sodium 115mg; Carbohydrate 9g (Dietary Fiber 1g); Protein 3g.*

Plantain Chips

Plantains look like bananas, but they're a starchy fruit that you must cook before eating. Here they're sliced and fried for an unusual snack sometimes referred to as *tostones*. Like all chips, these are best made close to serving time. Look for plantains in the produce department of your supermarket or at Latin American grocers.

Preparation time: *5 minutes*

Cooking time: *20 minutes*

Yield: *4 cups*

2 large green plantains (about 1 pound each)	*Salt*
Vegetable oil	

1 Peel the plantains and, using a knife or a mandoline, slice thinly, about ⅛-inch thick. Drop the slices in a bowl of ice water and let them soak for 30 minutes. Pat dry with a clean dish towel or paper towels.

2 Heat 2 to 3 inches of vegetable oil in a deep, heavy pot or deep-fat fryer to 375 degrees. Fry the chips, about a dozen at a time, turning them occasionally with a slotted spoon. Fry until golden, about 3 minutes. Transfer to several layers of paper towels set on a work surface to drain and blot the excess oil. Repeat with the remaining slices. Season with salt and serve warm or at room temperature. They may be held at room temperature for a few hours. Serve mounded in a bowl or basket as a snack by themselves or with dips.

Tip: *Some high-quality black bean dips on the market are great with these chips. Look for the dip next to the salsa in your supermarket.*

Remember: *A mandoline is a gadget that helps produce perfectly even, thin slices from vegetables and fruit. See Chapter 3 for a complete treatise on this great kitchen tool.*

Per serving: *Calories 105 (From Fat 63); Fat 7g (Saturated 1g); Cholesterol 0mg; Sodium 38mg; Carbohydrate 12g (Dietary Fiber 1g); Protein 1g.*

Chapter 6

Tried and True: Classic Appetizers

● ●

In This Chapter

▶ Preparing crudités

▶ Making crab cakes

▶ Wrapping pigs in a blanket

▶ Giving eggs the deviled touch

▶ Stuffing mushrooms

▶ Feasting on shrimp cocktail

▶ Setting up a raw bar

● ●

Recipes in This Chapter

▶ Cheddar, Port, and Blue Cheese Ball

▶ Crab Cakes

▶ Deviled Eggs

▶ Spinach and Blue Cheese Stuffed Mushrooms

▶ Shrimp Cocktail with Two Sauces

▶ Mignonette Sauce

🎔 🥒 🍳 🍴 🌶 🥕

The word "classic" denotes that something is timeless — that it is a standard in its category. When it comes to classic American appetizers, almost everyone likes foods such as shrimp cocktail, deviled eggs, and veggies for dipping, and comes to expect them at events such as cocktail parties and picnics. This chapter is all about those types of classics. I present recipes that you should have at your disposal so that you're ready for any occasion.

Just like the classic little black dress or the pinstriped suit that fits in almost anywhere, classic foods are welcome in many situations. For example, if you know how to make a tasty cheese ball, you'll be ready for myriad occasions, whether it's a holiday family gathering or a potluck dinner with your neighbors.

Because this chapter is packed with recipes that suit so many occasions, I suggest that you read through it and refer to it when you need to whip up an appetizer. I'm sure that you'll find a recipe to suit your particular occasion.

Crudités

Crudités is a fancy word for the raw and lightly cooked vegetables that are usually served on platters and accompanied by dips. Pronounced kru-di-tay, these vegetables are always popular. It's an easy, one-word name for a whole assortment of vegetables. They provide color and texture and, without the dips, are low-calorie and lowfat choices for your guests.

I always serve crudités along with whatever else I'm serving. That way, people who are dieting can nibble along with everyone else. But don't limit your veggies to carrot and celery sticks and cherry tomatoes; offer some more interesting veggies, such as asparagus, sugar-snap peas, or radishes.

Washing those vegetables

When you bring your veggies home, you need to wash them first, before doing any other prep work. Some have been sprayed with pesticides and herbicides, and most of them have been handled by dozens of people and may have residual dirt from many sources. The dirty condition of your fresh produce may sound gross to you, but it's a problem that's easy to fix.

For years, cooks have simply washed their veggies in water, which I think is just fine. Scrub your veggies with a soft brush as you rinse them with water. (Use this brush only for washing vegetables; keep a separate brush for washing your dishes.) You can find vegetable scrubbers in just about any grocery or cookware store. They should be labeled as such. Or you can use any soft brush that's delicate enough to not bruise the veggie but firm enough to remove the dirt.

Prepping raw vegetables

To prepare raw vegetables, you really don't have to do much. Fresh veggies usually need only a little washing and scrubbing (covered in the previous section) and trimming or cutting (as described in the following sections) to show them off to their best advantage.

Try these veggies with your favorite dip (for a whole assortment of dips, see Chapter 7).

"Baby" carrots

The "baby" carrots found in most supermarkets aren't really baby carrots at all. They're actually grown-up carrots that have been whittled down to baby size. You can find them in 1- and 2-pound bags in most supermarkets, and they come ready to eat.

You can occasionally find real baby carrots, often at a farmer's market or specialty foods store in the summer and fall. If you can find 'em, try 'em. Otherwise, I think the "baby" carrots that are packaged in the regular supermarket are great. You pay a bit more for them, but there's no prep time and no waste, so I think they're worth it.

Belgian endive

Endive is a lettucelike green that you can find with the other types of lettuce in your supermarket. It's a pale yellow-green — almost white — with a bullet-shaped head. Simply wash and dry it, cut off the thick root end, and separate the leaves, or spears. The spears form a perfect scoop for dips, as shown in Figure 6-1.

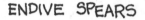

ENDIVE SPEARS

Figure 6-1:
Use endive spears as scoops for dips.

WHEN EACH LEAF IS SEPARATED FROM THE HEAD, THEY FORM A PERFECT SCOOP FOR DIPS.

Big carrots

Look for carrots with the lively green tops attached. These are usually the freshest. If the tops, or the carrots themselves, are limp, pass them by. The carrots should be a vivid orange and have a moist, stiff texture. A stiff texture gives you a crisp carrot, one of this vegetable's best qualities.

Some well-stocked markets now carry a maroon/burgundy carrot that is consistently really, really sweet. They're sometimes called beta carrots because they have a high level of beta carotene. This unusual vegetable is definitely worth checking out.

Here are two ways to prepare big carrots for the crudité platter:

✔ If the carrots are somewhat small and slender, wash and lightly peel them, trim off any rootlike appendage from the pointed end, and trim the green to about ½ inch. The portion that's left is the quintessential carrot — one that Peter Rabbit would have been proud to risk his neck for. The little bit of greenery that remains acts like a tiny handle and looks adorable, but make sure that you provide your guests a place to discard them, because you don't eat the greenery. Alternatively, you can remove all the green part so that the entire carrot is edible.

✔ If you're using larger carrots, wash and peel them and trim off both ends. Make ¼-inch-thick slices on a deep diagonal to create large ovals. These shapes add some variety to your crudité platter.

Celery

Celery is usually good year round. Look for bunches of celery that still have their leafy tops attached; these are usually the freshest. To prepare celery, remove any outer stalks that are bruised or damaged or look tough and stringy. Wash the innermost stalks, separating them gently from one another. Trim large, tough bottoms and leafy tops and cut the stalks into lengths suitable for finger food — about 3 to 4 inches. You may also cut them lengthwise to make thinner celery sticks.

Cherry and grape tomatoes

Cherry tomatoes can be served just as they are. All you need to do is give them a rinse. You can leave their tops on to use as little handles, if you like. In the summer, you can sometimes find yellow and orange cherry tomatoes, too. Grape tomatoes are relatively new. They're essentially the same size as the cherry tomatoes, but they have an elegant, oval, grapelike shape. Look for all these types of tomatoes in little plastic baskets in the produce department.

Cucumber slices

You need to consider a few things when it comes to cucumbers. In the summertime, good-quality cucumbers are easy to find. They're usually quite crisp and not wax coated. During the colder months, cucumbers can be flabby and so overwaxed that they're downright shiny, making them a not-so-great choice. If you're shopping for cucumbers at the time of year when you can't get the farm-fresh variety, look for the English hothouse cucumbers. These somewhat slender, super-long cucumbers are shrink-wrapped with plastic. You can usually find them right next to the other cucumbers. They have a thin skin and very few seeds, making them a good choice for crudité platters.

There are many ways to prepare cucumbers. Here's what to do with waxy winter cucumbers (a process you can see illustrated in Figure 6-2):

1. **Wash and scrub them a bit to remove any waxy coating.**

2. **Use a vegetable peeler to remove some strips of skin along the length of the cucumber, leaving some skin in between the exposed parts.**

   Each stripe will be about ½ inch wide. This technique makes this type of cucumber more pleasant to eat because part of the tough skin is gone and the cucumber has a decorative look.

3. **Remove the ends and slice into ¼-inch-thick rounds.**

   The slices should be thick enough so that they're not too floppy when you hold them. The little bit of skin left on also gives them some stiffness so that you can easily pick them up.

You can also peel the cucumber completely, trim the ends, and slice the cucumber once or twice crosswise and then a few times lengthwise into stick shapes.

STRIPED CUCUMBER ROUNDS

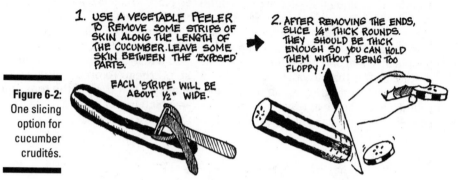

1. USE A VEGETABLE PEELER TO REMOVE SOME STRIPS OF SKIN ALONG THE LENGTH OF THE CUCUMBER. LEAVE SOME SKIN BETWEEN THE 'EXPOSED' PARTS.

EACH 'STRIPE' WILL BE ABOUT ½" WIDE.

2. AFTER REMOVING THE ENDS, SLICE ¼" THICK ROUNDS. THEY SHOULD BE THICK ENOUGH SO YOU CAN HOLD THEM WITHOUT BEING TOO FLOPPY!

Figure 6-2: One slicing option for cucumber crudités.

Here's a fancier way to present cucumbers. Cut very thick slices, about 1 to 1½ inches thick, and use a melon baller to remove part of the center of each slice. Now you have a circular depression that you can fill with softened goat cheese, thick dips, such as blue cheese (Chapter 7), or even purchased white-fish salad from the deli or smoked trout or salmon mousse, both of which you can find in many seafood markets. As an alternative, you can cut a cucumber in half lengthwise and then remove the seedy portion with a melon baller, as shown in Figure 6-3.

CUCUMBER CUPS

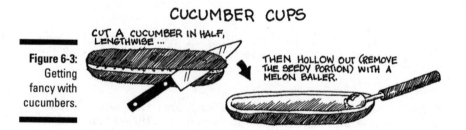

Figure 6-3: Getting fancy with cucumbers.

CUT A CUCUMBER IN HALF, LENGTHWISE ...

THEN HOLLOW OUT (REMOVE THE SEEDY PORTION) WITH A MELON BALLER.

Mushrooms

If you want mushrooms for your vegetable platter, look no farther than the regular white variety. You don't need exotics like shiitake or portobello mushrooms. Look for white button mushrooms that are light in color, blemish free, and no bigger than a walnut, preferably smaller. I simply wipe them clean with a damp cloth, making sure to remove any dirt clinging to them. Then simply trim off the end of the stem. Their color and shape add immensely to the visual presentation of a varied crudité platter.

Radishes

The most common radishes are the round red kind, which is what I discuss here. You might overlook radishes when shopping for vegetables because they're somewhat misunderstood. What do they taste like? What do you do with them? They're clean and crisp with a spicy peppery bite, which some people love and some find too strong. They add a taste and texture to your crudité platter that no other vegetable can, so try them! To prepare them, simply wash and lightly scrub them if they're dirty. Then trim off the tops and rootlike ends. You can leave the small ones — which have almost a heart shape — as is or make little roses, as shown in Figure 6-4.

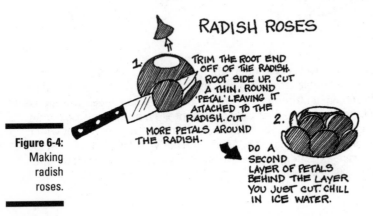

RADISH ROSES

1. TRIM THE ROOT END OFF OF THE RADISH. ROOT SIDE UP, CUT A THIN, ROUND 'PETAL' LEAVING IT ATTACHED TO THE RADISH. CUT MORE PETALS AROUND THE RADISH.

2. DO A SECOND LAYER OF PETALS BEHIND THE LAYER YOU JUST CUT. CHILL IN ICE WATER.

Figure 6-4:
Making radish roses.

You can store prepared radishes (as well as carrots and celery) in ice water in the refrigerator until needed. They stay nice and crisp for at least 3 days.

Scallions

These slender vegetables from the onion family are terrific raw. To prepare them for serving, give them a quick rinse and trim off the root end and about one-half to two-thirds of the greens. Leave some of the white bulbous end and some of the crisp green tops.

For a really pretty presentation, make vertical cuts into the green scallion tops and place the whole stalk in ice water. After a bit, the tops will curl back over on themselves and make a pretty shape. Drain before serving.

Snow peas and sugar snap peas

Both of these veggies add color and crunch to the crudité platter. When shopping for either type of pea, look for crisp, bright green pods. Simply rinse them, break off the stem end, and remove the tough string that goes along one side, as shown in Figure 6-5. They're ready to eat.

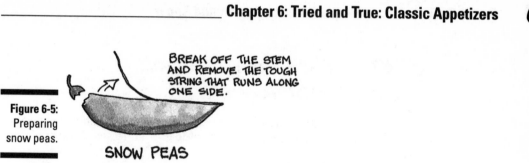

BREAK OFF THE STEM AND REMOVE THE TOUGH STRING THAT RUNS ALONG ONE SIDE.

SNOW PEAS

Figure 6-5:
Preparing snow peas.

Sweet peppers

Sweet peppers come in an assortment of colors — green, red, yellow, orange, and even chocolate brown and purple. You probably can find most of these peppers in your produce department. Simply wash and lightly scrub them if necessary and remove the core, as shown in Figure 6-6. Slice them in half and remove any seeds and the white flesh attached to the "ribs" of the pepper. Then slice them into thin or thick strips that are easy to hold and dip.

Green and red peppers are actually the same pepper. The red ones have just been allowed to ripen further and develop their characteristic color and sweetness.

How to Core and Seed a Pepper

1. cut out stem — twist and pull out
2. cut in ½ — remove membranes
3. Cut into lengthwise strips

Figure 6-6:
Coring and seeding a pepper.

Zucchini and yellow summer squash

Both of these types of summer squash make nice additions to the crudité platter. Whichever you choose, look for smaller ones with unblemished skin. Give them a quick wash, trim both ends, and then slice them about ¼-inch thick on a steep diagonal. You can also slice them as rounds or cut them into stick shapes.

Knowing when to serve what: Seasonal menu ideas

Crudités are a great appetizer to serve year round, but your choice of vegetables may vary somewhat. Here's a quick guide to what to serve when:

- **Year-round:** Broccoli, carrots, cauliflower, celery, bell peppers, cherry and grape tomatoes, endive, mushrooms, potatoes, and scallions.

- **Spring and summer:** Artichokes, asparagus (blanched), snow and sugar snap peas, zucchini, and yellow summer squash

- **Fall and winter:** Whatever looks good! Ask your produce supplier for suggestions. I find packaged "baby" carrots, hot-house cucumbers, broccoli, and tiny potatoes (steamed) to be reliable this time of year. In early fall, you can find almost any of the summer veggies, too.

Cheese Balls

I love a perfectly ripe cheese presented on a plate, but sometimes a cheese ball, made from one or more cheeses and other tasty ingredients, is the way to go. In some families, a cheese ball is reserved for holidays, but they're so easy to make. Why not give my recipe a go the next time you need a cheese appetizer?

The cheese ball recipe that follows is coated with toasted, chopped walnuts. Toasting nuts brings out their flavors and is a worthwhile technique to learn. It is also very easy.

Preheat the oven to 350 degrees. Spread the nuts in a single layer on a jelly roll pan and bake for about 5 minutes, stirring once. After 5 minutes, some nuts will already be toasted. You'll know when they're done because they'll just begin to be fragrant and will have turned a very light golden brown. Some nuts may take twice as long; the cooking time depends on the oil content of the nuts, so watch them carefully and rely on visual cues more than time. For instance, macadamia nuts are very high in oil and toast quite quickly. Also, the larger the pieces (such as whole nuts), the longer they will take to toast. Cool before chopping.

Cheddar, Port, and Blue Cheese Ball

The flavors of cheddar, port wine, blue cheese, and walnuts are all rolled into one, literally, in the form of the classic cheese ball. This is a great dish to make ahead. Kids love to play with food, so rolling the cheese ball in the nuts is a perfect way for them to help.

Preparation time: *5 minutes, plus 2 hours refrigeration*

Yield: *10 servings, or one 5-inch ball*

8 ounces full-fat cream cheese

5 ounces sharp cheddar cheese, grated

5 ounces blue cheese, crumbled

1 tablespoon port wine

½ cup walnuts, toasted and chopped

1 Mix the cream cheese, cheddar cheese, blue cheese, and port wine in the bowl of a stand mixer on low-medium speed, using the flat paddle attachment, until combined. Scrape onto a piece of plastic wrap, form into a ball, and refrigerate until firm, at least 2 hours or up to 4 days.

2 Roll in the walnuts and serve immediately.

Tip: *Serve with celery sticks, apple slices, and crackers. You can slice the apples ahead of time and place them in water with a little lemon juice (a mixture known as acidulated water) to keep them from discoloring.*

Vary It! *You can double this recipe and mold it into a large log rather than a ball. Simply double the ingredients, follow the original recipe instructions, and shape the mixture into a log about 9 inches long. It will serve twice as many people and is great for a buffet.*

Per serving: *Calories 228 (From Fat 185); Fat 21g (Saturated 11g); Cholesterol 50mg; Sodium 353mg; Carbohydrate 2g (Dietary Fiber 0g); Protein 9g.*

Crab Cakes in a Pinch

Have you ever eaten a fresh, steamed crab? It's a deliciously messy affair. You take a crab, slap it down in front of you on a paper-covered table, and whack it with a mallet. Then you dig in with your fingers to extract all the tender, flaky, sweet flesh. Although this is a classic American food experience that everyone should have at least once, it's probably not the best item to serve at an elegant dinner party. Crab cakes are more appropriate for such an occasion, and when it comes to my crab cakes, you don't have to kill or crack fresh crab yourself.

To make my crab cakes, I don't ask you to wrestle a live (or even departed) crab. Prepared crab is available in several different ways in your grocery store. Stay away from the canned variety, found near the canned tuna, for this dish. Just as canned tuna bears little resemblance to fresh tuna, canned crab doesn't hold a candle to fresh. (However, Chapter 7 includes a crab dip in which it's okay to used canned crab.)

Sometimes you can find frozen crab, which is okay, but the best prepared crabmeat is the kind found in the seafood department or at the fish store. It's usually packed in a small plastic container, and it has a good texture for crab cake purposes. Use this type for the following recipe. If it's labeled *lump* crabmeat, it's in big chunks. If it's called *flaked,* it is, well, flaked. Because you need it flaked anyway before mixing it with other ingredients, buy it either way.

Crab Cakes

The key to making tasty crab cakes is to use a high proportion of crab to other ingredients — let the crab shine on its own. Do not, I repeat, do not, add any salt to either the crab cakes or tartar sauce before tasting. Both of these dishes already contain a lot of sodium. However, if you can't find the Old Bay Seasoning, then you can season to taste with additional salt and pepper, too. Serve these crab cakes while they're still warm and accompany them with the Tangy Tartar Sauce. Don't forget the napkins.

Preparation time: *10 minutes*

Cooking time: *About 4 minutes per batch*

Yield: *About 24 crab cakes*

2 tablespoons prepared mayonnaise

2 tablespoons finely chopped flat-leaf parsley

1 tablespoon Dijon mustard

2 teaspoons Old Bay Seasoning

2 teaspoons lemon juice

1 scallion, minced

1 egg, whisked well

1 pound crabmeat, picked free of cartilage and flaked (shredded into small pieces with your fingers)

1 to 2 cups fresh bread crumbs (see Chapter 8 for instructions)

Pepper

Tabasco (optional)

⅓ cup clarified butter or vegetable oil

Tangy Tartar Sauce (see the following recipe)

1 Place the mayonnaise, parsley, mustard, Old Bay Seasoning, lemon juice, scallion, and egg in a mixing bowl and stir well to combine. Add the crabmeat and bread crumbs and stir just until combined. If you want a luxe, crab-filled version, use only 1 cup of bread crumbs. If you want to get a little more bang for your buck, use up to 2 cups of bread crumbs. Season with the pepper and a few dashes of Tabasco (if desired). Do not overmix, or the mixture will become compacted, resulting in heavily textured crab cakes.

2 Using about 2 tablespoons of the mixture for each crab cake, shape the crabmeat into small patties, about ½-inch thick and 1½ inches across. Heat about ¼ cup of clarified butter or oil in a heavy-bottomed sauté pan, or just enough to generously coat the bottom. Over medium-high heat, sauté the crab cakes, several at a time, for about 2 minutes, or until golden brown. Flip over and continue to cook until the other side is browned, about 2 minutes more. Add more clarified butter or oil as you cook subsequent batches, if necessary.

3 Transfer the crab cakes to paper towels to absorb excess oil and serve immediately with the Tangy Tartar Sauce. You also can make them ahead and reheat them in a 325-degree oven for a few minutes. Just place them on a sheet pan and bake until warmed through. (The heating time varies depending on whether or not they're straight out of the refrigerator.) Crab cakes may be held at room temperature for an hour and then reheated. Or you can place them on a tray, wrap them well with plastic wrap, and refrigerate them overnight. Rewarm before serving.

Tip: *Using clarified butter gives these crab cakes a rich, buttery flavor that accents the crab beautifully. Alternatively, you can use a neutral flavored vegetable oil, if you like.*

Vary It! *Made as suggested, these crab cakes are basically bite-size hors d'oeuvres. If you want to turn these into larger appetizers, do the following: Shape the crab cakes into larger patties, about 3 inches across; you'll get about 8 crab cakes. Toss some mesclun (which I describe in Chapter 11) with your favorite vinaigrette, place 2 warm crab cakes per person on top of a mound of the dressed salad on each plate, and add a dollop of the Tangy Tartar Sauce on the side. The contrast of the fresh vinegary greens, warm crab cakes, and creamy sauce makes a delicious starter.*

Tip: *Because of the bread content in the crab cakes, don't serve them before a meal that has a breaded component, such as breaded veal or breaded fish fillets.*

Per serving: *Calories 55 (From Fat 33); Fat 4g (Saturated 2g); Cholesterol 32mg; Sodium 153mg; Carbohydrate 1g (Dietary Fiber 0g); Protein 4g.*

Tangy Tartar Sauce

1½ cups mayonnaise (I like Hellman's)	1 tablespoon plus 1 teaspoon Dijon mustard
¼ cup chopped capers	1 tablespoon chopped shallot
¼ cup finely chopped flat-leaf parsley	2 teaspoons lemon juice

Stir all the sauce ingredients together in a bowl. Use immediately or pack into an airtight container and refrigerate until needed. You can make this sauce up to 2 days ahead.

Tip: *Although you can use the tartar sauce right away, the flavors meld and even improve with an hour's rest. If you can plan to make it ahead, do so.*

Per serving: *Calories 201 (From Fat 199); Fat 22g (Saturated 3g); Cholesterol 16mg; Sodium 305mg; Carbohydrate 1g (Dietary Fiber 0g); Protein 1g.*

Pigs in a Blanket

I daresay that I don't know anyone my age (having grown up in the '60s) who has not encountered pigs in a blanket. The recipe is comprised of those little hot dogs, called cocktail franks, that are about 2 inches long, and refrigerated crescent dinner roll dough. In brief, you separate the dough into triangles and cut each triangle into thirds lengthwise. Then you wrap the dough around the little dogs by placing the franks on the shortest end of the triangle and rolling them up. Bake them on an ungreased jelly roll pan at 375 degrees for about 12 minutes or until golden brown. Serve them speared with the requisite toothpicks and accompanied by ketchup, mustard, or a sweet sauce.

And if you invite Regis Philbin, of *Live with Regis and Kelly* fame, over for appetizers, include pigs in a blanket on your menu. I happened to catch him on TV one day saying, " If you invite me to a party, you should have pigs in a blanket. Just give me pigs in a blanket, but you've got to have the mustard."

Pigs in a blanket are such a part of the American landscape that to try and improve upon them would amount to culinary blasphemy. So I'm not even going to try. You can find more-complete recipes in old cookbooks from the '50s and '60s, and the Pillsbury Web site (www.pillsbury.com) has a recipe for pigs in a blanket called Sausage Snack Wraps. If you want a nostalgic treat, pick up some mini franks and biscuit dough and go to town.

If you're preparing a meal for kids, pigs in a blanket are usually popular. Don't forget the ketchup.

Hard-Cooked Eggs: Devilishly Delicious

Deviled eggs are a classic American appetizer that requires you to start with a perfect hard-cooked egg. At their simplest, deviled eggs are hard-cooked eggs with the yolks removed, flavored, and packed back in. But they offer so many more opportunities if you consider that the neutral egg is a perfect backdrop for a variety of flavor experiences.

Hard-cooked eggs lend themselves to flavors, both simple and exotic. Giving your deviled eggs some added pizzazz is relatively simple. Try any or all of the following. An assortment on a tray looks most inviting.

- Add herbs such as minced fresh tarragon, dill, or chives to the egg yolk.
- Give your eggs a sprinkling of curry powder rather than the parsley and paprika topping.
- Instead of mayonnaise, use sour cream, yogurt, or crème fraîche.
- Use mild softened goat cheese, such as Montrachet, in place of the mayonnaise.
- Instead of mustard, add some salsa and top with chopped cilantro.
- Use chutney instead of the mustard and add a tablespoon of currants or chopped nuts.
- Add minced, sun-dried tomatoes to the basic version.
- Add minced black olives, such as kalamata, to the original filling recipe.
- Add a sprinkling of crispy crumbled bacon to the filling.

The devil made me do it

The term *deviled,* sometimes spelled *devilled,* is used in the food world to describe a dish that has some hot seasonings, such as cayenne, mustard, or a hot paprika. Because hell is reportedly hot and the devil is its main resident, that's why recipes with hot seasonings often use the term "deviled."

Deviled Eggs

If you take care in cooking your eggs, you'll be rewarded with a tender white and a silky yolk, ready to be flavored. Each ingredient is important in this basic version of deviled eggs. Don't overlook the power of a little salt and pepper and a dash or two of Tabasco. Without them, these eggs will be bland.

If you're toting your eggs to a picnic or a potluck supper, you may want to consider buying a platter specifically designed for deviled eggs. These types of platters have oval indentations to help prevent the eggs from rolling around.

Preparation time: *15 minutes*

Cooking time: *10 minutes to cook, plus 12 minutes to rest*

Yield: *12 deviled egg halves*

6 eggs	*Salt and pepper to taste*
Lettuce, such as green leaf or red leaf (optional)	*Tabasco*
	Minced flat-leaf parsley for garnish
1 tablespoon mayonnaise	*Paprika for garnish*
2¼ teaspoons Dijon mustard	

1 Place the eggs in a pot and fill with enough cold water to cover the eggs by an inch. Place over medium-high heat and bring to a simmer, uncovered. Just when the water comes to a simmer, cover the pot and remove it from the heat. Let the eggs sit in the hot water for 12 minutes. Set a timer and don't let them sit any less or any more than 12 minutes.

2 Immediately drain the water out of the pot and run cold water over the eggs, refilling the pot several times to diffuse the heat. Let the eggs sit in the cold water until they're cool to the touch, about 5 minutes.

3 To peel, tap the rounded end of the egg against your work surface or rap firmly with a spoon to crack the egg, and return it to the pot of water. The water will seep in between the egg and the shell, making it easier to peel. Then, one by one, roll the eggs around on your work surface until they're cracked all over. Carefully peel the egg, discarding the shell. If the shell is stubborn, run the egg under cold running water to help remove it. At this point, you can put the eggs in a bowl, cover them tightly with plastic wrap, and refrigerate them for up to a day.

4 When you're ready to make the deviled eggs, slice each egg vertically, from top to bottom, and place the yolks in a small mixing bowl. They should pop out easily when you turn the egg half upside down over the bowl and give a little squeeze. Or you can gently scoop out the yolk with a spoon, being careful not to break the white. Place the whites, cut side up, on a serving platter. If desired, you can set them on a bed of curly lettuce to prevent them from rolling around.

5 Mash the yolks with a fork, add the mayonnaise and mustard, and mix well. Season with salt, pepper, and Tabasco and beat with a wooden spoon until light and fluffy.

6 Carefully spoon some filling into each egg white half, rounding the tops. Sprinkle with parsley and paprika and serve immediately, or cover them with plastic wrap and refrigerate up to 6 hours.

Vary It! *Pack the deviled egg mixture into a small resealable plastic bag and snip off one of the corners from the bottom of the bag. Seal the top closed and press the yolk mixture out of the hole and pipe decoratively into the egg white halves. If you have a pastry bag (see Figure 6-7), you can use that, too, fitted with a coupler and plain round or star tip.*

Per serving: Calories 47 (From Fat 32); Fat 4g (Saturated 1g); Cholesterol 107mg; Sodium 111mg; Carbohydrate 1g (Dietary Fiber 0g); Protein 3g.

Figure 6-7:
You can use a pastry bag and tips to fill deviled eggs.

Making Room for Stuffed Mushrooms

Mushroom caps make delicious containers for everything from sausage to crab to cheese. It was hard to pick one recipe as a basic stuffed mushroom recipe, but I decided to offer a veggie version so that you can add this to your vegetarian repertoire.

You don't need to buy fancy or exotic mushrooms — simple white mushrooms are fine. Try to find ones that are all about 2 inches in diameter. This way, they'll be easy to pick up with the fingers and eat, and they'll all cook for the same length of time.

Spinach and Blue Cheese Stuffed Mushrooms

These mushrooms are filled with spinach and blue cheese and are very easy to prepare. If you want to make your last-minute party preparations easier, take advantage of the several make-ahead options in this recipe.

Preparation time: *10 minutes*

Cooking time: *20 minutes*

Yield: *24 stuffed mushrooms*

3 tablespoons olive oil

1 cup finely chopped white or yellow onion

10-ounce package frozen chopped spinach, thawed and squeezed dry

Salt and pepper

24 white mushrooms, about 2 inches across

¼ cup crumbled blue cheese

2 tablespoons chopped, toasted walnuts

1 Place 1 tablespoon of the olive oil and the onion in a sauté pan and cook over medium heat until the onions are translucent, stirring occasionally, about 5 minutes. Add the spinach, stir to combine, and season with salt and pepper. You can make the filling the night before and refrigerate it in an airtight container, if desired.

2 Preheat the oven to 400 degrees. Clean the mushrooms by wiping them off with a damp cloth. Carefully remove the stems and discard them. (Or chop them up, sauté them, and add them to scrambled eggs.) If you snap the stems off with your fingers, the stems usually come off whole, including the piece nestled down in the cap. If you need to dig in with your fingertips to remove this part, do so, but make sure to keep the caps intact. Place the caps in a roasting pan, rounded side up, drizzle with the remaining 2 tablespoons olive oil, and season lightly with salt and pepper. Roast the mushroom caps for about 10 minutes. They should start to soften and exude juices. Transfer the mushroom caps to paper towels, rounded side up, to drain. Discard any liquid from the roasting pan and wipe dry. Place the mushrooms, rounded side down, back in the roasting pan. Now they're ready to be stuffed.

3 Stuff the mushrooms with the onion/spinach mixture and either proceed to Step 4 or cover the pan tightly with plastic wrap and refrigerate for up to 2 days.

4 Sprinkle the tops of the mushrooms with the crumbled cheese and chopped nuts. Place in the oven until they're warm all the way through, about 8 minutes. Serve immediately.

Vary It! *If you're in a hurry or your oven is in use, try heating the stuffed mushrooms in the microwave for about 3 minutes. The heating time will vary depending on the strength of your microwave.*

Tip: *In the ingredient list, I call for thawed spinach that has been squeezed dry, which means that you have to squeeze all the water out of it. To do this, take a clean dish towel,* place the thawed chopped spinach inside of it, wrap it up, and squeeze the spinach dry over the sink. Quite a bit of water will drain out. There is really no other truly effective way to remove all the water from the spinach. If you use paper towels, they'll fall apart, and you'll have little bits of paper towels in your spinach. If you place the spinach in a colander and press the water out with a wooden spoon, you won't get it as dry. So go squeeze your spinach! I'm giving you an excuse to play with your food, all in the name of performing a kitchen duty properly.

Tip: I like to serve these mushrooms by passing them, along with cocktail napkins, while they're still hot. If you set them out on a table, they'll chill down quite quickly and lose part of their appeal. Alternatively, you can set them out on a warming tray or in a small chafing dish.

Per serving: Calories 34 (From Fat 24); Fat 3g (Saturated 1g); Cholesterol 1mg; Sodium 54mg; Carbohydrate 2g (Dietary Fiber 1g); Protein 2g.

The Best Shrimp Cocktail

This section is dedicated to shrimp. I love shrimp. Guests love shrimp. Shrimp are special, and when you serve them, you make a statement to your guests that they're worth the effort and expense. Shrimp aren't cheap, so offering shrimp to your guests can signify a special occasion, or just that you think they're special! You should be aware of a few things when buying shrimp and also should become acquainted with a few techniques so that you can prepare and serve them to their best advantage. I spell out everything you need to know right here.

Buying shrimp

What size do you buy? How many shrimp per person? Fresh or frozen? You need to consider all these questions when buying shrimp. You may think that this a lot to know, but the following sections make your shrimp shopping trip (say that three times fast) as easy as possible.

Figuring out shrimp sizes: Is large shrimp an oxymoron?

Have you ever noticed that olives come in large, extra-large, and jumbo? They don't come in small, medium, and large. I guess they have fragile egos that must be protected. Not so with shrimp. They know that they're so fantastic that they don't have to hide behind such word play.

FYI: IQF

I hope the "IQF" in the title of this sidebar captured your attention. It simply means "individually quick frozen," a process that involves spreading out the food — such as shrimp or peas — in a single layer and flash-freezing them before packaging. IQF is used primarily with foodstuffs such as shrimp, fruits, and vegetables. You know how sometimes you pick up a bag of frozen blueberries and all the berries are separate and loose? Those are IQF. Blocks of frozen shrimp or peas are not IQF; they are, as you might expect, referred to as "block frozen."

The benefit of IQF is that the food usually retains its shape and integrity. You want your food to have integrity, don't you? Seriously, the food will be less bruised with IQF. Buy IQF if you can. Here's what to look for with IQF:

✔ Each shrimp, blueberry, or pea should be separate from the rest, with no large ice crystals.

✔ Large ice crystal formation indicates that somewhere along the way the food partially defrosted and was refrozen.

✔ If some of the food is in clumps, it, too, has been defrosted and refrozen.

However, they do come in various sizes, so you probably should become familiar with what the terms mean. You'll see labels such as "26/30's" or "U-15's." The former means that there are 26 to 30 shrimp per pound, while the later means that there are less than 15 shrimp per pound. They may also be labeled "medium" or "large," but these terms are much less accurate than the number identification system. So go by the numbers, if possible. If the numbers aren't out there for you to see, ask the fishmonger. He should be able to give you this information.

Deciding whether to buy fresh or frozen

There's a very simple answer to the question of whether to buy fresh or frozen shrimp. Basically, unless you live near a community that has fleets of shrimp boats, frozen is what you're going to find. But frozen shrimp are okay. The flash-freezing techniques that most fishermen use these days produce very high-quality shrimp and fish. This process, called IQF (for "individually quick frozen"), is described in the sidebar "FYI: IQF?"

Here are a few things to consider when buying shrimp:

✔ Non-frozen shrimp are probably defrosted, previously frozen shrimp, which should also be clearly labeled as such.

✔ Never refreeze shrimp that have been previously frozen.

> ✔ Shrimp, like any fish, should have a fresh, briny smell. Avoid shrimp that smells fishy.
>
> ✔ If a recipe calls for 1 pound of shrimp with the shell, you'll end up with ¾ pound shelled shrimp.

Some shrimp, especially shrimp found at wholesale suppliers and at some wholesale buying clubs, come in a large frozen block. It may seem heavy as a cinderblock, but in reality, these blocks usually weigh about 5 pounds. This can be an economical way to buy shrimp if you need that much. Use the whole 5 pounds at a time and don't try to partially thaw the block.

Defrosting shrimp

If you buy frozen shrimp in bulk from the seafood case or grab a bag from the freezer section of your supermarket, chances are that the shrimp will be IQF and, therefore, all separate from one another. Defrosting these types of shrimp is easy. Simply place the shrimp in a clean resealable plastic bag and place in a bowl filled with cold water. Rotate the bag occasionally until the shrimp defrost.

If you have to defrost a large block of shrimp, plan ahead and do it in the refrigerator. You want the shrimp to defrost slowly and gently. Place the block in a large bowl in the refrigerator overnight, or up to 2 days, until completely defrosted.

Resist the temptation to plunge any kind of frozen shrimp in boiling water or to soak it in hot water. These techniques will all but guarantee you tough, chewy shrimp.

Cleaning shrimp

Before cooking your shrimp, you need to do a little preparation. I briefly describe the deveining process here, but a diagram is worth a thousand words, so check out Figure 6-8, too.

1. **Hold each shrimp by the tail, using it as a handle.**

2. **Using the fingers of the other hand, pull off all of the legs and shell.**

   A tiny bit of shell will remain covering the tail; that's okay.

3. **Using a small knife, make a slit along the back (outer curve) of the shrimp, exposing the "vein," which looks like a dark string; remove the vein.**

4. **Rinse under cold water.**

Some shrimp come already deveined, even though they still have the shell on, thus making your job easier. Sometimes the vein is almost nonexistent or very light in color, so make sure that you find and remove it if it's there.

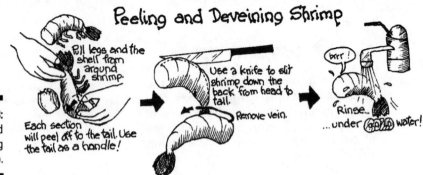

Figure 6-8:
Peeling and
deveining
shrimp.

Cooking and chilling shrimp

In the following recipe for Shrimp Cocktail with Two Sauces, you simply throw the shrimp in a pot of boiling water, briefly cook them, and then quick-chill them in ice water to halt the cooking. Cooking shrimp is just that easy, but here are a few things to remember:

✔ You can use plain water, but the bay leaf and peppercorns that I suggest adding to the water do add some flavor, so use them if you can.

✔ Don't actually let the shrimp "boil," which toughens them. While the shrimp are added to boiling water, you don't really want them to be bouncing around in rapidly boiling water, and you certainly don't want to cook them for very long. When you add the shrimp to the boiling water, the water stops boiling, which is just what you want. Then, as the temperature slowly comes back up, the shrimp will cook, which you can see because they slowly turn an opaque pink color.

When they're done, drain them immediately and then plunge them into an icy water bath as described in Figure 6-9. Doing so immediately stops the cooking process, further ensuring that your shrimpies will be tender.

Create an Icy Bath

1. Fill a large bowl half with cold water and half with ice cubes and place bowl in sink.

2. Immediately drain shrimp in a colander (or remove shrimp with a slotted spoon) and stir into ice water bath. Let stand for 2 minutes!

3. Drain shrimp, cover, and refrigerate if not using IMMEDIATELY!

Figure 6-9: Chilling shrimp.

Large supermarkets often have ready-to-go platters of shrimp, complete with cocktail sauce. In a pinch, those are better than going without if you really want shrimp for your party.

Getting down to business: Making shrimp cocktail

When I was a kid, I thought shrimp cocktail was the epitome of fancy food. It seemed elegant, partially because I found it only in restaurants. And it was always a little more expensive than any of the other appetizers, so I figured it must be good! Well, it always was tasty, and there's no reason you can't make it at home. I include a recipe for shrimp with the typical red tomato-based spicy cocktail sauce, and then for good measure, I add a creamy herb sauce for variety. Use one or both of the sauces as you see fit. Personally, I do think variety is the spice of life.

Shrimp Cocktail with Two Sauces

You can never go wrong when you give your guests a choice, so this recipe includes two sauces to serve with the shrimp: a classic red cocktail sauce and a creamy, garlicky herb sauce.

Preparation time: *30 minutes*

Cooking time: *10 minutes*

Yield: *10 servings*

12 cups water

1 large bay leaf

5 black peppercorns

2 pounds large shrimp, shell on (20 to 25 per pound)

1 Fill a large stockpot with the water, bay leaf, and peppercorns. Cover and bring to a boil over high heat. Add the shrimp, cover the pot, and bring back to a boil, stirring the shrimp up from the bottom once or twice so that they cook evenly. Boil the shrimp until they just begin to turn pink, about 2 to 3 minutes. Keep covered, turn off the heat, and let sit a few more minutes, until the shrimp are cooked through.

2 Drain in a colander and rinse under cold water to stop the cooking. Peel the shrimp. You may refrigerate them in an airtight container overnight.

3 To serve, arrange the shrimp in a bowl set in a larger bowl filled with ice. Serve with the Cocktail Sauce and the Fresh Herb and Garlic Sauce in separate bowls and provide lots of paper napkins.

Tip: *When figuring out the proper amount of shrimp to offer, the only thing that you can count on is that the more shrimp you serve, the more your guests will eat. Shrimp is one of those dishes where a bottomless bowl is necessary, but not attainable. Figure about 4 shrimp per person and hope for the best. Some folks will want more, but your guests will be thrilled to have had any at all, so you come out ahead.*

Per serving: *Calories 55 (From Fat 5); Fat 1g (Saturated 0g); Cholesterol 108mg; Sodium 124mg; Carbohydrate 0g (Dietary Fiber 0g); Protein 12g.*

Cocktail Sauce

½ cup chili sauce

1 tablespoon horseradish

1½ teaspoons lemon juice

Salt and pepper to taste

Whisk together all the ingredients in a bowl. Cover with plastic wrap and refrigerate for at least 6 hours for the flavors to develop.

Per serving: *Calories 15 (From Fat 0); Fat 0g (Saturated 0g); Cholesterol 0mg; Sodium 245mg; Carbohydrate 4g (Dietary Fiber 0g); Protein 0g.*

Fresh Herb and Garlic Sauce

⅔ cup mayonnaise

⅔ cup sour cream

1 tablespoon minced garlic

1 tablespoon minced fresh chives

1 tablespoon minced flat-leaf parsley

1 tablespoon minced fresh tarragon

2 teaspoons freshly squeezed lemon juice

Salt and pepper to taste

Stir together all the ingredients in a small bowl. Cover with plastic wrap and refrigerate for at least 1 hour for the flavors to develop.

Simplify: *You can always find fresh parsley, so use that, but if you can't find fresh chives or tarragon, consider the following. Substitute 1 tablespoon minced scallion for the chives and substitute 1 teaspoon dried tarragon for the 1 tablespoon of fresh tarragon. Or, for the chives, you can sometimes find dried chives where bulk herbs are sold, and they're really quite good. Use tablespoon for tablespoon as called for with fresh herbs.*

Per serving: *Calories 141 (From Fat 135); Fat 15g (Saturated 4g); Cholesterol 16mg; Sodium 151mg; Carbohydrate 2g (Dietary Fiber 0g); Protein 1g.*

Bellying Up to the Raw Bar

Some restaurants, usually ones near the coast or in larger metropolitan areas, specialize in serving oysters and clams on the half shell. A selection of raw shellfish, as well as some cooked shrimp, is often collectively referred to as a "raw bar." Restaurants are perfectly set up to serve this kind of appetizer because they have a good relationship with their seafood vendor, ensuring the freshest seafood possible, and they know how to keep the shellfish in peak condition. All these things are important when serving raw shellfish.

Presenting your own raw bar at home is simple to do. Just make sure to buy your seafood from a reputable fishmonger. I suggest shopping at an independent seafood market rather than at a supermarket seafood department. Wherever you shop, ask ahead of time when the store will have a fresh delivery of the items you want and then plan your purchases accordingly. With any kind of seafood, whether you plan to serve it raw or cooked, the fresher the better.

Buying fresh shellfish

If you make your own raw bar, you must buy the freshest shellfish possible. I discuss shrimp earlier in this chapters, and because you'll be cooking the shrimp, buying frozen is perfectly okay. But for clams and oysters, the approach is a bit different. Here are some tips:

- ✔ Shellfish is best served raw during the winter months; they spawn during the summer months, and some aficionados think that they have a poorer texture at this time. An old saying warns against eating oysters in any month without an *R* in it — in other words, May through August aren't great times to indulge. But this very old saying may no longer apply now that refrigeration is more plentiful and better than it was when the saying was made popular. In fact, there's nothing better than sitting seaside on a dock during a summer sunset while slurping raw clams and oysters and sipping a cocktail, but I digress.

- ✔ Many varieties of oysters and clams are available in the United States, and devotees have their favorites. Again, ask the fish seller for suggestions for your raw bar.

- ✔ If a store specializing in seafood is located near you, definitely do your shopping there. If not, you may have to make do with the supermarket seafood department. Either way, ask what day the store gets fresh deliveries of the items you're looking for. Then shop and serve on those days. Tell your grocer or fishmonger that you plan to serve your seafood raw and ask for guidance. Believe me, your seafood supplier wants you to be happy and come back, so he'll probably be truthful in his assessment of his store's product. No one wants a customer to fall ill from a bad clam.

- ✔ If you need extra help with shucking the shellfish, ask the fishmonger to give you a mini-tutorial. He should be able to pick up a clam or oyster and show you how to do it. I describe the process in the section "Shucking clams and oysters," later in this chapter.

- ✔ Ask the fish seller to package the seafood with a bag of crushed ice to keep it cold on the way home.

- ✔ As soon as you get home, place the seafood in the refrigerator and keep it there until you're ready to shuck and serve. The seafood probably will be packed in a heavy-duty paper bag, which is fine for brief storage. If the seafood is in plastic bags, remove it from the plastic bags as soon as you get home, place it in a bowl covered with a damp towel, and refrigerate.

Choosing oysters

Four major kinds of oysters are available, and you may be lucky enough to find more than one kind at your seafood market. Each kind has its fans. Here are the individual species you may come across:

- ✔ **Eastern:** Blue Point, Malpeque, and Wellfleet.
- ✔ **Pacific:** Kumamoto, Snow Creek, and Penn Cove.

✔ **European flat:** Belon and Wescott.

✔ **Olympia:** These are the only oysters native to the West Coast of the United States.

The term "Eastern" does indeed refer to the fact that those types of oysters are from the eastern seaboard and are most often found on the east coast of the United States. Likewise, Pacific oysters are found most often on the west coast of the United States. My suggestion is to eat oysters that are indigenous to your region, if possible, because they're usually the freshest.

The exception to this rule is that occasionally you may find a fish market that caters to the oyster lovers out there and has a selection of oysters from around the globe. If the market can vouch for the oysters' freshness, then go ahead and indulge.

When in doubt, buy the freshest oysters available.

Choosing clams

If you're going to eat raw clams, look for the hard-shell variety. Soft shell clams are usually cooked and are the clams you eat when you order "steamers." Hard-shell clams are categorized by size, with littlenecks being the smallest and cherrystones being the largest you would ever want to eat raw. (Save the larger clams, called quahogs, for chowdas, er, I mean chowders.) I like both littlenecks and cherrystones and suggest you start with those. Manila clams, a good type to eat raw, are the size of littlenecks and are a particular kind in that size category. Mahogany clams, which have a gorgeous golden brown color, are usually the same size as cherrystones and, again, are a specific type of that size.

No matter what type of clams you're going to eat, about an hour before you need them, place them in a bowl or bucket of water that has a handful of cornmeal added to it. Doing so encourages the clams to spit out any grit they're holding inside.

Assembling your raw materials

If you want to serve a mini raw bar at home, you can do it successfully if you follow a few pieces of advice. Although you do have to be careful when handling raw shellfish, a raw bar actually comes together easily and quickly, and you get a big wow factor out of the presentation. (See Figure 6-10 for a look at how to set up your raw bar.) The following is an overview of how to put a raw bar together:

✔ Start with the largest deep-rimmed platter or pan you can find.

✔ Fill up the container with crushed ice.

✔ Make sure that whatever platter or pan you use is deep enough to hold the water as the ice melts. I know you probably won't go to such measures, but when I was catering a lot, a metalworker made a large rectangular galvanized metal tray, with deep sides, for me. In the back of it, right along the bottom edge, he drilled a hole large enough to accommodate a hose. Then, after I set up the buffet table, the hose drained into a large bucket beneath the table, where no one could see it. The water from the melting ice drained away as it accumulated. If you're adventurous enough to be hosting a very large party and can figure out a way to rig something up like this, then by all means, go for it. You also can ask your local rental company whether it has anything like this that you could rent for the day.

✔ Ask the fishmonger for some seaweed to act as a bed for the seafood. Simply arrange it here and there on top of the ice. You don't absolutely need seaweed, but it does look cool (and not just because it's on ice).

✔ Scrub and shuck the clams and oysters (explained later in this chapter) and place the "on-the-half-shell" seafood all over the platter.

✔ Place some cooked shrimp on the platter, too. You may even want to add cooked crab legs, which you can find in some fish stores. Use the same dipping sauces for both the shrimp and the crab.

✔ Tuck lemon wedges here and there.

✔ Include a bowl of cocktail sauce as well as the Mignonette Sauce. (See the recipe later in this chapter.)

✔ Have a bottle of Tabasco and a pepper mill handy.

✔ Offer small plates, cocktail napkins, and, if you have them, cocktail forks.

✔ Demonstrate to your guests how to enjoy the raw bar: Take a clam or oyster, add a dash of Tabasco, squeeze on some lemon and/or add a little Mignonette Sauce, and slurp it down! The cocktail sauce goes great with the shrimp and crab.

✔ The whole shebang can sit out for 1 hour for leisurely slurping.

Shucking clams and oysters

Most shellfish have a little grit attached, so before you shuck them (as shown in Figure 6-11), wash and scrub the shells with a medium-stiff brush. Then follow my shucking instructions:

1. **Place the oyster or clam on a thick or folded cloth towel in the palm of your hand. Place the oysters rounded side down.**

2. **Insert a small, stiff, sturdy knife, preferably an oyster knife, near the hinge of the shell, pry the top shell off, and discard it. (A clam knife is safer because it's built so that it won't snap in two or cut you as easily.)**

For oysters, slip the knife underneath the oyster to dislodge it from its shell. Remove any small shell pieces that have flaked off.

For clams, first move the knife underneath the top shell to dislodge any meat sticking to it. Scoop the knife underneath the clam to dislodge it from the bottom and then cut the "neck" skin and remove.

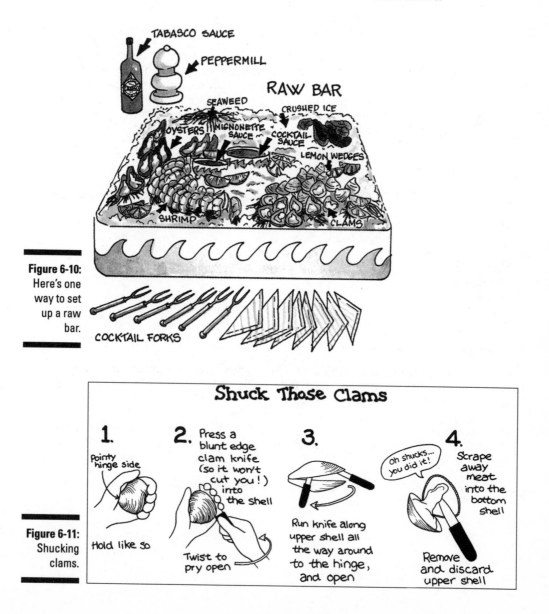

Figure 6-10: Here's one way to set up a raw bar.

Figure 6-11: Shucking clams.

You do need to shuck the shellfish yourself when you're serving them raw. For safety reasons, you can't ask your fishmonger to do it ahead of time. It is best to serve oysters and clams as soon as possible after shucking. If you're serving them on ice, you can do this up to one hour ahead.

Saucing things up

A perfectly fresh, briny raw clam or oyster is a thing of beauty, but a little embellishment can add greatly to the experience. Mignonette sauce is the classic French accompaniment. It is basically a flavored vinegar. The acidic tang provided from the vinegar complements the rich, velvety texture and taste of the shellfish beautifully. It is extremely easy to make and worth offering with your shellfish.

Mignonette Sauce

This is a classic sauce to eat with raw oysters. Although it would be an unconventional usage, try it with raw clams, too.

Preparation time: *10 minutes*

Yield: *½ cup*

½ cup red wine vinegar

2 tablespoons minced shallots

1 tablespoon minced flat-leaf parsley

Salt to taste

Coarsely cracked pepper to taste

Combine all the ingredients. Don't skimp when seasoning with the salt and pepper. Place a tiny bit on an oyster and slurp it down! Serve immediately or refrigerate the sauce in an airtight container overnight.

Tip: *You need very coarsely cracked pepper for this sauce. If your pepper mill doesn't allow you to adjust the coarseness, place black peppercorns in a heavy plastic bag, set on a work surface, and whack with a hammer until they're coarsely crushed.*

Per serving: *Calories 4 (From Fat 0); Fat 0g (Saturated 0g); Cholesterol 0mg; Sodium 147mg; Carbohydrate 1g (Dietary Fiber 0g); Protein 0g.*

Chapter 7

Dips and Dippers

In This Chapter

▶ Dishing up delicious dips
▶ Designing delectable dippers

*W*hat's a party without a dip? I take you far beyond that onion dip made from dry soup mix. I have an onion dip for you that's so delicious you'll never go back to the old kind. And I also have guacamole, hummus, a fresh salsa, and a selection of hot dips that will be the talk of your next party.

If you have dips, then you need dippers — those things you use to sample the dips. Sure, you can always serve store-bought potato chips or pretzels, but why not wow your guests with homemade potato chips, corn chips, and bagel chips. I explain how to make all of them in this chapter.

Dip-itty Do-Dah, Dip-itty Yea

This section may become the most popular in the book because it has great recipes that you'll probably come to rely on whenever you entertain. Check here for recipes such as The Best Onion Dip, Blue Cheese Dip, Guacamole, and more.

The Best Onion Dip

Are you still making onion dip from dry soup mix? Toss it out, pick up a bunch of onions, and prepare this dip instead. It's easy; you're gonna cook the onions, combine them with sour cream, season, and — voilà! — homemade onion dip that's light years ahead of the packaged kind.

Preparation time: *5 minutes*

Cooking time: *30 minutes*

Yield: *1¼ cups dip*

2 cups chopped yellow onions	*1 cup sour cream*
3 tablespoons light olive oil	*Salt and pepper*

1 Cook the onions in the olive oil over medium heat in a heavy-bottomed sauté pan until they're a rich golden brown, stirring frequently. Be patient; the onions need to caramelize and turn a deep golden brown. Caramelization is what happens when the natural sugars in the onions cook, helping to turn the mixture into a golden brown color.

2 Cool the onions to room temperature and then fold in the sour cream. Season liberally with salt and pepper. You may serve immediately or store it in an airtight container up to 3 days. The flavor actually improves if it sits overnight. Serve with an assortment of crudités (raw vegetables) and chips. (See Chapter 6 for more about crudités.)

Tip: To turn this dip into a lowfat recipe, substitute no-fat sour cream.

Vary It! Season the dip with the following herbs to give it an international flair: a pinch or two of curry powder for an Indian touch, herbes de Provence (which I describe in Chapter 3) for a taste of France, and a little basil or oregano for an Italian flavor.

Per serving: *Calories 94 (From Fat 80); Fat 9g (Saturated 4g); Cholesterol 10mg; Sodium 71mg; Carbohydrate 3g (Dietary Fiber 0g); Protein 1g.*

Guacamole

Almost everyone has had some version of this classic Mexican avocado relish. What makes a great guacamole? Ripe avocados and restraint with additional ingredients.

Preparation time: *15 minutes*

Yield: *2½ cups*

3 medium-sized ripe Haas avocados (about 1¼ pounds total)

1 fresh jalapeño pepper

¼ cup diced onion

¼ cup finely chopped fresh cilantro

1 to 2 tablespoons lime juice

Salt to taste

1 Cut the avocados in half lengthwise around the large center pit. Twist apart and discard the pit. Cup each avocado half in your palm and, using a butter knife, make a ½-inch crosshatch pattern in the avocado; take care not to slice through the skin. Using a teaspoon, scoop the avocado dices into a medium mixing bowl.

2 Slice the jalapeño lengthwise and remove the seeds and the ribs of pepper. Mince and add to the avocado along with the onion and cilantro. Toss to combine, coarsely mashing the avocado with a wooden spoon.

3 Season with the lime juice and salt. Letting the dip sit for at least 30 minutes before serving improves the flavor but isn't necessary. Press a sheet of plastic wrap directly on the surface of the guacamole while it is sitting to minimize discoloration. You can use the guacamole immediately or store it in an airtight container for up to 4 hours. You can store it longer (up to 8 hours), but the flavor won't be as good and the color will darken, making the whole dish less appealing.

Per serving: *Calories 43 (From Fat 34); Fat 4g (Saturated 1g); Cholesterol 0mg; Sodium 30mg; Carbohydrate 3g (Dietary Fiber 2g); Protein 1g.*

Seven-Layer Southwestern Dip

I bet you've encountered this dip at parties. It's a delicious layered creation of refried beans, sour cream, cheese, avocado, and tomatoes. How can you go wrong?

When selecting refried beans, remember that they're not all created equal. Some contain lard, which gives them a certain flavor. You may or may not like that flavor, but regardless, they're full of fat that you don't need. Look for ones labeled fat-free or vegetarian. I think they work best.

Preparation time: *10 minutes*

Yield: *10 servings*

2 cans (16 ounces each) refried beans, preferably vegetarian

1¼-ounce package seasoning mix

1½ cups sour cream

2 cups shredded cheddar cheese

4 ripe Haas avocados, cut into ½-inch dice

2 tablespoons lime or lemon juice, bottled or fresh

3 large tomatoes, seeded and chopped

½ cup pitted, sliced black olives

4 scallions, thinly sliced

Corn chips

Crudités

1 Stir together the refried beans and taco seasoning mix in a small bowl to combine. Using a rubber spatula, spread the bean mixture in a 10-inch deep-dish pie plate or a dish of a similar size. Top with a layer of sour cream, spreading to cover the refried beans. Sprinkle the cheese over the sour cream in an even layer.

2 Toss the avocados with the lime juice in a small bowl and sprinkle over the cheese. Top with a layer of diced tomatoes, followed by the olives and scallions. You can serve the dip immediately or cover it with plastic wrap and refrigerate it overnight. Bring to room temperature before serving. You an also zap this in a microwave for about 3 minutes (more or less, depending on your machine) if you want a hot dip. Serve with corn chips, and crudités if you like.

Tip: *The taco seasoning adds a lot of flavor, including salt, to this recipe. If you use chips for dipping, some of them are also very salty, resulting in an unhealthy dosage of sodium in your diet. Try unsalted corn chips for a change of pace.*

Tip: *Cheddar cheese is available in several varieties. You can find orange and pale yellow cheeses as well as mild and sharp flavors. I prefer sharp orange cheddar for this dip, but any type works well.*

Per serving: *Calories 384 (From Fat 234); Fat 26g (Saturated 11g); Cholesterol 39mg; Sodium 979mg; Carbohydrate 27g (Dietary Fiber 12g); Protein 14g.*

Pico de Gallo

This fresh-tasting salsa is colorful and easy to make. Use the best-tasting tomatoes you can find; it makes a difference. By the way, the name *pico de gallo,* literally translated, means "beak of the rooster." Well, all I can tell you is that a rooster's beak is red and so is this fresh salsa. Isn't that cool?

Preparation time: *10 minutes*

Yield: *4 cups*

6 medium, ripe tomatoes

1 fresh jalapeño pepper

½ cup diced yellow or white onion

½ cup diced red onion

½ cup minced fresh cilantro

¼ cup lime juice

Salt to taste

1 Seed the tomatoes as follows: Slice them in half crosswise and squeeze the halves over the sink to release the seeds. Scrap out any stubborn seeds with your fingers. Chop the seeded tomatoes into ¼-inch dices and place in a medium-size mixing bowl.

2 Slice the jalapeño lengthwise and remove the seeds and ribs of pepper. Mince and add to the tomatoes. Add the onions and cilantro to the mixture. Add the lime juice and toss. Season with salt. Letting the salsa sit for at least 30 minutes before serving improves the flavor but isn't necessary. You can use the salsa immediately or store it in the refrigerator in an airtight container for up to 3 days.

Per serving: *Calories 5 (From Fat 0); Fat 0g (Saturated 0g); Cholesterol 0mg; Sodium 20mg; Carbohydrate 1g (Dietary Fiber 0g); Protein 0g.*

Hummus

This creamy, tangy, pureed chickpea dip works as well with raw veggies as it does with pita bread. Look for cans labeled chickpeas or garbanzo beans; they're the same thing. With canned beans, you can make the recipe right away because the beans are already cooked and ready to use. By the way, I'm not a fan of overly salted foods, but trust me, this dish needs at least some, so don't skip it. Just taste as you go so that you don't overdo it.

Preparation time: *10 minutes*

Yield: *3 cups*

2 cans (15 ounces each) chickpeas

3 garlic cloves

¼ cup lemon juice

2 tablespoons tahini

Salt to taste

1 Drain the chickpeas, reserving the liquid. Set the chickpeas and liquid aside.

2 Place the garlic cloves in a food processor fitted with a metal blade and pulse on and off until the garlic is minced. Add the chickpeas, lemon juice, and tahini and process the mixture until smooth. Add the reserved liquid a tablespoon at a time if needed to make a smooth fluid paste. You will most likely need some of the liquid.

3 Season with salt. Letting the hummus sit for at least 30 minutes before serving will improve the flavor but isn't necessary. Serve the hummus immediately or store it in an airtight container and refrigerate for up to 3 days.

Tip: *Tahini, which is a sesame paste, is similar to peanut butter in texture. It is used frequently in Middle Eastern cuisine, and nothing can duplicate its unique, nutty taste. Look for it in your supermarket where the other ethnic ingredients are stocked.*

Tip: *My Mom was an expert hummus maker. Although her version was untraditional, it was incredibly flavorful. She added about four times the usual amount of tahini, twice the usual amount of lemon juice, and a good-size dose of cayenne. She occasionally stirred in some minced parsley right before serving, and she almost always floated a little extra-virgin olive oil on top and a sprinkling of paprika. My point is that she made the dip her own, and you should, too. This dip is truly a sum of its parts, so feel free to play around with the proportions and come up with a hummus that tickles your taste buds.*

Per serving: *Calories 29 (From Fat 9); Fat 1g (Saturated 0g); Cholesterol 0mg; Sodium 96mg; Carbohydrate 4g (Dietary Fiber 1g); Protein 1g.*

Roasted Eggplant Dip

The simple technique of roasting whole eggplant in an oven at high heat lends a smoky flavor to this easy dip.

Preparation time: *10 minutes*

Cooking time: *1 hour*

Yield: *About 2 cups*

4 pounds purple eggplant

3 garlic cloves

4 teaspoons lemon juice

1 tablespoon tahini

1 tablespoon light olive oil (optional)

Salt to taste

Fresh flat-leaf parsley, chopped (optional)

1 Preheat the oven to 400 degrees. Line a baking sheet with foil. Prick the eggplant in a few places with a fork or knife and place on the baking sheet. Bake for 50 to 60 minutes or until easily pierced with a knife. The inside should be completely soft. Let the eggplant cool. Scoop the flesh out and place in a colander set in the sink to let any excess liquid drain off.

2 Meanwhile, place the garlic cloves in the bowl of a food processor fitted with the metal blade. Pulse on and off until minced. Add the eggplant pulp along with the lemon juice and tahini. Pulse on and off just until smooth. Add the olive oil, if desired, to obtain a richer dip. Season with salt.

3 To serve, present in a bowl along with pita bread. Sprinkle with the chopped parsley right before serving, if desired. Serve the dip immediately or store it in an airtight container in the refrigerator for up to 3 days.

Remember: *You can find tahini in your supermarket along with the other ethnic ingredients or in natural food stores.*

Per serving: *Calories 36 (From Fat 7); Fat 1g (Saturated 0g); Cholesterol 0mg; Sodium 40mg; Carbohydrate 8g (Dietary Fiber 3g); Protein 1g.*

Blue Cheese Dip

This easy-to-make dip works well with French bread, crudités, or slices of fruit, such as apples and pears. Grapes on toothpicks work well, too. If you have sour cream in the refrigerator, use that. If you have yogurt, stir that in. Both are equally good, but the yogurt version is a bit tangier.

Preparation time: *10 minutes*

Yield: *About 2 cups*

8 ounces Neufchâtel cheese, at room temperature	*¼ cup finely chopped scallions*
4 ounces blue cheese	*French bread*
⅔ cup sour cream or yogurt	*Crudités*
¼ cup mayonnaise	*Fruit*

1 Place the Neufchâtel cheese and the blue cheese in a mixing bowl and mash together with a wooden spoon. Work the mixture until smooth and stir in the sour cream, mayonnaise, and scallions.

2 To serve, present it in a bowl and accompany with sliced French bread, crudités, and fruit. You can serve the dip immediately or store it in an airtight container in the refrigerator for up to 3 days.

Tip: *Neufchâtel cheese is cream cheese with less fat. It is a lighter, creamier version of cream cheese that you can find next to the regular cream cheese in the supermarket dairy case.*

Tip: *If offering slices of apples and pears, which I suggest you try, here's how to make sure that they don't turn brown. Fill a bowl with a quart of water and add 1 tablespoon lemon juice. Use ripe but firm fruit and slice into ¼-inch-thick slices with the skins on. Add the fruit slices to the water as you go. Let the fruit soak until needed and then dry before serving. The acid in the lemon juice prevents the fruit from discoloring.*

Vary It! *Toasted walnuts go fantastically well with blue cheese. For a nice variation, top this dip with ½ cup chopped, toasted walnuts. Or sandwich some dip between two walnut halves and set them out as finger food.*

Per serving: *Calories 106 (From Fat 89); Fat 10g (Saturated 5g); Cholesterol 22mg; Sodium 185mg; Carbohydrate 1g (Dietary Fiber 0g); Protein 3g.*

Cheese Fondue

How can you resist a hot, melted cheese dip? And, you don't even need a fondue pot to make it! (See the suggestions earlier in this section on fondue.) Kirsch, a cherry liqueur, is traditional in many fondue recipes, but you can substitute apple cider if you want.

Preparation time: *10 minutes*

Cooking time: *5 minutes*

Yield: *4 to 6 servings*

1 garlic clove, peeled and sliced in half lengthwise

1 cup dry white wine

2 teaspoons lemon juice

10 ounces Gruyère cheese, shredded (about 2⅔ cups)

10 ounces Emmentaler cheese, shredded (about 2⅔ cups)

4 teaspoons cornstarch

1 tablespoon kirsch or apple cider

2 loaves crusty French bread (each approximately 24 inches long and 12 to 14 ounces), cubed so that each piece has some crust

1 Rub the inside of a heavy-bottomed pot with the garlic clove halves, using the cut sides against the pot. Discard the cloves. Add the wine and lemon juice to the pot and bring to a low simmer over medium heat.

2 Toss the cheeses together with the cornstarch and add a little at a time to the hot liquid. Do this in about three or four batches, stirring all the while and allowing each batch to melt before adding the next. After the entire mixture is smooth, stir in the kirsch. Transfer the fondue to a fondue pot, if using, and set over a fuel source. If you're not using a fondue pot, serve immediately with the French bread cubes. Fondue doesn't sit well. Be prepared to serve it as soon as you finish making it, so have your bread and any other accompaniments ready.

Tip: *Gruyère and Emmentaler cheeses are both types of Swiss cheeses. The blend of the two creates a deliciously balanced dish. Plain supermarket-type Swiss cheese just won't cut it. Look for these two cheeses in the gourmet cheese section of your supermarket or at a specialty food store.*

Vary It! *Cubes of crusty French bread are a necessity with cheese fondue, but plenty of other foods go well with it, too. Try offering a platter of sausages (such as Italian sausage, cooked and thickly sliced), skinless chicken breast (cooked and cubed), or steamed broccoli, asparagus, carrots, or potatoes. Make sure that all the spearable food is bite-sized. And don't overlook multigrain breads, pretzels, slices of pears or apples, and grapes. Just think about what you like to eat with cheese.*

Per serving: *Calories 699 (From Fat 285); Fat 32g (Saturated 18g); Cholesterol 95mg; Sodium 973mg; Carbohydrate 63g (Dietary Fiber 3g); Protein 38g.*

Growing fond of fondue

Fondue dining has its own rules of etiquette. Fondue pots come with long-handled forks. Each guest should receive one of these forks and a plate. To eat fondue, simply spear a piece of bread with the long-handled fork and dip it into the cheese fondue. Then use a regular dinner fork to push the cheese-dipped bread off the long-handled fork and onto your plate. You also use the dinner fork to eat your bread. By following these guidelines, the long-handled fork doesn't touch your mouth and then go back into the pot.

Tapenade

This bold-flavored dip from the Provençal region of France always contains capers, which are the immature flower buds of the caper plant.

Preparation time: *10 minutes*

Yield: *About 1¾ cups*

3 garlic cloves

½ cup flat-leaf parsley

2 cups oil-cured pitted black olives, such as kalamata or other Mediterranean olives

3 tablespoons capers, rinsed and drained

3 tablespoons light olive oil

2 tablespoons lemon juice

2 anchovy fillets in oil, drained

Salt and pepper to taste

French bread (approximately 24 inches long and 12 to 14 ounces), thinly sliced

Crudités, for dipping

1 Place the garlic and parsley in the bowl of a food processor fitted with the metal blade and pulse on and off until minced.

2 Add the olives, capers, olive oil, lemon juice, and anchovy fillets to the processor bowl and pulse on and off until the mixture is smooth but still a bit textured. Season with salt and pepper. Taste before seasoning because some of the other ingredients already contain a lot of salt. You can use the dip immediately or store it in an airtight container in the refrigerator for up to 1 week. The flavor actually improves if it sits overnight.

3 Serve with crusty French bread and crudités.

Vary It! Once you have added the olives, anchovies, and capers, which are the basis of this dip, you can vary it a bit. Try adding one or more of the following: 1 teaspoon thyme, 2 tablespoons chopped fresh basil, or 2 tablespoons chopped sun-dried tomatoes. You also can replace 1 cup of the black olives with green olives.

Per serving: Calories 97 (From Fat 73); Fat 8g (Saturated 1g); Cholesterol 1mg; Sodium 345mg; Carbohydrate 3g (Dietary Fiber 1g); Protein 0g.

Spinach Dip

This dip is usually served in a hollowed-out bread bowl. Dark rye and pumpernickel go especially well with this recipe. (See Chapter 8 for instructions on making your own bread bowl.) The original spinach dip uses a packaged soup mix, but mine is from scratch and just as easy.

Preparation time: *5 minutes*

Yield: *About 2 cups*

10-ounce package frozen chopped spinach, thawed

½ cup mayonnaise

½ cup sour cream

¼ cup minced carrots

¼ cup minced red pepper

¼ cup Parmesan cheese

3 tablespoons minced white or yellow onion

1 teaspoon minced garlic

Salt and pepper to taste

1 Place the spinach in a colander and press as much water out of the spinach as possible. Use your hands to squeeze it dry. This method may be messy, but it works. You must squeeze the spinach dry, or the dip will be watery. Place the spinach in a mixing bowl.

2 Add the mayonnaise, sour cream, carrots, red pepper, Parmesan cheese, onion, and garlic to the spinach and mix well. Season with salt and pepper. Use the dip immediately or store it in an airtight container in the refrigerator for up to 3 days. The flavor actually improves if it sits overnight.

3 Serve with crudités or in a bread bowl.

Tip: *You may be tempted to cook spinach from scratch, but believe me, for this dip, you would be wasting your time. Convenience products rarely are as good as fresh products, but in this case, take advantage of using the frozen chopped spinach.*

Tip: *The dip is very spinachy, which I like. If you want to extend the recipe to serve more people and to have more of a creamy texture, simply double the mayonnaise, sour cream, and Parmesan cheese.*

Simplify: *I have a mini food processor, which is great for chopping and mincing small amounts of food. I use it to chop the carrots, red pepper, and onion, which makes this dip very quick to put together. If you have one, by all means, use it for this recipe.*

Per serving: *Calories 78 (From Fat 68); Fat 8g (Saturated 2g); Cholesterol 9mg; Sodium 122mg; Carbohydrate 2g (Dietary Fiber 1g); Protein 2g.*

Hot Crab Dip

This classic hot crab dip has a number of ingredients but comes together quickly. Old Bay Seasoning is a spice mix that you can find in many supermarket seafood departments or with the other herbs and spices. It's a classic pairing with crab.

Preparation time: *10 minutes*

Cooking time: *25 minutes*

Yield: *12 servings*

2 packages (8 ounces each) cream cheese, at room temperature

½ cup mayonnaise

¼ cup minced onion

1 tablespoon lemon juice

2 teaspoons Worcestershire sauce

½ teaspoon Old Bay Seasoning

Pinch cayenne

4 tablespoons chopped flat-leaf parsley

2 cans (6 ounces each) lump crabmeat

Paprika

French bread (approximately 24 inches long and 12 to 14 ounces), thinly sliced

1 Preheat the oven to 375 degrees. Spray a 9-inch pie plate with nonstick cooking spray.

2 Place the cream cheese, mayonnaise, onion, lemon juice, Worcestershire sauce, Old Bay Seasoning, cayenne, and 3 tablespoons of the parsley in a bowl and stir vigorously with a wooden spoon until combined.

3 Drain the crabmeat and remove any cartilage (the hard, white, bonelike material). Fold into the dip. (The dip can be made ahead up to this point. Cover with plastic wrap and refrigerate up to 1 day. Bring to room temperature while the oven preheats.)

4 Bake for about 25 minutes or until hot, bubbling, and lightly browned. Top with a light dusting of paprika and the remaining 1 tablespoon parsley. Serve with thin slices of French bread, toasted or plain.

Simplify: *You can make this dip without turning on your oven. Instead, microwave it on 50 percent power until hot and bubbly. The timing depends on your own microwave's wattage. It will not brown, but it will be hot and ready to eat very quickly.*

Remember: *I know that in Chapter 6, I strongly oppose using canned crab for the crab cakes. But in this dip recipe, canned crabmeat is acceptable because the cream cheese and the seasonings provide lots of flavor. With the crab cakes, the taste of the crab is paramount, so the fresher crab is essential. Here, the dip is about the combination of crab, mayonnaise, cream cheese, and seasonings, so the canned crabmeat works just fine.*

Per serving: *Calories 243 (From Fat 189); Fat 21g (Saturated 10g); Cholesterol 85mg; Sodium 343mg; Carbohydrate 2g (Dietary Fiber 0g); Protein 12g.*

Making Big and Little Dippers the Stars of Your Party

To accompany your zesty, creamy, chunky, and smooth dips, you need a selection of dippers — that is, the foods that you use to dip into the dips. Dippers, such as the colorful sweet potato chips and homemade corn chips in this chapter, are more than mere vehicles for transporting dips to our lips. They're tasty in their own right. For tips on using crudités or raw and steamed vegetables as dippers, see Chapter 6.

Baked Corn Chips

I was dubious about baking these, but you can hardly tell the difference between these and the fried. But with these, you save calories and leave more room in your tummy for extra salsa and guacamole.

Preparation time: 5 minutes

Cooking time: 10 minutes

Yield: Almost 50 chips

6 corn tortillas, 6- to 8-inch size (yellow, white, or blue corn, or a mixture)

Vegetable oil

Salt (optional)

1 Preheat the oven to 375 degrees. Brush the front and back of each tortilla with a thin layer of vegetable oil. Stack about 4 tortillas at a time and cut them into 8 equal wedges.

2 Spread the chips out in a single layer on baking sheets. Bake for 5 minutes, flip them over, and bake for 5 minutes more or until they turn light golden brown. Repeat if you can't fit all the chips on the baking sheet the first time around.

3 Sprinkle with salt, if desired, and serve immediately for best results. You can hold the corn chips at room temperature for a few hours if necessary.

Per serving: *Calories 12 (From Fat 6); Fat 1g (Saturated 0g); Cholesterol 0mg; Sodium 0mg; Carbohydrate 2g (Dietary Fiber 0g); Protein 0g.*

Homemade Potato Chips

Yummy! Homemade potato chips are crunchy, like the packaged ones, but they're so much more potato-ier. The flavor of the spud really shines through. If you like even more potato flavor per chip, you can slice them a little thicker so that you get more potato per bite.

Specialty tools: *Long, sharp knife, mandoline, or food processor; deep-fat fryer, electric fryer, or deep, heavy pot; thermometer with range up to 400 degrees*

Preparation time: *10 minutes*

Cooking time: *3 minutes for each batch*

Yield: *8 servings*

3 pounds russet potatoes	Salt (optional)
2 to 4 quarts vegetable oil	

1 Scrub the potatoes; you don't need to peel them. Slice them as thinly as possible, using a sharp knife, mandoline, or food processor fitted with a thin slicing blade. Try to keep the potato slices round and whole.

2 Place the slices in a bowl of ice water and soak for 1 hour. Drain and pat dry.

3 Meanwhile, fill a deep-fat fryer or heavy pot with oil to at least a 3-inch depth. (I give you a range for the amount of oil because the amount all depends on the size of your pot. You need the 3-inch depth of oil, so that is what you should use to gauge how much oil to use.) Use a thermometer if the unit isn't equipped with one and heat the oil to 375 degrees.

4 Fry the slices in small batches until golden brown, turning them frequently with a slotted spoon. The slices should move freely around the pot and have room to be evenly bathed in the oil. This process takes about 3 minutes. Remove with the slotted spoon and drain on paper towels. Sprinkle with salt, if desired, and serve immediately for best results. You can hold the chips at room temperature for a few hours if necessary.

Tip: *You can choose from several types of oil to fry the chips. Peanut oil is an excellent frying medium. It holds a high temperature well and provides a wonderful flavor. However, so many people have peanut allergies these days that it's better to err on the side of caution and not use peanut oil, especially if you're making these for a party and you don't know everyone's health history. A vegetable oil blend, canola oil, and a light olive oil are all fine choices.*

Vary It! *You can flavor your homemade potato chips to taste just like the expensive chips in the supermarket. Here are some ideas to get you started: Try slicing a bit thicker for a chewier chip. Sprinkle with garlic salt or an herb such as rosemary, being sure to crush the herb first. Or sprinkle with a spice such as chili powder or taco seasoning.*

Per serving: *Calories 512 (From Fat 369); Fat 41g (Saturated 3g); Cholesterol 0mg; Sodium 11mg; Carbohydrate 35g (Dietary Fiber 3g); Protein 3g.*

Bagel Chips

Bagels, even slightly stale ones, can easily be turned into sturdy chips. Because bagels are so popular these days, you may find that you always have a few around the house, but they can go stale quickly. You don't need to throw them out, however; just convert them into bagel chips!

Preparation time: *10 minutes*

Cooking time: *20 minutes*

Yield: *About 100 bagel chips*

6 plain bagels, about 5 inches across   *Salt (optional)*

⅓ cup light olive oil

1 Preheat the oven to 325 degrees. Line 3 baking sheets with parchment paper or foil.

2 Slice the bagels as follows (see Figure 7-1): Place a whole bagel on a cutting surface and cut in half down through the center vertically (in other words, not the usual way you cut a bagel, which is horizontally). Then take each half and place the cut ends down on the work surface, with the rounded edge facing up. Cut thin ⅛-inch slices from top to bottom. You end up with slices that have the shape of half a bagel.

3 Place the bagel slices on the baking sheets in a single layer and lightly brush with the olive oil. Sprinkle with salt, if desired. Depending on the size of your pans, you may have to bake the chips in batches.

4 Bake for about 15 minutes or until they begin to brown. Turn the chips over and continue to bake until thoroughly crisp. Allow to cool on the baking sheets and then transfer to an airtight container. The chips will keep up to 1 week.

Per serving: *Calories 25 (From Fat 7); Fat 1g (Saturated 0g); Cholesterol 0mg; Sodium 35mg; Carbohydrate 4g (Dietary Fiber 0g); Protein 1g.*

BAGEL SLICING 101...

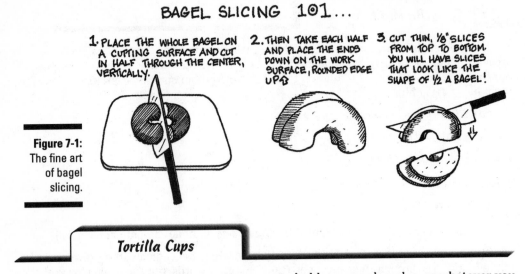

1. PLACE THE WHOLE BAGEL ON A CUTTING SURFACE AND CUT IN HALF THROUGH THE CENTER, VERTICALLY.

2. THEN TAKE EACH HALF AND PLACE THE ENDS DOWN ON THE WORK SURFACE, ROUNDED EDGE UP

3. CUT THIN, ⅛" SLICES FROM TOP TO BOTTOM. YOU WILL HAVE SLICES THAT LOOK LIKE THE SHAPE OF ½ A BAGEL!

Figure 7-1:
The fine art
of bagel
slicing.

Tortilla Cups

You can convert corn tortillas into tiny cups to hold guacamole, salsa, or whatever you fancy. You press tortilla rounds into mini muffin tins and bake them to get these crispy cups. These are perfect at a party because they're easy to pick up and eat with your fingers.

Specialty tools: *Mini muffin tin; 2½-inch round biscuit cutter*

Preparation time: *5 minutes*

Cooking time: *10 minutes*

Yield: *About 18 cups*

6 corn tortillas, 6- to 8-inch size   Vegetable oil

1 Preheat the oven to 350 degrees. Brush both sides of the tortillas lightly with the oil. Cut as many rounds as possible out of each tortilla with the 2½-inch round biscuit cutter. Press the rounds into the mini muffin tins. (You will need several pans, or you can make these in batches.)

2 Bake for about 10 minutes or until golden brown. Let cool slightly in the muffin pan. The cups will hold their shape and are now ready for filling. These are best if used right away, but you can hold them at room temperature for a few hours if necessary.

Tip: Fill these cups with guacamole topped with a little bit of crabmeat for a sophisticated appetizer.

Per serving: *Calories 33 (From Fat 16); Fat 2g (Saturated 0g); Cholesterol 0mg; Sodium 1mg; Carbohydrate 4g (Dietary Fiber 1g); Protein 1g.*

Sweet Potato Chips

This recipe is a worthwhile variation on regular potato chips. While essentially made the same way as plain potato chips, sweet potato chips add a whole different flavor and a whole lot of color to your array of dippers.

Specialty tools: Long, sharp knife, mandoline, or food processor; deep-fat fryer, electric fryer, or deep, heavy pot; thermometer with a range up to 400 degrees

Preparation time: 10 minutes

Cooking time: 3 minutes for each batch

Yield: 8 servings

3 pounds orange-fleshed sweet potatoes (sometimes called yams)

2 to 4 quarts vegetable oil

Salt (optional)

1 Scrub the sweet potatoes; you don't need to peel them. Slice them as thinly as possible, using a sharp knife, mandoline, or food processor fitted with a thin slicing blade. Try to keep the potato slices round and whole.

2 Place the slices in a bowl of ice water and soak for 1 hour. Drain and pat dry.

3 Meanwhile, fill a fryer or heavy pot with oil to at least a 3-inch depth. Use a thermometer if the unit isn't equipped with one and heat the oil to 375 degrees.

4 Fry the slices in small batches until golden brown, turning them frequently with a slotted spoon. The slices should move freely around the pot and have room to be evenly bathed in the oil. This process takes about 3 minutes. Remove with a slotted spoon and drain on paper towels. Sprinkle with salt, if desired, and serve immediately for best results. You may hold the chips at room temperature for a few hours if necessary.

Vary It! Try one of the following ideas for a change of pace: Try slicing the potatoes a bit thicker for a chewier chip. Sprinkle the chips with spices such as chili powder or taco seasoning. Make the chips sweet by sprinkling them with a little cinnamon and sugar.

Per serving: *Calories 572 (From Fat 369); Fat 41g (Saturated 3g); Cholesterol 0mg; Sodium 21mg; Carbohydrate 49g (Dietary Fiber 7g); Protein 4g.*

Root Veggie Chips

Root vegetables, such as carrots, beets, rutabagas, turnips, and parsnips, can make delicious fried chips that are very different from ones made from potatoes. The trick is to fry only one kind of vegetable at a time because they fry at different rates.

Specialty tools: *Long, sharp knife, mandoline, or food processor; deep-fat fryer, electric fryer, or deep, heavy pot; thermometer with a range up to 400 degrees*

Preparation time: *10 minutes*

Cooking time: *3 minutes for each batch*

Yield: *8 servings*

3 pounds assorted root vegetables, such as carrots, beets, rutabagas, parsnips, turnips, Jerusalem artichokes, or celery root

2 to 4 quarts vegetable oil

Salt (optional)

1 Scrub and peel the vegetables. Slice them as thinly as possible, using a sharp knife, mandoline, or food processor fitted with a thin slicing blade. Try to keep the slices round and whole.

2 Place the slices in a bowl of ice water and soak for 1 hour. Drain and pat dry.

3 Meanwhile, fill a fryer or heavy pot with oil to at least a 3-inch depth. Use a thermometer if the unit isn't equipped with one and heat the oil to 375 degrees.

4 Fry the slices, one variety at a time, in small batches until golden brown, turning them frequently with a slotted spoon. The slices should move freely around the pot and have room to be evenly bathed in the oil. This process takes about 3 minutes. Remove with a slotted spoon and drain on paper towels. Sprinkle with salt, if desired, and serve immediately for best results. You may hold the chips at room temperature for a few hours if necessary.

Tip: *For very narrow vegetables, such as carrots, you can slice them on the diagonal to make ovals, and give them a larger surface area.*

Per serving: *Calories 446 (From Fat 370); Fat 41g (Saturated 3g); Cholesterol 0mg; Sodium 76mg; Carbohydrate 20g (Dietary Fiber 5g); Protein 2g.*

Fried Corn Chips

Sure, you can buy corn chips, but these are fresher and really delicious and will enhance your homemade guacamole.

Specialty tools: *Long, sharp knife; deep-fat fryer, electric fryer, or deep, heavy pot; thermometer with a range up to 400 degrees*

Preparation time: *5 minutes*

Cooking time: *1½ minutes for each batch*

Yield: *Almost 100 chips*

12 corn tortillas, 6- to 8-inch size (yellow, white, or blue corn, or a mixture)

2 to 4 quarts vegetable oil

Salt (optional)

1 Stack about 4 tortillas at a time and cut them into 8 equal wedges.

2 Meanwhile, fill a fryer or heavy pot with oil to at least a 3-inch depth. Use a thermometer if the unit isn't equipped with one and heat the oil to 375 degrees.

3 Fry the chips in small batches until golden brown, turning them frequently with a slotted spoon. The slices should move freely around the pot and have room to be evenly bathed in the oil. This process takes about 1 minute. Remove with a slotted spoon and drain on paper towels. Sprinkle with salt, if desired, and serve immediately for best results. You may hold them at room temperature for a few hours if necessary.

Tip: *Some corn chips are thicker than others. Both thick and thin make good chips, but you may prefer one over the other. Experiment to find out which you like best.*

Per serving: *Calories 27 (From Fat 21); Fat 2g (Saturated 0g); Cholesterol 0mg; Sodium 0mg; Carbohydrate 2g (Dietary Fiber 0g); Protein 0g.*

Fried Flour Tortilla Chips

These end up being crispy and flaky — they're much more than a sum of their parts. Try them!

Specialty tools: *Deep-fat fryer, electric fryer, or deep, heavy pot; thermometer with a range up to 400 degrees*

Preparation time: *5 minutes*

Cooking time: *1½ minutes for each batch*

Yield: *Almost 100 chips*

12 flour tortillas, 6- to 8-inch size	Salt (optional)
2 to 4 quarts vegetable oil	

1 Stack about 4 tortillas at a time and cut them into 8 equal wedges.

2 Meanwhile, fill a fryer or heavy pot with oil to at least a 3-inch depth. Use a thermometer if the unit isn't equipped with one and heat the oil to 375 degrees.

3 Fry the chips in small batches until golden brown, turning them frequently with a slotted spoon. The slices should move freely around the pot and have room to be evenly bathed in the oil. This process takes about 1 minute. Remove with a slotted spoon and drain on paper towels. Sprinkle with salt, if desired, and serve immediately for best results. You can hold the chips at room temperature for a few hours if necessary.

Tip: *You can find the plain, white, flour tortillas in any supermarket, and they're fine for this recipe. But with a little searching, you can find sun-dried tomato tortillas, pesto or spinach tortillas, red pepper tortillas, and others. My supermarket, for some reason, has the regular kind in the refrigerated section, but the flavored ones are in the international foods section. Look around or ask at the customer service desk if you can't find what you're looking for.*

Per serving: *Calories 33 (From Fat 24); Fat 3g (Saturated 0g); Cholesterol 0mg; Sodium 4mg; Carbohydrate 2g (Dietary Fiber 0g); Protein 1g.*

Part III
Special Touches:
Recipes to Impress

The 5th Wave   By Rich Tennant

"Oooo, what's in here? Is that sun-dried eye of newt? How gourmet!"

In this part . . .

If you're looking for appetizers beyond the basics, this part is for you. The chapter on bread-based bites includes such tempting treats as canapés, tea sandwiches, crostini, tartlets, biscuits, and muffins. If you want your menu to include hot hors d'oeuvres, you can find recipes for such dishes as Stuffed Potato Skins with Horseradish Sour Cream and Chive Dip, Glazed Chicken Wings, and Bacon-Wrapped Scallops. This part also includes recipes with an international touch, including favorites like calamari, spring rolls, and Swedish meatballs.

Chapter 8

Bread-Based Bites

• •

In This Chapter

▶ Concocting canapés and tea sandwiches

▶ Making quesadillas, crostini, tartlets, and biscuits

▶ Assembling appetizers made from puff pastry and phyllo

• •

Many appetizers have some sort of bread as a base, be it French bread, a tortilla, puff pastry, or plain old sandwich bread. Yet partygoers can't seem to get enough of them. Because there is such variety in bread-based appetizers, I devote an entire chapter to them.

This is the chapter to refer to if you want recipes for canapés, tea sandwiches, crostini, quesadillas, tartlets, muffins, biscuits, and appetizers using puff pastry or phyllo dough. These bread-based appetizers add delicious variety to almost any occasion.

Canapés and Tea Sandwiches

Canapés are tiny open-faced sandwiches. I don't know who came up with the term "open-faced." Sandwiches don't have a face that I know of. What this literally means is that a single piece of bread is covered with toppings, but no second piece of bread is on top. (Should we call them topless sandwiches? Maybe that's too provocative. I'll stick with the standard description.)

Tea sandwiches are small sandwiches — just a bite or two in size — that have fillings in between two pieces of bread. They're called "tea sandwiches" because they often accompany tea wherever afternoon tea is served. They are meant to be delicate and often have the crusts removed.

Both canapés and tea sandwiches are usually made with regular sandwich bread — white, wheat, or even rye or pumpernickel. As far as toppings and fillings are concerned, your imagination is the limit. I present some popular toppings and fillings and also give you a list of creative ingredients that you can mix and match on your own.

Choosing your shape

Squares, triangles, rectangles, and rounds are the most common shapes of canapés, but they're by no means the only shapes these appetizers can take. You sometimes need to cut the canapés before applying toppings, sometimes after; tea sandwiches are usually cut after they're filled. Follow specific instructions in individual recipes.

Here are some tips on creating the different shapes:

- **Rectangles:** To make long, skinny rectangles, often called finger shapes, simply remove the crusts from sandwich bread, square off the ends, and cut pieces that are the length of the bread and an inch across. You can usually get about 4 rectangles per slice of bread.

- **Rounds:** To make these shapes, you need to have a round cookie or biscuit cutter. A cutter that's 2 inches in diameter is a good size, but you can make them a little larger or smaller if you like.

- **Squares:** To make square sandwiches, use sandwich bread, whether it's squareish white or whole-wheat bread or the more rounded rye or pumpernickel breads. Remove the crusts and cut each slice into fourths. If using the rounder-shaped breads, you need to trim some bread to square the shape.

- **Triangles:** Remove the crusts from sandwich bread and make two diagonal cuts through each slice to create the triangles.

You're not limited to those basic shapes, however. Try petals, stars, hearts, diamonds, even bunnies, if you're so inclined. You can cut canapés and tea sandwiches with any shape of cookie cutter that you like. But unless you're making peanut butter sandwiches for a toddler's birthday party, stick with the simpler shapes. Small details often get lost in fancier shapes.

Building a canapé

A canapé is less of a recipe than of an assemblage of ingredients. Here are some basic steps to creating canapés:

1. **Spread a piece of sandwich bread with a flavored butter, flavored cream cheese, soft cheese, mustard, chutney, or other condiment.**

2. **Trim off the crusts and cut the bread into squares, triangles, or rectangles with a sharp knife, or cut into rounds or fancier shapes with a cookie cutter, as shown in Figure 8-1.**

3. **Add a layer of a firm cheese, a piece of meat or seafood, seafood salad, vegetable, or some other topping of your choice. (See the section "Topping canapés," later in this chapter, for more ideas.)**

4. **Finally, crown the canapé with an edible flourish by adding a fresh herb sprig, an ultrathin strip of lemon, a sprinkling of curry powder, or some other embellishment. You can even add an edible flower or a dollop of chutney or other condiment on top.**

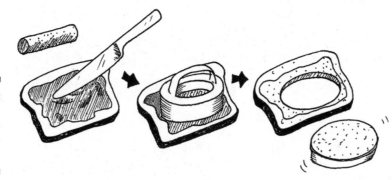

Figure 8-1:
Using a
cutter to
make
canapés.

 Canapés and tea sandwiches are best when assembled within 6 hours of serving, but you can make some of the components ahead. The following section, "Spreading some flavor," tells how to make flavored spreads and store them until you need them. You can chop herbs for toppings ahead and store them overnight in a covered plastic container. You can slice pieces of cheese and wrap and store them until it's time to assemble the canapés. You also can prepare ahead of time a seafood salad or guacamole to dollop on top of a canapé. Think about each ingredient in your canapé and take advantage of any do-ahead steps.

Spreading some flavor

Butter and cream cheese serve as the basic ingredient in two basic spreads for your canapés and some tea sandwiches. Both types of spreads are easy to make. The flavored butters are often referred to as "compound butters," so if you see this term elsewhere, now you'll know what it means. Both butter and cream cheese are fairly high in fat, but that's a good thing in this case. Fat adds flavor, and when you add curry, for instance, to butter or cream cheese, the flavor is wonderfully pronounced. And don't worry about the calories — you're using only a little bit of spread on your canapés.

In either case, begin with softened, unsalted butter or cream cheese. When using cream cheese, I actually prefer to use Neufchâtel, a lower-fat cream cheese, but you can use regular cream cheese, too. Neufchâtel is smoother and creamier, but it is still quite flavorful and has a good texture.

Please don't use fat-free cream cheese. It has a very odd taste and a shiny, plasticlike texture. I repeat: Do not use it!

To make a spread, choose your favorite herbs, spices, condiments, and other flavorings. You simply put the softened butter or cream cheese in a bowl, add the flavoring ingredients, and beat with a wooden spoon until creamy and combined. If you're making a butter spread, you can scrape the mixture onto a piece of wax paper, parchment paper, or plastic wrap and form into a roll. Twist the ends tightly and store in the freezer for up to a month. Then just slice off what you need as you need it, defrost it, and you're ready to go. You also can refrigerate the butter spread for up to 4 days. For a cream cheese spread, pack it into an airtight container and refrigerate up to 4 days until needed.

Your spreads should be creamy so that they form a smooth base for the next layer. So mince your herbs, finely chop your nuts and anchovies, and make sure, in general, that whatever you add to your butter or cream cheese will blend in easily.

Topping canapés

Canapés can be as colorful and flavorful as the toppings you use. The brilliant greens of fresh herbs and vegetables, the deep red of roasted peppers or beets, the sheer orange of a smattering of salmon roe, the deep amber of a dollop of chutney — they all really dress up a canapé. The list of ingredients is meant to inspire you to pick and choose and make your own combinations. For extra help, I also give you some tried-and-true combinations that are sure to please.

Many of the items that I list as toppings are the same ingredients that you can mix into butter and cream cheese for your base spread. However, when making the spreads, you need to mince or chop the ingredients so that they're as fine as possible. Here are some topping suggestions:

- Anchovies
- Bacon, cooked and crisp
- Blue cheese
- Capers
- Caviar
- Cherry tomato halves or slices
- Chutney

- ✔ Crab
- ✔ Cucumber slices
- ✔ Dried fruit, such as figs, dates, raisins, or candied orange peel
- ✔ Feta cheese
- ✔ Fresh herbs
- ✔ Guacamole
- ✔ Ham and smoked ham
- ✔ Hard-cooked egg slices
- ✔ Hummus
- ✔ Jalapeño pepper jelly
- ✔ Nuts (walnut halves, almond slices, or roughly chopped pecans, for example)
- ✔ Olives, black or green
- ✔ Onions (yellow, white, red, or sweet; thinly sliced)
- ✔ Pesto
- ✔ Prosciutto
- ✔ Radish slices
- ✔ Roast beef
- ✔ Roasted red pepper
- ✔ Salsa
- ✔ Seafood salad
- ✔ Shrimp
- ✔ Smoked salmon
- ✔ Smoked trout
- ✔ Soft goat cheese, such as Montrachet
- ✔ Sun-dried tomatoes
- ✔ Tapenade
- ✔ Turkey and smoked turkey
- ✔ Watercress

Trying some sure-fire canapé combinations

My ultimate goal is to get you to make up your own combinations, but I never leave you high and dry. Here are some canapé combinations that I have served to very grateful guests:

- ✔ Pumpernickel bread topped with lemon-flavored cream cheese, a piece of smoked salmon, a piece of chive, and a caper or two.

- ✔ Whole-wheat bread spread with Dijon mustard and then topped with a layer of thick hummus and a slice or curl of roasted red pepper.

- ✔ White bread spread with goat cheese, topped with a dollop of tapenade, and crowned with a parsley sprig.

- ✔ Rye bread spread with mango or cranberry chutney and topped with a piece of smoked turkey and a walnut or pecan half. Or put the turkey right on the bread, add a dollop of the chutney, and top with the pecan. Be flexible!

- ✔ Whole-wheat bread spread with honey-flavored cream cheese and topped with a walnut half and a few slivers of date.

- ✔ White bread spread with blue cheese and topped with a tiny slice of apple. (Don't forget to soak the apple in lemon water to prevent browning.)

- ✔ White bread spread with mayonnaise and topped with a piece of lettuce, a piece of bacon, and a cherry tomato slice — a BLT!

- ✔ White bread spread with pesto and topped with a slice of mozzarella, a perfect basil leaf, and a sliver of fresh or sun-dried tomato.

Making tea sandwiches: The tea is optional

Tea sandwiches are just like regular sandwiches in that there are two pieces of bread sandwiching the fillings. The difference is that tea sandwiches are smaller and usually have the crusts removed. If you can make a sandwich, you can make a tea sandwich.

You can make a tea sandwich with a prepared filling, such as the ones I provide in the recipes in this section. Or you can make a sandwich filling from the canapé topping ideas I provide earlier in this chapter, but instead of adding a visually attractive topping, simply add the second piece of bread.

Serve tea sandwiches as soon as possible after making them. You can make them up to 6 hours ahead, stack them together in a long log shape, and then wrap the whole stack in plastic wrap. Or you can assemble them on serving platters and cover them tightly. Leave at room temperature if serving within the hour. Otherwise, refrigerate the sandwiches. Bring to room temperature before serving.

Tarragon Chicken Tea Sandwiches

This is a simple chicken salad recipe that you can vary with different herbs, if you like. For example, try dill or chervil instead of the tarragon.

Getting the cooked chicken for this recipe isn't as hard as you may think. If you made roasted chicken last night and have some left over, then you're in luck. If not, you can pick up a roasted chicken in the supermarket deli. Cooking the chicken just for this recipe is another option — and very easy. Place boneless, skinless chicken breasts in a pan with enough water to cover and add a bay leaf, a couple peppercorns, an onion slice, and a carrot. Then bring the water to a simmer and cook until done. To determine when the chicken is done, remove a breast, cut into it, and make sure that the meat is completely opaque and there are no pink juices.

Preparation time: 10 minutes

Yield: 20 square or triangular sandwiches

2 cups finely shredded or diced cooked chicken	1 tablespoon chopped fresh tarragon or 1 teaspoon dried tarragon
½ cup finely chopped celery	Salt and pepper to taste
¾ cup mayonnaise	10 slices white or whole-wheat sandwich bread

1 Combine the chicken, celery, mayonnaise, and tarragon in a bowl. Season with salt and pepper.

2 Spread the chicken salad on 5 slices of bread all the way to the edges and top each one with another slice of bread.

3 Trim off the crusts and cut into 4 squares or triangles. Or cut the sandwiches out with cookie cutters in shapes of your choice. If you use cookie cutters, be sure to cut inside the crusts. Serve the sandwiches as soon as possible after making them.

Vary It! *For a very easy way to vary this recipe, make half the sandwiches with white bread and half with whole-wheat bread.*

Tip: *For this recipe, it's important that your chicken be shredded, not in cubes or chunks. Shred the chicken with your fingers. Tea sandwiches are so delicate that larger cubes or chunks of chicken just won't do. The larger pieces of chicken may be okay for large sandwiches, but not here.*

Vary It! *To make these sandwiches even more appealing visually, you need some extra mayonnaise and about 2 cups of minced parsley. After you cut the sandwiches, spread the thinnest possible film of mayonnaise on all the cut surfaces and then dip them in a plate filled with the minced parsley. The parsley will stick to the mayonnaise and make a pretty border all around the sandwiches. You also can mix in some fresh chopped herbs of your choice, but parsley should comprise the bulk of the mixture.*

Per serving: Calories 133 (From Fat 79); Fat 9g (Saturated 2g); Cholesterol 17mg; Sodium 170mg; Carbohydrate 8g (Dietary Fiber 0g); Protein 6g.

Egg Salad Tea Sandwiches

This basic egg salad recipe contains a little bit of Dijon mustard for a kick. See Chapter 6 for instructions on how to hard-cook your eggs.

Preparation time: *10 minutes*

Yield: *16 square or triangular sandwiches*

¼ cup mayonnaise

1 tablespoon minced celery

1 tablespoon minced scallions, green and white parts

1 teaspoon Dijon mustard

4 hard-cooked eggs, cooled and peeled

Salt and pepper to taste

8 slices white or whole-wheat sandwich bread

1 Combine the mayonnaise, celery, scallions, and Dijon mustard in a bowl. Chop the hard-cooked eggs to about a ¼-inch dice. Add to the mayonnaise mixture and stir gently. Season with salt and pepper.

2 Spread the egg salad on 4 slices of bread all the way to the edges and then top each one with another slice of bread.

3 Trim off the crusts and cut each into 4 squares or triangles. Or cut the sandwiches out with cookie cutters in shapes of your choice. If you use cookie cutters, be sure to cut inside the crusts. Serve the sandwiches as soon as possible after making them.

Per serving: Calories 85 (From Fat 42); Fat 5g (Saturated 1g); Cholesterol 55mg; Sodium 161mg; Carbohydrate 8g (Dietary Fiber 0g); Protein 3g.

Cucumber and Watercress Tea Sandwiches

This recipe combines the best of both worlds. The clean, crisp flavor of the cucumber pairs perfectly with the peppery watercress. And it's all cushioned by a smear of sweet (that's unsalted) butter. The salt and pepper really add to the flavor of these sandwiches, so don't leave them out!

Preparation time: *10 minutes*

Yield: *24 square or triangular sandwiches*

12 slices white or whole-wheat sandwich bread

6 tablespoons (¾ stick) unsalted butter, very soft

36 very thin slices peeled cucumber

1 bunch watercress

Salt and pepper to taste

1 Spread about 1½ teaspoons butter on each piece of bread. Arrange about 6 slices of cucumber on each of 6 bread slices. The exact number will be determined by the size of your bread; the cucumber slices can overlap somewhat. Tear the tender leaves from the stalks of watercress and make an even layer over the cucumbers. Season with salt and pepper and cover with the remaining slices of bread, butter side down.

2 Trim off the crusts and cut into 4 squares or triangles. Or cut sandwiches out with cookie cutters in shapes of your choice. If you use cookie cutters, be sure to cut inside the crusts. Serve the sandwiches as soon as possible after making them.

Tip: You can tear bread even if you're using room-temperature butter. To soften the butter further, you can zap it briefly in the microwave oven. I do this all the time, such as when I need softened butter to cream for cakes or cookies. The key is knowing how to work with your microwave. Some are so powerful that you get melted butter before you know it. Start with a 5- or 10-second burst on full power. It is worth sacrificing a stick of butter to acquaint yourself with your individual microwave because, once you're comfortable with it, you'll use it all the time for tasks like this.

Tip: If you have very fresh and/or very tender-skinned cucumber, you may leave the skin on. Use your own judgment.

Per serving: *Calories 67 (From Fat 31); Fat 3g (Saturated 2g); Cholesterol 8mg; Sodium 106mg; Carbohydrate 8g (Dietary Fiber 0g); Protein 1g.*

Bowl 'em over with bread bowls

Large round breads, such as a French bread round or a large black bread, make perfect bowls for dips after they've been hollowed out. Carving out the middle of the bread is very easy to do, and the resulting bowl makes a nice addition to your hors d'oeuvres table. Follow these steps:

1. **Find a bread round that is about 8 inches across and about 6 inches high.**

2. **Take a small, sharp knife, such as a paring knife, and cut out a circle from the top of the bread, about 6 inches around and about 1 inch deep.**

3. **Lift off this round piece of bread with your fingers. Remove the bread from the center of the loaf, again using your fingers, and create a bowl-like cavity.**

   Be careful as you hollow out the bread, making sure to leave the sides and bottom intact. You'll probably be able to tell if your fingers are getting close to the sides and bottom, so trust your sense of touch. You may want to try to remove as much of the inner bread as possible in one big piece. Then you can cube the bread and serve it along with your dip-filled bread bowl. You also can use the hollowed-out bread to make bread crumbs, or you can snack on it as you go.

4. **Fill the bread with a dip or spread.**

You can make your bread bowl right before you need it, or you can hollow the bread out the day before and store it in a resealable plastic bag.

If you're bringing dip to a party, pack it into a bread bowl instead of a "real" bowl. That way, you don't have to worry about leaving a serving dish behind.

Quesadillas: Grilled Cheese, Mexican Style

Quesadillas are the Mexican version of a grilled cheese sandwich. At their simplest, they're made from two flour tortillas and contain a cheese, such as Monterey Jack or sharp cheddar, in the middle. You also add ingredients such as refried beans, scallions, or spicy jalapeño peppers. As you gently cook them in a cast-iron skillet, the cheese melts, the tortillas lightly brown, and you get a satisfying taste treat in less than 5 minutes, including prep time. I offer you two versions of quesadillas, but feel free to mix and match the ingredients or come up with ideas of your own. These recipes are very forgiving and flexible, so have fun with them.

Monterey Jack and Scallion Quesadillas

These quesadillas are quick to make, which is a good thing, because you need to serve them almost immediately. Use small tortillas, about 7 to 8 inches in diameter, if you can find them. If you use larger tortillas, the resulting wedges will be long and floppy and difficult to eat.

For variety, you may want to replace the Monterey Jack cheese with pepper jack cheese, which is Monterey Jack cheese that has flecks of hot pepper throughout. You can usually find it near the regular Monterey Jack cheese. It not only provides a spicy bite but is colorful, too.

Preparation time: *5 minutes*

Cooking time: *About 5 minutes per quesadilla*

Yield: *32 quesadilla wedges*

8 flour tortillas (7- to 8-inch size)

2 cups (8 ounces) shredded Monterey Jack cheese

½ cup thinly sliced scallions, both green and white parts

Vegetable oil

Salsa

1 Place 4 of the tortillas on your work surface and divide the cheese among them in an even layer. Sprinkle the scallions evenly over the cheese. Top each tortilla with one of the remaining tortillas.

2 Place a heavy skillet (such as one made from cast-iron) over medium-high heat and add enough oil to lightly coat the surface. Tilt the skillet so that the pan is evenly coated with the oil. If you have an oil mister (a gadget that I describe in Chapter 5), use it to coat the skillet. It provides the perfect amount of oil for this recipe.

3 One at a time, place the quesadillas in the skillet and cook until the bottom is lightly browned. Use a spatula to lift up an edge and take a peak. If it's browned, turn it over. A trick that helps ensure that you flip the quesadilla over without losing the filling is to gently press the top tortilla down onto the cheese first. Doing so makes the tortilla stick to the cheese so that the quesadilla is less prone to fall apart when you turn it over. Cook the second side until golden brown and the cheese is melted. You may need to add more cooking oil before cooking each of the remaining quesadillas.

4 Remove the quesadilla from the skillet, place it on a cutting board, and cut into 8 wedges, using a sharp chef's knife, a rolling pizza cutter, or kitchen shears. Serve immediately with salsa.

Tip: *If you're good at doing more than one thing at a time and you have two skillets, by all means cook two — or three or four — quesadillas at once. You're limited only by the number of burners on your stove, the number of skillets, and your ambidexterity.*

Per serving: *Calories 55 (From Fat 19); Fat 2g (Saturated 1g); Cholesterol 3mg; Sodium 78mg; Carbohydrate 7g (Dietary Fiber 0g); Protein 2g.*

Refried Beans and Chile Quesadillas

This recipe calls for canned refried beans, so taste a couple brands first to see which you like. I look for vegetarian versions because the others sometimes have lard, and I just don't need that extra fat. I'd rather load up on the cheese!

Preparation time: *5 minutes*

Cooking time: *About 5 minutes per quesadilla*

Yield: *32 quesadilla wedges*

8 flour tortillas (7- to 8-inch size)

1 cup refried beans

2 cups (8 ounces) shredded sharp cheddar cheese

2 to 4 teaspoons minced jalapeño pepper

Vegetable oil

Salsa

1 Place 4 of the tortillas on a work surface and divide the refried beans among them, spreading the beans to the edges with a butter knife. Sprinkle the cheese evenly over the beans. Sprinkle the jalapeños on top of the cheese. Top each with one of the remaining tortillas.

2 Place a skillet over medium-high heat and add enough oil to lightly coat the surface. Tilt the skillet so that the pan is evenly coated with the oil.

3 One at a time, place the quesadillas in the skillet and cook until the bottom is lightly browned. Use a spatula to lift up an edge and take a peak. If it's browned, turn it over. A trick that helps ensure that you flip the quesadilla over without losing the filling is to gently press the top tortilla down onto the cheese first. Doing so makes the tortilla stick to the cheese so the quesadilla is less prone to fall apart when you turn it over. Cook the second side until golden brown and the cheese is melted. You may need to add more cooking oil before cooking each of the remaining quesadillas.

4 Remove the quesadilla from the pan, place it on a cutting board, cut into 8 wedges, and serve immediately with salsa.

Remember: *Take care when handling jalapeños or any type of chile peppers. Remove the seeds and the ribs before mincing and don't touch your eyes! For more advice on working with jalapeños, see Chapter 7.*

Per serving: *Calories 60 (From Fat 21); Fat 2g (Saturated 1g); Cholesterol 4mg; Sodium 92mg; Carbohydrate 8g (Dietary Fiber 1g); Protein 2g.*

French-Bread Appetizers: Bon Appétit!

I love French bread. Good French bread is ultra-crusty on the outside and tender on the inside. The fresh wheat flavor comes through whether you slather it with perfectly ripe, runny brie or just tear off a hunk to eat on the way home.

If you have a local bakery nearby, buy your French bread there. Many supermarkets have in-house bakeries where you can find French bread, but chances are that it won't be as high quality as the loaves made in an independent bakery. But this recommendation isn't a foolproof method of bread buying. Taste loaves from different bakeries and buy the best loaf you can find. If the bread has a soft exterior that isn't very distinct from the inside, keep searching. A good French loaf has a distinctive crusty crust.

Baguette is another name for French bread. If you were in France, your baguette-buying forays would be simple. The size, shape, and ingredients are monitored by the government! There's no fooling around over there with their beloved loaf. But in the United States, there is no such thing as a federal baguette committee. One bakery can sell a baguette that's twice as large (or twice as small) as the baguette from the bakery down the street. So what is a recipe writer to do? In this book I include several recipes that call for "1 loaf French bread." Most full-size French breads are about 24 inches long and weigh somewhere between 12 and 14 ounces. Try to find a bread that is as close to this size as possible for these recipes.

Pesto and Sun-Dried Tomato Baguette

This appetizer is easy to make. You make a long sandwich with the French bread and cut it into small pieces, giving you many servings for very little prep time. You can either buy your own pesto or make it. The red, white, and green filling is very colorful and makes a great addition to the appetizer table.

Preparation time: *5 minutes*

Yield: *24 small sandwiches*

1 loaf French bread (about 24 inches long and 12 to 14 ounces)

2 tablespoons plus 2 teaspoons balsamic vinegar

⅓ cup pesto

7 ounces fresh mozzarella (2 ovoline size), thinly sliced

14 sun-dried tomato halves in oil

1 Shortly before serving, slice the bread in half horizontally almost all the way through from one side to the other, leaving one long side still attached. It will look like a clam shell; you'll be able to open the top as if a hinge were attached, as shown in Figure 8-2.

DO NOT CUT ALL THE WAY THROUGH! LEAVE ONE LONG SIDE ATTACHED.

YOU WILL BE ABLE TO HINGE OPEN THE TOP, LIKE A CLAM SHELL!

Figure 8-2:
Slicing a baguette.

2 Dab the vinegar evenly on both the top and bottom halves of the bread, using a pastry brush. Spread the pesto on the bottom half of the loaf. Lay the mozzarella slices evenly down the length of the bread. Top the cheese evenly with the sun-dried tomatoes, which should cover the length of the loaf.

3 Close up the sandwich and cut into 1-inch slices. Lay individual sandwiches on a platter on their sides so you can see the pretty colors of the fillings. They stack easily into a pyramid shape. These are best served as soon as possible, but you can wrap the platter with two layers of plastic wrap and store it at room temperature for up to 2 hours.

Tip: *To apply the balsamic vinegar without a pastry brush, you can use a spoon and slowly dribble it over the loaf. Or you can do what I do. I place my thumb over the vinegar bottle's opening and shake the bottle over the loaf, letting just a little bit of the vinegar out at a time. Obviously, you can't measure the vinegar if you use this technique. But if you trust your cooking skills, you can try this method.*

Tip: *As with so many recipes, the exact amount of the ingredients isn't important. What you want is a light, even layer of vinegar (which will be absorbed by the bread), an even layer of pesto, thin slices of mozzarella in a single layer down the length of the bread, and a single layer of tomatoes. If your bread is a little longer, shorter, wider, or thinner, the amounts may vary.*

Per serving: *Calories 87 (From Fat 39); Fat 4g (Saturated 2g); Cholesterol 7mg; Sodium 171mg; Carbohydrate 8g (Dietary Fiber 1g); Protein 4g.*

A Toast to Crostini

Crostini refers to the Italian version of canapés in that they combine a bread base with a topping. Literally, *crostini* means "toast," but that's a bland description for an appetizer that can be elegant, rustic, hearty, or delicate. After you start with an Italian or French bread base, the toppings are up to your imagination. One difference between crostini and canapés is that while the latter can be fussy and precise, the best crostini recipes are more casual. For example, consider a small heap of creamy white beans drizzled with extra-virgin olive oil and crushed rosemary. Or how about slices of deep red tomatoes and a perfect fresh basil leaf? I include recipes using those ingredients in this chapter, but you can also find a list of delicious options if you want to experiment with other flavors.

Crostini is all about the bread, so you need to find a good loaf. You need a loaf that's firm and crusty on the outside and chewy in the middle. The center of the slices should be tender enough to provide a good chewy bite, but resilient enough to soak up the juices from the toppings and not fall apart. Your best bet is to find a bakery and describe what you need. The owner should be able to suggest a suitable type of bread.

Here's the trick to serving crostini: Toast crostini right before serving and have the toppings made ahead of time. That way, assembling them right before serving will go quickly.

Basic Crostini

Use this recipe to prepare the different versions of crostini. Then proceed with the following recipes or refer to my list of ideas to make up your own version.

Preparation time: *1 minute*

Cooking time: *10 minutes*

Yield: *40 crostini*

1 crusty, chewy loaf of Italian or French bread
(about 24 inches long and 12 to 14 ounces)

Preheat the oven to 400 degrees. Cut the bread in ½-inch slices and place the slices, cut side down, on a baking sheet. Toast for 5 minutes, flip the slices over, and toast for 5 minutes more or until just lightly golden. Use immediately.

Tip: *Bread for crostini must be very lightly toasted. If it's toasted all the way through, it will be too crunchy and become brittle. So use the recipe times as mere suggestions and go for the proper looks and texture above all else.*

Tip: *The number of crostini that you get per loaf will vary. I suggest ½-inch slices as a good size, but I don't mean for you to pull out a ruler. Just strive for some uniformity. Also, the ends don't make good crostini, so eat them while you work.*

Per serving: *Calories 23 (From Fat 2); Fat 0g (Saturated 0g); Cholesterol 0mg; Sodium 52mg; Carbohydrate 4g (Dietary Fiber 0g); Protein 1g.*

Tomato-Basil Crostini

Use the Basic Crostini recipe as the base for this summer crostini. Make this appetizer only in late summer, when tomatoes and basil are at their peak.

Preparation time: *5 minutes*

Yield: *40 crostini*

8 medium-size ripe tomatoes, seeded and chopped into ¼-inch dice (about 4 cups)

½ cup extra-virgin olive oil

Salt and pepper

1 Basic Crostini recipe (see the recipe earlier in this chapter)

2 pounds fresh mozzarella (4 to 5 ovoline size), thinly sliced

40 large fresh basil leaves

1 Place the tomatoes and olive oil in a small bowl and season well with salt and pepper, tossing gently. Let sit for about 15 minutes to allow the flavors to develop. You may prepare the recipe up to this point 3 hours ahead. Just cover the bowl with plastic wrap and let it sit at room temperature.

2 When you're ready to serve, make the Basic Crostini recipe and arrange the bread slices on a serving platter. Place a slice of mozzarella on each bread slice and top with a whole basil leaf and a small spoonful of the seasoned tomatoes. Serve immediately. Don't forget to provide napkins to sop up the delicious tomato juices that may drip down your chin.

Tip: *The best size basil leaves for this dish are approximately the same size as the bread slices. That way, they conveniently cover each slice.*

Vary It! *These days, particularly at farmers markets, you can find tomatoes in a rainbow of colors, including orange, yellow, green, and all shades of red. You may even be lucky enough to find burgundy ones or striped ones. If you gather together a varied selection of tomatoes, you can easily make crostini with a kaleidoscope of color.*

Per serving: *Calories 124 (From Fat 78); Fat 9g (Saturated 5g); Cholesterol 16mg; Sodium 214mg; Carbohydrate 6g (Dietary Fiber 1g); Protein 6g.*

White Beans with Rosemary Crostini

This recipe is a perfect winter appetizer because you don't need any fresh ingredients. Use the Basic Crostini recipe as the base for this easy crostini that pairs creamy cannellini beans (a type of white bean) with rosemary. Cannellini beans are different from white kidney beans and Great Northern beans, which are other kinds of white beans, so make sure that the label says "cannellini."

Preparation time: 5 minutes

Yield: 40 crostini

4 cans (15 ounces each) cannellini beans

2 tablespoons plus 2 teaspoons minced garlic

2 tablespoons plus 2 teaspoons crushed rosemary

1 cup extra-virgin olive oil

Salt and pepper

1 recipe Basic Crostini (earlier in this chapter)

1 Place the beans, garlic, rosemary, and olive oil in a small bowl and gently stir to combine, taking care not to mash the beans. Season well with salt and pepper. You may store this mixture at room temperature (being sure to cover the bowl with plastic wrap) for up to 3 hours.

2 When you're ready to serve, make the Basic Crostini recipe, arrange the bread slices on a serving platter, and top each one with a small mound of beans. Serve immediately.

Per serving: Calories 105 (From Fat 53); Fat 6g (Saturated 1g); Cholesterol 0mg; Sodium 155mg; Carbohydrate 11g (Dietary Fiber 2g); Protein 2g.

Frozen Puff Pastry Magic

Certain convenience products are high quality and really help save time in the kitchen. Frozen puff pastry is on that list. Every supermarket carries frozen puff pastry; look for an all-butter version and use it if you find it. The instructions are usually fairly simple. You let it sit at room temperature for about 25 minutes, carefully unfold the frozen sheets of pastry, and proceed with the recipe.

In the hors d'oeuvres world, puff pastry is used in myriad ways. I show you how to make some crispy, flaky, cheesy, stick-shaped treats as well as butterfly-shaped hors d'oeuvres flavored with pesto and filled with sun-dried tomatoes.

If you want to make your own puff pastry, by all means, go for it! Most baking books, including *Desserts For Dummies* by Bill Yosses and Bryan Miller (Wiley), have a recipe. Making puff pastry isn't very hard, but it is time consuming. So read the recipe thoroughly and make sure that you have the time to handle it.

Spicy Cheese Straws

If you use purchased puff pastry, these cheese straws come together quite easily.

Preparation time: *10 minutes*

Cooking time: *12 minutes*

Yield: *40 cheese straws, 6 inches each*

½ pound frozen puff pastry

¾ cup Parmesan cheese

1½ ounces (½ cup, lightly packed) sharp cheddar cheese, finely grated

¼ teaspoon cayenne

Pinch of salt

Pepper

Flour for dusting work surface

1 egg, beaten until frothy

1 Remove the puff pastry from the freezer and let it sit at room temperature for 25 minutes (or have homemade puff pastry ready to go). Line 2 baking sheets with parchment paper and set aside.

2 While the pastry is defrosting, combine the Parmesan cheese, cheddar cheese, cayenne, salt, and a few grinds of black pepper in a bowl. Toss gently.

3 Dust the work surface with flour and roll out 1 piece of dough to approximately ⅛-inch thickness and to a rectangle approximately 13 x 16 inches. Arrange the rectangle so that the shorter edges are positioned horizontally.

4 Brush the surface of the pastry with some egg. Sprinkle half of the cheese mixture on the bottom half of the dough. Fold the top half over the bottom half. Roll the pastry into a 13-x-16-inch rectangle again. Brush with egg (you will have some egg left over) and sprinkle the remaining cheese mixture over the entire surface. Gently roll a rolling pin over the cheese to help it adhere.

5 Trim the edges with a sharp knife to create an even shape and to free the individual layers so that they'll puff in the oven. (That's why they call it puff pastry!) Cut the pastry into ¾-inch strips from one long side to the other. Then divide the pastry in half from short end to short end. You should have about 40 pieces that are about 6 inches long. Place the strips on sheet pans so that they aren't touching. Pick up each strip by the ends, twist the ends in opposite directions to create a spiral, and place back on the baking sheet. Place the baking sheets in the refrigerator to chill for 30 minutes.

6 Preheat the oven to 400 degrees. Bake the cheese straws for about 12 minutes or until uniformly golden brown. Let them cool on the baking sheet for 5 minutes. You may serve them warm or cool them completely on a wire rack.

Tip: Pepperidge Farm Puff Pastry is the most widely available puff pastry. The box holds 2 sheets, with a total weight of 17¼ ounces. (Who comes up with these amounts, anyway?) So if you use this brand of puff pastry for this recipe, use only 1 sheet, or half the box.

Per serving: Calories 45 (From Fat 28); Fat 3g (Saturated 1g); Cholesterol 8mg; Sodium 59mg; Carbohydrate 3g (Dietary Fiber 0g); Protein 2g.

Pesto Sun-Dried Tomato Palmiers

Palmiers, pronounced palm-ee-yay, is the French word for palm leaves, which these small pastries are said to resemble. For this recipe, you need prepared pesto, which you can find in the supermarket near the packaged fresh pasta. You also need sun-dried tomato paste, which comes in a tube, like a tube of toothpaste; if your supermarket has it, it will be near the tomato sauce or in a gourmet section. If you can't find it, start with oil-packed sun-dried tomatoes and whir them around in a food processor with additional olive oil to make a smooth paste and proceed from there.

Preparation time: *10 minutes*

Cooking time: *12 minutes*

Yield: *About 40 palmiers*

½ pound frozen puff pastry (see the tip at the end of the Spicy Cheese Straws recipe)

Flour for dusting work surface

3 tablespoons sun-dried tomato paste

½ cup pesto

¼ cup Parmesan cheese

1 Remove the puff pastry from the freezer and let it sit at room temperature for 25 minutes (or have homemade puff pastry ready to go). Line 2 baking sheets with parchment paper and set aside.

2 Dust the work surface with flour and roll out dough to approximately ⅛-inch thickness and to a rectangle approximately 12 x 18 inches. Arrange the rectangle so that the longer edges are positioned horizontally.

3 Spread the sun-dried tomato paste over the pastry. Then spread the pesto over the tomato paste and sprinkle evenly with the Parmesan cheese. Starting with the bottom, long edge, roll tightly into a spiral log up to the center. Then roll the top down to the center so that you have 2 equal spiral logs meeting in the middle. Brush the center seam where the rolls meet with water, using a pastry brush. Gently press the rolls together; the water helps seal the pastry. Place on a baking sheet and refrigerate for 30 minutes. At this point, you can double-wrap the roll in plastic and freeze for up to 2 weeks. Defrost the roll in the refrigerator overnight before proceeding.

4 Preheat the oven to 375 degrees. Transfer the roll to a cutting board and slice into ⅓-inch slices, using a thin, sharp knife. Place the slices on the baking sheets, evenly spaced apart. Bake for about 6 minutes or until lightly golden and puffed. Flip them over and bake for about another 6 minutes or until golden and puffed on the second side.

5 Transfer to a stack of paper towels to briefly blot up any excess moisture. Serve warm.

Warning: *You need to use a thin, sharp knife to slice the pastry because you'll probably crush it if you use a heavy chef's knife, giving you misshapen pastries. A dull knife will drag through the pastry, leaving you with unsightly pinwheels. Don't use a serrated knife either because it will also tear the pastry.*

Per serving: *Calories 50 (From Fat 34); Fat 4g (Saturated 1g); Cholesterol 2mg; Sodium 53mg; Carbohydrate 3g (Dietary Fiber 0g); Protein 1g.*

Having Phun with Phyllo

Phyllo is an ultrathin, almost transparent, pastry dough that originally hails from Greece; translated, it means "leaf." It's a simple mixture of flour and water — no yeast, no sugar, no eggs, no butter. But the process of making phyllo can be difficult. Kneading and resting and stretching the dough to its thinnest possible thickness take some skill, and the task is most easily accomplished with at least two people. For this reason, most people use purchased frozen phyllo dough, even in traditional Greek homes.

Frozen phyllo dough is available in most supermarkets — right near the frozen puff pastry. If you live near a large Greek community, ask around. You may be able to find a source of fresh phyllo dough. I've never been lucky enough to use it, but you may be!

All pastry, be it pie dough or puff pastry or phyllo, has its own quirky nature. With phyllo, the main pitfall is that it dries out easily. Check the instructions on the particular brand's box, but here are some general tips on working with phyllo:

- ✔ Thaw the phyllo, in the box, in the refrigerator overnight.
- ✔ When you're ready to make your recipe, have the filling and melted butter ready to go.
- ✔ Have a baking sheet covered with a clean, damp kitchen towel and have another clean, damp kitchen towel nearby.
- ✔ Remove the phyllo, wrapped in a sealed plastic bag, from the box.

✔ Open the plastic bag and carefully and completely unfold the dough to its full size, placing it on the damp towel on the baking sheet. Immediately cover with the other damp towel.

✔ As you're making the recipe, always keep the phyllo covered with a damp towel.

If you don't keep the phyllo covered, it will dry out within a minute — literally — and become so dry that it cracks and tears and becomes impossible to use. Phyllo dries out so quickly because it's so thin. Take advantage of my experience and make sure to always replace the damp towel on top of the stack of phyllo as you're preparing your recipe.

✔ Even experienced phyllo users encounter a few tears and cracks in the pastry. Don't panic. Simply patch some pieces together the best you can.

Tiropetes

Tiropetes (tee-rope-pee-tahs) are crispy, flaky, cheese-filled pastries that are a hit at all sorts of parties. You can even assemble them a day ahead, refrigerate them, and bake them right before serving. Or you can bake them 6 hours ahead and rewarm them in the oven as guests arrive.

Preparation time: *20 minutes*

Cooking time: *17 minutes*

Yield: *32 triangles*

2 eggs	*2 teaspoons minced fresh flat-leaf parsley*
½ pound cottage cheese (not fat-free)	*Pepper*
½ pound feta cheese, crumbled	*16 sheets phyllo dough (part of a 1-pound box)*
2 teaspoons dill	*¾ cup (1½ sticks) unsalted butter, melted*

1 Line 2 baking sheets with parchment paper.

2 Place the eggs in a large bowl and whisk until blended. Add the cottage cheese, feta cheese, dill, parsley, and a few grinds of pepper.

3 Place one sheet of phyllo on a work surface, with the long sides positioned horizontally. Brush with the butter, place another sheet on top, and brush with butter again. Remember to keep the unused phyllo covered with a clean, damp kitchen towel or plastic wrap so that it doesn't dry out and become unusable.

4 Cut the phyllo dough lengthwise into four long strips, as shown in Figure 8-3. Each strip should be about 3 inches wide. Place about a tablespoon of filling on a bottom corner of each strip and fold over on the diagonal to form a triangle. Continue folding, back and forth, retaining the triangular shape, until you reach the end of the strip. Brush the tops of the pastries with more butter and repeat the process, using the remaining phyllo and filling. Place the triangles on a baking sheet so that they don't touch.

5 At this point, you may bake them, or cover the tray with plastic wrap and refrigerate overnight. You also can wrap them tightly and freeze for up to a month. When you're ready to bake them, preheat the oven to 375 degrees. (Take the tiropetes out of the refrigerator or freezer while the oven preheats.) Bake for about 17 minutes or until golden brown. Serve warm. You may also bake them up to 6 hours ahead, store them at room temperature, and rewarm them in a 350-degree oven for a few minutes before serving.

Tip: Don't heat tiropetes in the microwave oven. The delicate, crispy nature of the pastries, one of the best features of phyllo, will be obliterated, and you'll most likely end up with soggy pastries.

Per serving: Calories 97 (From Fat 63); Fat 7g (Saturated 4g); Cholesterol 32mg; Sodium 158mg; Carbohydrate 6g (Dietary Fiber 0g); Protein 3g.

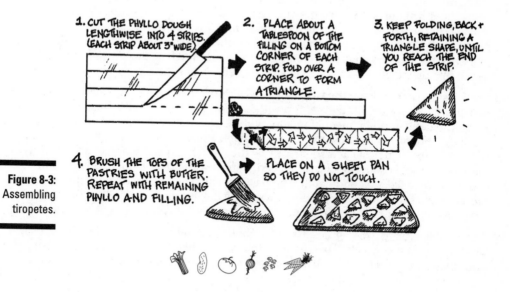

Figure 8-3:
Assembling
tiropetes.

Beggar's Purses with Lamb and Feta

Beggar's purses are little pouches, in this case filled with lamb and feta cheese. As with the tiropetes, you can assemble them a day ahead and bake them right before serving them. Or you can bake them 6 hours ahead and rewarm them as guests arrive.

Preparation time: *20 minutes, including sauce*

Cooking time: *13 minutes*

Yield: *40 appetizers*

¼ cup minced onion

1½ teaspoons light olive oil

¾ pound ground lamb

½ teaspoon crushed rosemary

Pepper

4 ounces feta cheese, finely crumbled

6 sheets phyllo dough

6 tablespoons (¾ stick) unsalted butter, melted

Garlic-Yogurt Dipping Sauce (see the following recipe)

1 Line a baking sheet with parchment paper.

2 Sauté the onions with the olive oil over medium heat in a large sauté pan until translucent, about 5 minutes. Remove the onions from the pan and set aside. Crumble the lamb and add to the pan. Sauté over medium heat until it is uniformly cooked through and no longer pink. Drain any fat or moisture and add the onions back in. Season with the rosemary and pepper and cook for 1 minute more. Stir in the feta cheese. (You don't need salt in this recipe because the feta is already very salty.)

3 Place 1 sheet of phyllo on the work surface, with the long edges positioned horizontally. Brush with the melted butter and top with a second piece of phyllo. Repeat once more with butter and another sheet of phyllo. Cut the phyllo into fourths horizontally and vertically into fifths. You now have twenty 3-inch squares. Place a heaping teaspoon of filling in the center of each square. Draw the corners up and pinch to seal the top. Place on the baking sheets, evenly spaced. Repeat with the remaining phyllo, butter, and filling to make a second batch. The pastries can be made up to a day ahead and refrigerated at this point until needed. Wrap the baking sheet carefully with plastic wrap, taking care not to crush the pastries. Or you can bake them right away.

4 Preheat the oven to 375 degrees. Bake for about 13 minutes or until light golden brown. Serve warm. You may also bake them up to 6 hours ahead, store them at room temperature, and rewarm them in a 350-degree oven for a few minutes before serving. Serve with the Garlic-Yogurt Dipping Sauce.

Per serving: Calories 58 (From Fat 36); Fat 4g (Saturated 2g); Cholesterol 13mg; Sodium 64mg; Carbohydrate 3g (Dietary Fiber 0g); Protein 2g.

Garlic-Yogurt Dipping Sauce

1 cup full-fat plain yogurt

1 teaspoon minced garlic

Salt and pepper to taste

Combine the yogurt and garlic and season with salt and pepper.

Tip: *You may use a lowfat or nonfat version of yogurt, if you like; I happen to like the texture of the full-fat version.*

Per serving: *Calories 4 (From Fat 0); Fat 0g (Saturated 0g); Cholesterol 1mg; Sodium 17mg; Carbohydrate 0g (Dietary Fiber 0g); Protein 0g.*

Tempting Your Guests with Tartlets

Savory tarts and tartlets provide welcome variety for your hors d'oeuvres table. The very smallest ones, about 2 inches in diameter, make a fine addition to a bridal shower or a New Year's Eve celebration. Large ones, such as an 11-inch mushroom tart, can be made in one pan and then sliced for individual servings. Tarts also come in between those sizes, such as the variation for the mushroom tart, which gives you individual tartlets about 4 inches in diameter.

Whatever their size, tarts consist of a basic dough with some sort of filling. Tarts, unlike pies, are unmolded from the tins in which they're baked, so the crust has to be firm enough to retain its shape. This dough is easy to work with, so don't shy away from trying these recipes.

The first tart recipe, which makes 2-inch onion tartlets, features a crust that is baked blind, which means it is completely baked without filling. Then, right before serving, you add the filling. The second recipe is for a larger tart that has a filling baked into it. I provide you with these two options so that you can use either technique to come up with variations of your own.

For these recipes, you need special tartlet tins for the larger versions and mini muffin tins for the smaller ones. You can find these pans at most kitchenware shops or through mail order catalogs. You can't make these recipes without them, so plan ahead. Both the 11-inch tart tin and 3-inch tartlet tins have fluted edges and are about 1 inch deep. Some have removable bottoms, which make for easy unmolding; buy those if you can find them. The mini muffin tins are one solid piece, but if you follow my instructions, the baked pastry will unmold easily. When working with solid pans, make sure to butter and flour the tartlet tins thoroughly or, better yet, use a nonstick version.

Caramelized Onion Tartlets with Crème Fraîche

These miniature tartlets start with a prebaked tartlet. Then you fill them right before serving. Although this recipe reads long, it is really quite simple. You make the tart dough, make the filling, and assemble it — that's it!

You do need crème fraîche, which is a cultured cream product, like sour cream, but has a slightly different flavor. You can find it in some cheese departments or near the sour cream in upscale supermarkets and specialty stores. If you want to substitute full-fat sour cream, you can.

Specialty tools: *2¼-inch cookie cutter, 1½-inch, 12-well mini muffin tins (you need 36 mini muffin wells)*

Preparation time: *20 minutes, plus 15 minutes freezing time*

Cooking time: *30 minutes*

Yield: *Thirty-six 2-inch tartlets*

1 recipe Basic Tart Dough (at the end of this section)	*¼ teaspoon thyme*
	2 tablespoons dry vermouth
2 cups very thinly sliced onions (about 2 small onions)	*Salt and pepper to taste*
½ teaspoon minced garlic	*⅓ cup crème fraîche or sour cream*
2 tablespoons plus 1½ teaspoons olive oil	*Fresh thyme sprigs (optional)*

1 Thoroughly and evenly butter and flour the pans. If you're using nonstick pans, you can skip this step.

2 Roll out the tart dough to ⅛-inch thickness. Cut out 2¼-inch circles using a cookie cutter. Gather the dough together, reroll, and cut out circles until you have 36, using all the dough. Press each circle into a muffin well and prick the bottoms. Freeze for 15 minutes (or refrigerate for 30 minutes).

3 Preheat the oven to 400 degrees. Bake the tartlets for about 5 minutes or until very light golden brown. They should be dry to the touch. The edges should have a tiny bit of color, whereas the center will remain almost white. Let them cool in the tins for 5 minutes and then carefully pop them out of the tins. When you invert a tin, the tartlet should pop out. If it doesn't, try tapping the bottom with a spoon or gently rapping the tin on your work surface. Cool the tartlets completely on a wire rack. Repeat with the remaining dough, if necessary. The tartlets are now ready to use. Or you may place them in an airtight container and store them up to 3 days at room temperature.

4 To make the filling, sauté the onions and garlic in the olive oil in a large heavy-bottomed, deep-sided pan over medium-high heat. Stir frequently, allowing the onions to soften slowly and not burn. Once they have reduced by about half, turn the heat down to low-medium and continue to cook until they're well caramelized, about 20 minutes.

5 Add the thyme. Turn the heat to high and add the vermouth. Cook for 2 minutes, stirring constantly. Season with salt and pepper. You can use this mixture immediately or pack it into an airtight container and refrigerate for up to 3 days. Bring it back to room temperature before proceeding.

6 Right before serving, place about ½ teaspoon crème fraîche in the bottom of each tartlet and top with a heaping teaspoon of onions. Garnish with fresh thyme leaves, if desired. These are best if served immediately, but you may hold them at room temperature for up to 4 hours.

Tip: When you're ready to assemble the tartlets, zap the onions in the microwave to warm them if you made them ahead of time.

Per serving: Calories 45 (From Fat 30); Fat 3g (Saturated 2g); Cholesterol 6mg; Sodium 22mg; Carbohydrate 3g (Dietary Fiber 0g); Protein 1g.

Blind baking with your eyes wide open

In all the tart recipes in this book, the pastry is either partially baked or fully baked without any fillings, which is called "baked blind" or "blind baked." The purpose is to bake the crust so that it is dried out a bit, or is baked completely, and holds its shape. To make sure that the crust meets these criteria, you must bake it for the proper amount of time. But, to help the crust hold its shape, it sometimes needs a little help.

You sometimes see the term "pie weights" or "line the tart shell with foil and weights" in recipes. They're not talking about gym equipment here. Pie weights are small ceramic or metal beads that, once the tart is lined with foil, you pour into the crust to weigh down the crust to help hold up the sides. Instead of buying these items, however, you can use rice or dried beans — or even pennies. The idea is that you need something that is heavy enough to weigh down the crust, small enough to fit within the crust, and capable of withstanding oven temperatures.

Exotic Mushroom Tart

This tart is 11 inches across, which you can slice to make an attractive plated appetizer before a formal meal. It combines white button mushrooms with a blend of exotic mushrooms and a rich custard.

Specialty tools: *One 11-inch tart pan with a removable bottom or six 3-inch tartlet pans with removable bottoms*

Preparation time: *20 minutes, plus 15 minutes freezing time and 30 minutes resting time*

Cooking time: *50 minutes for the larger tart, 30 minutes for smaller tartlets*

Yield: *One 11½-inch tart to yield 8 servings or six 3-inch tartlets*

1 recipe Basic Tart Dough (at the end of this section)	*2 tablespoons cognac or brandy*
	Salt and pepper to taste
⅓ ounce dried porcini mushrooms	*2 tablespoons minced flat-leaf parsley*
⅓ ounce dried shiitake mushrooms	*1¼ cups heavy cream*
¼ cup (½ stick) unsalted butter, cut into pieces	*3 eggs*
	2 egg yolks
⅓ cup minced onion	*1½ cups (5½ ounces) grated Gruyère cheese*
10 ounces button mushrooms, sliced	

1 Thoroughly and evenly butter and flour the pans. If you're using nonstick pans, you can skip this step.

2 Roll out the tart dough to an ⅛-inch thickness. Press the dough into the pan or into the individual pans, pressing it into the fluted shapes. Trim away any excess and prick the bottoms all over. Freeze for 15 minutes (or refrigerate for 30 minutes).

3 Meanwhile, place both the porcini and shiitake dried mushrooms in a small bowl and cover with boiling water; let them sit for 30 minutes or until softened. Drain, remove any hard stems, and finely chop.

4 Melt the butter in a heavy-bottomed sauté pan over medium heat, add the onions, and sauté until translucent, about 3 minutes, stirring occasionally. Add the dried and button mushrooms and cook over medium-high heat for about 3 minutes or until starting to reduce. Add the cognac, cover, and cook for an additional 4 minutes, stirring occasionally, until completely softened and lightly browned. Uncover and cook for 1 minute more, until the liquid is absorbed. Season with salt and pepper and stir in the parsley.

5 Preheat the oven to 375 degrees. If you're using individual tarts, place them on a baking sheet so that they're easy to take in and out of the oven. Line the tart or tarts with foil and fill with weights. (See the sidebar "Blind baking with your eyes wide open," earlier in this chapter.) Bake the 11-inch tart for about 10 to 12 minutes; remove the foil and weights. If the pastry bubbles up, prick it with a fork and press it back down. Bake for about 6 minutes more or until it begins to turn light brown. For the 3-inch tartlets, bake them for about 5 minutes with the foil and weights and for about 3 minutes without. Remove the tarts from the oven.

6 While the tarts are prebaking, whisk together the cream, eggs, and egg yolks; season with salt and pepper. Scatter the cheese over the tart bottom or divide the cheese among the tartlets; cover with the mushrooms. Top with the cream mixture.

7 Bake for about 20 to 25 minutes for the 11-inch tart and about 12 minutes for the 3-inch tarts or until the filling is set and the top and edges are tinged with brown. Transfer the tarts to a rack to cool for at least 10 minutes before serving. You may also serve them at room temperature or rewarm them before serving.

8 To unmold the tarts, press the solid bottom up, and the sides should release. For the large tart, slice into wedges and serve the wedges on plates. For individual tarts, use a broad spatula to remove the tartlets and gently place on a plate for serving.

Vary It! *Try Emmentaler or fontina cheese in place of the Gruyère cheese.*

Per serving: *Calories 458 (From Fat 344); Fat 38g (Saturated 22g); Cholesterol 245mg; Sodium 203mg; Carbohydrate 17g (Dietary Fiber 1g); Protein 13g.*

Basic Tart Dough

You can use this pastry dough for either of the tartlet recipes in this chapter. It freezes very well, too. I like to make this pastry in the food processor, but you may also make it by hand. The directions for making it by hand are in the tip at the end of the recipe. You may double this recipe.

Preparation time: *10 minutes, plus 2 hours for the dough to rest*

Yield: *One 11-inch tart, five 4-inch tartlets, or thirty-six 2-inch tartlets made in muffin tins*

1 cup all-purpose flour	6 tablespoons (¾ stick) cold unsalted butter, cut into small pieces
Pinch of salt	2 to 3 tablespoons ice water

1 Place the flour and salt in the bowl of a food processor fitted with the metal blade. Pulse on and off twice to combine. Add the butter pieces and pulse on and off several times to break up the butter. Turn the machine on briefly, until the dough is the texture of coarse meal. Turn the machine off and slowly add 2 tablespoons of water, pulsing on and off until the dough just comes together. Add more water if necessary.

2 Gather the dough together, shape into a flattened disk, and wrap in plastic wrap. Refrigerate for at least 2 hours. You may double-wrap the dough and freeze for up to a month. Or keep it refrigerated overnight, in which case it needs to soften slightly before rolling. Proceed with one of the following tartlet recipes.

Tip: *You may make this pastry dough by hand. Simply place the flour and salt in a bowl and scatter the butter on top. Cut the butter in, using a pastry blender or your fingers, and work the mixture until it resembles a coarse meal. Drizzle in the water a little at a time and mix just until the dough is moistened. Form the dough into a ball. Proceed as in the recipe.*

Tip: *The two-hour rest in the refrigerator is important. Not only does it firm up the pastry so that it's easier to roll, but the gluten (protein) in the flour has a chance to relax. As a result, the tartlets shrink less when you bake them, and the crust is more tender.*

Per serving: *Calories 133 (From Fat 79); Fat 9g (Saturated 5g); Cholesterol 23mg; Sodium 19mg; Carbohydrate 12g (Dietary Fiber 0g); Protein 0g.*

Loading Biscuits and Miniature Muffins with Flavor

I encourage you to explore the magnificence of miniature muffins. Prepared as tiny, almost bite-sized morsels, they provide a delicious foil for a variety of fillings. I give you a corn muffin recipe that, paired up with smoked ham and honey mustard, makes a tasty appetizer. If you like, you can make them full size for your breakfast, too.

I also present some biscuit recipes in this section. Biscuits are often best when they're eaten fresh and hot out of the oven, and for this reason, they're almost always made at home and not bought in a bakery or supermarket. Other than the fact that you want to make them close to serving time, they're actually very easy to make. They do come saddled with a mystique similar to pie crust; some cooks just seem to have the right touch, but other cooks find them difficult to make well.

For the biscuit recipe in this chapter, I suggest that you use a 2-inch biscuit cutter, not a cookie cutter, which isn't deep enough to cut through biscuit dough. When you cut out the biscuits, make sure that you go straight down with your cutter and then straight back up. Cooks tend to want to twist the cutter to make sure that they've cut all the way through. Do not do this! When you twist the cutter, you seal the edges of the biscuits. The layers smoosh together, and the pastry self-seals with itself; as a result, the individual layers aren't free to rise as high as possible in the oven.

Buttermilk Biscuits with Cranberry Chutney and Turkey

Biscuits are best eaten soon after they're made. You can make them up to 2 hours ahead, but they're extraordinary if served within the hour. Be gentle with the dough, and the biscuits will come out nice and light. The cranberry chutney makes more than you need. But it keeps well, and you'll find many uses for it — try it with roast chicken for a weeknight dinner.

Specialty tools: *2-inch biscuit cutter*

Preparation time: *15 minutes, plus 30 minutes resting time*

Cooking time: *20 minutes*

4 cups all-purpose flour

1½ teaspoons salt

2 tablespoons baking powder

½ teaspoon baking soda

12 tablespoons shortening, cut into 1-inch pieces

1½ cups buttermilk

1 Preheat the oven to 450 degrees. Have ready 1 large baking sheet.

2 Whisk together the flour, salt, baking powder, and baking soda in a large bowl. Cut in the shortening with a pastry blender or two knives until the mixture is uniform and the texture of coarse meal. Gently stir in the buttermilk just until the dough comes together and is evenly moistened. Take care not to overwork the dough. Cover with a damp kitchen towel or plastic wrap and let sit at room temperature for 30 minutes.

3 Turn the dough out onto a work surface and gently pat out to a ½-inch thickness. Cut out biscuits as close together as possible. Gently gather together any scraps and cut out the last few biscuits.

4 Transfer the biscuits to the baking sheet, arranging them so that they're not touching. Bake for about 10 minutes or until just tinged with brown on the bottom. Biscuits are best served as soon as possible. You may, however, make these up to 2 hours ahead, if necessary. Cover the baking sheet with a clean kitchen towel and let stand at room temperature until needed.

Cranberry Chutney

½ cup chopped onions

1 tablespoon vegetable oil

1 teaspoon minced garlic

12-ounce bag fresh or frozen cranberries

½ cup dried cranberries

⅔ cup sugar

¼ cup cider vinegar

1 teaspoon minced fresh ginger

Salt and pepper to taste

1 Combine the onions and oil in a large sauté pan. Cook over medium-high heat for about 4 minutes, until the onions have softened. Add the garlic and sauté for 1 minute more.

2 Add the fresh and dried cranberries, sugar, vinegar, and ginger and stir to combine. Cook over high heat, stirring frequently, for about 5 minutes, or until the raw cranberries have popped and the mixture has thickened. Season with salt and pepper. Cool to room temperature. You can use the cranberry chutney immediately or pack it in an airtight container and refrigerate for up to 1 week.

Assembly

10 ounces sliced turkey breast

Split each biscuit horizontally with a knife. Spread the bottom half with 1 teaspoon cranberry chutney and top with a folded piece of turkey, about ½ ounce meat per biscuit. Cap off with biscuit tops and serve immediately. You may also arrange the biscuit sandwiches in a pyramid on a serving platter and cover with plastic wrap for up to an hour before serving.

Simplify: *Many jarred chutneys are available, and some are quite good. In the supermarket, somewhere near the mustard, you'll most likely be able to locate a mango chutney, which is probably the most common kind.. Substitute it in this recipe if you want to simplify your approach.*

Per serving: Calories 231 (From Fat 82); Fat 9g (Saturated 2g); Cholesterol 6mg; Sodium 536mg; Carbohydrate 32g (Dietary Fiber 2g); Protein 6g.

Corn Muffins with Honey Mustard and Smoked Ham

This corn muffin recipe is a very basic one. Feel free to make the recipe in standard muffin tins if you want a larger muffin. The combination of butter and oil is important; the butter provides great flavor, and the oil keeps the muffins nice and soft at room temperature longer than if they were made with all butter.

Specialty tools: *Miniature muffin tin with 12 cups, each 1½ inches in diameter*

Preparation time: *10 minutes*

Cooking time: *10 minutes*

Yield: *48 miniature muffins*

1 ¾ cups stone ground yellow cornmeal	¼ cup (½ stick) unsalted butter, melted
1¼ cups all-purpose flour	¼ cup vegetable oil
½ cup sugar	2 eggs
4 teaspoons baking powder	½ cup honey mustard
1 teaspoon salt	20 ounces sliced smoked ham
1½ cups buttermilk	

1 Preheat the oven to 400 degrees. Generously coat the insides of the muffin tins with nonstick cooking spray.

2 Combine the cornmeal, flour, sugar, baking powder, and salt in a large bowl and whisk to blend. In a separate bowl, whisk the buttermilk, butter, vegetable oil, and eggs together. Add the buttermilk mixture to the cornmeal mixture and stir just until blended.

3 Fill the muffin tins about two-thirds full. Bake for 10 minutes or until they're puffed and slightly golden and a toothpick inserted in the center of a muffin comes out clean. Let the muffins cool for 5 minutes in their tins and then turn them out onto a rack to cool further. If you're using only one muffin tin, proceed with the remaining batter. The muffins may be used warm, or you can let them cool completely.

4 To assemble, cut the muffins in half horizontally. Spread the bottom halves with a little bit of mustard and top with a tiny bit of ham. Replace the top halves of the muffins and serve as soon as possible. You can stack the muffins in a pyramid on a serving platter, cover them tightly with plastic wrap, and hold for 1 hour before serving, if necessary.

Per serving: Calories 95 (From Fat 31); Fat 3g (Saturated 1g); Cholesterol 18mg; Sodium 217mg; Carbohydrate 10g (Dietary Fiber 1g); Protein 3g.

Dijon-Parmesan Almonds;
Herbed Popcorn (both in Chapter 5)

Shrimp Cocktail with Two Sauces:
Cocktail Sauce and Fresh Herb and Garlic Sauce
(all in Chapter 6)

Guacamole;
Fried and Baked Corn Chips
(all in Chapter 7)

Basic Appetizer Pizzas with toppings, front to back: mozzarella, tomato, and basil; mozzarella and yellow and green squash; provolone, olives, and prosciutto (Chapter 9)

Caramelized Onion Tartlets with
Crème Fraîche (Chapter 8)

Canapes, counterclockwise from front:
pumpernickel bread with egg and red onion;
rye bread with roasted turkey and cranberry chutney;
Corn Muffins with Honey Mustard and Smoked Ham (Chapter 8)

**Vietnamese Spring Rolls with Peanut Dipping Sauce
(Chapter 10)**

Seared Tuna with Wasabi-Ginger Dressing (Chapter 11)

Chapter 9

The Heat Is On: Hot Hors d'Oeuvres

● ●

In This Chapter

▶ Preparing potato skins

▶ Shelling out scallops and mussels

▶ Cheering for chicken wings

▶ Baking brie

▶ Cooking pizzas and nachos

● ●

*W*hen you go to a bar or restaurant and order an appetizer, chances are it's served warm or hot. Sure, you find cold offerings here and there, but a hot appetizer warms up your palates for what is to come. But you don't need to go to a restaurant for hot appetizers such as potato skins and chicken wings. You can make your own mouth-watering versions at home.

This chapter contains recipes for those appetizers, along with scallops wrapped in bacon, and garlicky mussels on the half shell. You can also find instructions for making a baked brie that will feed a crowd and an easy home-made pizza dough for your own hors d'oeuvres-size pizzas. And what appetizer cookbook would be complete without the author's favorite version of nachos? I promise that these recipes won't let you down.

Potato Skins: This Spud's for You

Potato skins are everywhere. I'm not talking about the peelings left over from your mashed potatoes. I'm talking about those delicious appetizers of baked or fried scooped-out potatoes that combine both crisp and tender textures all in one dish. Sometimes they're served with a dip, and sometimes they're filled with all sorts of luscious things — cheese, vegetables, bacon, you name it! You can get potato skins in bars, family-style restaurants, fancy restaurants (where I've seen them stuffed with caviar), and even in the frozen foods section of the supermarket. Potatoes have such a great flavor and texture that they lend themselves to many variations.

But have you made them at home? There's no mystery to making them. They're really quite easy to prepare, and they require ingredients that are easy to find. They're quite hearty and best served when you need something filling. How about at a Super Bowl party or a winter potluck dinner?

Stuffed Potato Skins with Horseradish Sour Cream and Chive Dip

These popular restaurant appetizers are very easy to make at home. The potato skins sometimes come out crisp enough to eat as finger food, and sometimes they come out floppy, so you need a fork and knife. The result all depends on how evenly and effectively you scoop out the potato flesh and how long you roast the skins. They taste great either way.

Preparation time: *15 minutes*

Cooking time: *60 minutes if using the oven, 25 minutes if using the microwave*

Yield: *6 servings*

6 medium russet potatoes, whole, scrubbed, and baked or cooked in microwave	Pinch of cayenne
¼ cup light olive oil	1 cup small broccoli florets, cooked just until done (they should be bite size)
1 teaspoon paprika	¾ cup shredded sharp cheddar cheese (about 2 ounces)
½ teaspoon cumin	¾ cup shredded Monterey Jack cheese (about 2 ounces)
½ teaspoon garlic powder	Horseradish Sour Cream and Chive Dip (see the following recipe)
½ teaspoon thyme	
½ teaspoon salt	
Pepper	

1 Preheat the oven to 425 degrees. Have ready a rimmed jelly roll pan.

2 Cut the potatoes in half lengthwise and scoop out the flesh, leaving a ⅛-inch shell of potato flesh and skin. Save the soft scooped-out flesh for mashed potatoes. Cut each half in half lengthwise. Brush the potatoes inside and out with olive oil.

3 Combine the paprika, cumin, garlic powder, thyme, salt, a few grinds of pepper, and cayenne in a small bowl. Sprinkle evenly over the potatoes, inside and out. Place them, flesh side down, on the baking pan and roast for about 8 minutes or until browned on the fleshy side. Flip them over and roast for another 10 minutes or until they're crisp on the skin side.

4 Remove the skins from the oven, scatter the broccoli over the potato "boats," and sprinkle both cheeses over all. Return them to the oven until the cheese is melted, about 3 minutes.

5 Serve hot on a platter surrounding the bowl of dip.

Horseradish Sour Cream and Chive Dip

1 cup sour cream

1 tablespoon snipped chives (dried or fresh)

1 tablespoon minced fresh flat-leaf parsley

2 teaspoons prepared horseradish

1 teaspoon lemon juice

Salt and pepper to taste

While the potato skins are roasting, make the dip by combining the sour cream, chives, parsley, horseradish, and lemon juice in a bowl and seasoning with salt and pepper.

Vary It! *To make a lighter version, without the broccoli and cheese topping, simply stop after Step 3 and serve the seasoned skins with the dip as is.*

Tip: *Take care when scooping out the flesh so that a thin, even layer of potato is left inside the skin. If you scoop all the way down to the skin, no potato will be left to hold it together. Also, make sure that you cook the skins long enough on both sides so that they crisp up nicely. But you know what? Even if you have to use a fork and knife to eat these potatoes, you're gonna love the way they taste.*

Per serving: *Calories 392 (From Fat 236); Fat 26g (Saturated 12g); Cholesterol 44mg; Sodium 496mg; Carbohydrate 30g (Dietary Fiber 5g); Protein 11g.*

Searching for Scallops: Watch Out for Sharks

Several types of scallops are available for your appetizer recipes, but the two most commonly found are sea scallops, which are large — about the size of half a golf ball — and smaller scallops, which might be bay scallops or another type called calico. The smaller scallops are the size of small marbles or smaller. For the Bacon-Wrapped Scallops recipe, the bacon can overpower the delicate, briny scallop all too easily, so I prefer using halved sea scallops. That way, there's a high scallop-to-bacon ratio.

Bacon-Wrapped Scallops

These appetizers were in vogue decades ago, so they may be considered a retro item. But there's a reason why they're still around. The smoky nature of the bacon complements the creamy, fresh taste of the sea scallops. My version is light on the bacon with a high scallop-per-bite ratio.

Getting these cooked just right may take a bit of practice on your part. You want to cook the bacon until crisp, but you don't want to overcook the scallops. The scallops can afford to stay on the lightly cooked side, and because they're wrapped in bacon, they most likely won't get overcooked. The bacon, however, needs a high heat and a position close to the heat source. You also need to turn the scallops over at least once so that all sides of the bacon get a chance to crisp up. Do a sample batch first to see whether you have the hang of it and then make adjustments for subsequent batches.

Preparation time: 5 minutes

Cooking time: 6 minutes

Yield: 6 servings

24 large sea scallops	Pepper
6 slices bacon	1 lemon, quartered

1 Rinse and dry the scallops and cut them in half; set aside.

2 Cut the bacon slices lengthwise and then crosswise. (In other words, quarter each slice.)

3 Wrap a piece of bacon around each scallop half and secure with a toothpick. Season with pepper and place on a shallow roasting pan. (You may make the recipe 6 hours ahead up to this point. Cover the pan with plastic wrap and refrigerate until needed.)

4 Preheat the broiler when ready to serve and set the oven rack to the highest position. Broil the scallops for about 3 minutes, turn them over, and broil for about 3 more minutes or until the bacon is crisp and the scallops are just cooked through.

5 Transfer to a serving platter, squirt some fresh lemon juice over all, and serve immediately.

Tip: Broilers are funny things, sort of like microwaves, in that some are just way more powerful than others. In addition, the closer the food, the hotter the heat. Because of these factors, it's difficult to give you exact broiling times in any recipe that requires broiling.

Tip: Don't overlook the squeeze of lemon — it brightens the flavors of the dish immeasurably.

Per serving: Calories 141 (From Fat 93); Fat 10g (Saturated 4g); Cholesterol 25mg; Sodium 358mg; Carbohydrate 1g (Dietary Fiber 0g); Protein 11g.

Garlic Mussels on the Half Shell

This very simple recipe is quite impressive — give it a try. The amount of filling may be more than you need, but I want to make sure that you have enough, because mussels can vary so much in size.

Preparation time: *15 minutes*

Cooking time: *2 minutes per batch*

Yield: *50 mussels*

50 mussels, cleaned

1 cup white wine

1 medium shallot, peeled

1 medium garlic clove

3 tablespoons minced flat-leaf parsley

¼ cup (1/2 stick) unsalted butter, at room temperature, cut into pieces

½ cup fresh bread crumbs (see Chapter 8 for instructions)

Salt and pepper to taste

1 Place the mussels and wine in a large covered pot. Bring to a boil over medium-high heat and steam the mussels until they open, about 5 minutes. Drain, discarding any mussels that haven't opened. Cool the mussels for a few minutes, until they're easy to handle.

2 While the mussels are cooling, place the shallot, garlic, and parsley in the bowl of a food processor fitted with the metal blade. Pulse on and off until the mixture is evenly minced. Add the butter and bread crumbs and pulse on and off to combine. Season with salt and pepper.

3 Line a rimmed baking sheet or roasting pan with crumpled foil. Remove the top shells of the mussels and discard. Scatter the bottom shells on top of the crumpled foil to keep them from falling over. Top each with a bit of bread crumb mixture. I find this easiest to do with my fingers. Just pick up some of the butter/bread mixture and smear it over the mussel to cover. (You may refrigerate the mussels overnight at this point. Just cover them with plastic wrap.)

4 Preheat the broiler with the rack in the top position. Broil the mussels for about 2 minutes or until the crumbs are lightly browned. Serve immediately.

Per serving: Calories 27 (From Fat 13); Fat 1g (Saturated 1g); Cholesterol 8mg; Sodium 71mg; Carbohydrate 1g (Dietary Fiber 0g); Protein 2g.

Chicken Wings Take Off

I could write a book just on chicken wings — spicy wings, barbecue wings, Asian-glazed wings. I love 'em all — and judging from their popularity, so do lots of other people. But I had to choose one basic recipe for you, so I decided on the Glazed Chicken Wings. They are easy to make; have that sticky, yummy, flavorful quality I love in a chicken wing; and are a great choice to feed a crowd.

A whole chicken wing has two joints connecting three pieces. The last joint attaches a very skinny wing tip, which has no meat and offers nothing to the chicken wing eater. If your chicken wings come with three parts, remove the last, bony wing tip and discard or use for chicken stock. You're not quite done yet! Now separate the last two pieces. This is best accomplished with a cleaver or a heavy knife. It will be much easier for you and your guests to nibble on single pieces at a time.

Most supermarkets have this entire procedure done for you. Read the labels and look for chicken wings labeled "chicken wings and drummettes" or something similar. Packages with that label contain a combination of these two meaty parts of the chicken wing with nary a bony wing tip in sight. If you have a butcher, or can find a butcher in a supermarket meat department, you can ask for your raw chicken wings to be prepared to your specifications. This request is very common and a perfectly acceptable thing to expect from a butcher.

Showing your mussels

If you're more familiar with clams and oysters than with mussels, I have a treat for you. Mussels are not only delicious and beautiful, with their blue-black shells, but they're often the least expensive *bivalve* (a soft-bodied mollusk encased between two bilateral shells) available. You can buy dozens and be set back only a few bucks.

When cleaning the mussels, look for a beard. This fuzzy strand curves around the shell, like a beard — hence its name. You won't always see a beard on mussels, but if you do, grab an end and pull it off. You may have to help it along with a sharp knife. This technique is called "bearding a mussel."

After removing the beard, scrub the shells, which may be muddy. If they're particularly heavy, they may be dead and/or meatless and filled with mud. Mussels can be the dirtiest shellfish, so don't skip these steps.

Glazed Chicken Wings

These wings are sticky, sweet, and tangy — making them positively addictive. They're great for so many events, whether it's a football game or a cocktail party. Either way, offer plenty of napkins. This is finger-lickin' food.

Preparation time: *15 minutes, plus at least 2 hours for marinating*

Cooking time: *27 minutes*

Yield: *About 15 chicken wings (tips removed), divided in half, yielding 30 pieces*

½ cup honey	1 tablespoon lime juice
½ cup orange marmalade	1 tablespoon minced garlic
¼ cup orange juice	2½ to 3 pounds chicken wings, tips removed
¼ cup soy sauce	3 scallions, thinly sliced, both green and white parts
1 tablespoon grated ginger	

1 Place the honey, orange marmalade, orange juice, soy sauce, ginger, lime juice, and garlic in a large mixing bowl and whisk to combine well. Divide the chicken wings into two pieces by cutting at the joint; use a cleaver or heavy chef's knife. Add all the chicken wings and toss well to coat. Let them marinate in the refrigerator for at least 2 hours or even overnight. If you can, stir them around once or twice.

2 Preheat the oven to 375 degrees. Lift the wings with tongs or a slotted spoon and place them in a roasting pan so that they don't touch. You'll probably need 2 roasting pans. Roast the wings for 15 minutes, flip them over, and roast for 10 more minutes. (The wings can be made up to a day ahead at this point and refrigerated or held at room temperature for 1 hour.)

3 Meanwhile, pour the marinade into a small saucepan and boil on high heat until it is reduced by half and has become thick and syrupy, about 8 minutes.

4 Preheat the broiler right before serving and set the oven rack to the top position. Brush the thickened marinade over the wings and broil for about 2 minutes or until browned. Sprinkle with the scallions and serve immediately.

Tip: This recipe gives you about 30 wings. My three kids demolished these in minutes. Okay, I did help a bit, but the point is that these go fast. I've never seen anyone eat fewer than 3 of these, so plan accordingly.

Per serving: *Calories 151 (From Fat 51); Fat 6g (Saturated 2g); Cholesterol 24mg; Sodium 305mg; Carbohydrate 18g (Dietary Fiber 0g); Protein 8g.*

Briefing You about Brie

Brie is one of the greatest cheeses in the world. No wonder chefs are always coming up with ways to serve it. I give you a baked brie recipe, but I certainly didn't invent baked brie. The dish has been around for years. Sometimes it's encased in brioche and sometimes in phyllo. Sometimes no pastry is involved at all, but instead, various ingredients are stuffed inside the brie, spread over the top, or served with the brie. The engaging, delicate flavor of the cheese makes it the perfect foil for so many flavors, from fruits to vegetables to pastry to condiments and seasonings.

But you have to start with a good brie, so here's what to look for. This baked brie recipe calls for an entire wheel of brie, so you need to know your whole brie options. Most cheese shops can get you a 2.2-pound brie, which is about 8 inches across, and a larger size that is twice as heavy and about 15 inches across. Both are about 1½ inches high. They have a creamy interior and an edible white rind. Some people cut the rind away, but try it — it's delicious. Look for Brie de Meaux, which is considered to be the best. It's made in the Meaux region of France, where the cow's diet seems to affect this cheese most favorably. Some domestic bries are produced as well. Any brie should have at least 50 to 60 percent butterfat. If you buy a wedge of cheese, you can assess the ripeness of the inside. But because you need a whole brie for the recipe in this chapter, you should ask your cheese purveyor to pick you out a ripe one. When gently pressed, the brie should be soft and yielding. It should never have any kind of ammonia smell, which signals that it is past its prime. You can usually smell this aroma only after the brie is cut, but I want you to be aware of this indicator anyway.

For the recipe in this chapter, I suggest a 2.2-pound brie, which fits perfectly inside a 9-inch deep-dish pie plate. This is an important point as it provides you with a convenient way to bake and serve the brie all in one dish. If you want to use the larger brie (and double the other ingredients), you certainly can, but you need to have a baking or roasting pan large enough to hold it. Some recipes tell you that you can wrap up the whole shebang in heavy-duty aluminum foil. But once the brie is baked and becomes soft and melting, how are you supposed to transfer it to a serving platter? Save yourself this last-minute messy work and take the time to find something you can bake and serve it in before you start.

If you happen to have a large pan that is perfect to bake and serve the larger size brie in, then you have the choice of proceeding in this way. However, if you have an extra-large crowd coming over, I suggest making two smaller bries, each in its own pie plate. You can stagger their baking times so that you can enjoy warm, runny brie for the length of your party.

Baked Brie with Dried Cranberries, Pecans, and Grand Marnier

This appetizer is as warm, melting, and inviting as a hot hors d'oeuvre can be. Try this for a winter party. You need a deep-dish pie plate; I use a Pyrex one.

I need to offer one word of caution before you start to make this recipe: Take care to heat the Grand Marnier gently. Its alcohol content is high, and it could burst into flames if heated to too high a temperature.

Preparation time: *25 minutes*

Cooking time: *35 minutes*

Yield: *20 servings*

¾ cup dried cranberries (try Craisins, which are available in most supermarkets)

⅓ cup Grand Marnier

2.2 pounds brie (about 8 inches across)

¼ cup chopped, toasted pecans

¼ cup toasted pecan halves

2 loaves French bread, cut in ½-inch slices

1 Preheat the oven to 350 degrees.

2 Combine ½ cup of the dried cranberries with the Grand Marnier in a small saucepan. Heat over medium heat until the liqueur is warmed. (Or if you want, you can combine the cranberries and Grand Marnier in a microwaveable bowl and zap them for a minute.) Remove from the heat and let sit for 15 minutes to plump the cranberries.

3 Slice the brie in half horizontally and place the bottom half, cut side up, in a 9-inch deep-dish pie plate. Prick the cheese all over with a fork so that it will absorb the liqueur. Carefully drizzle half of the Grand Marnier liquid all over the brie and scatter the dried cranberries evenly over the cheese. Sprinkle the chopped pecans over the cranberries and put the top half of cheese over the bottom half, cut side down. Press gently. Prick the top of the cheese and drizzle the remaining Grand Marnier over it. The brie may be wrapped tightly in plastic wrap and refrigerated for up to 2 days at this point, or you can bake it and serve it immediately.

4 Bake the brie for 35 minutes or until the cheese is melted and beginning to bubble gently. Scatter the remaining ¼ cup cranberries over the brie and arrange the pecan halves on top as a garnish. Serve immediately with sliced French bread.

Tip: *You can find, or order, a whole brie from any reputable supermarket cheese department or from a specialty food store.*

Tip: *Many orange liqueurs are on the market, and most are less expensive than Grand Marnier. What makes Grand Marnier so special is that it is based on cognac, which gives it a remarkable depth of flavor. You can try Triple Sec or curaçao, both orange-flavored liqueurs, but they won't have the same effect.*

Per serving: *Calories 301 (From Fat 152); Fat 17g (Saturated 9g); Cholesterol 50mg; Sodium 521mg; Carbohydrate 22g (Dietary Fiber 2g); Protein 14g.*

Putting Pizazz in Your Pizza

I actually know people who don't like chocolate; I don't understand them, but I know them. However, I've never met a person who doesn't like pizza. Maybe that's because it's so chameleon-like. It can be thin and crispy, or thick and chewy. It can be topped with tomato sauce and mozzarella, or a white clam sauce. It can be slathered with pesto or loaded up with sautéed mushrooms, olives, sun-dried tomatoes, or caramelized onions. What's not to love? And you even get to eat it with your fingers, which just clinches the deal.

When served in small pieces, pizza is perfect as an hors d'oeuvre. If the only kind of pizza that you have ever made is with English muffins, jarred tomato sauce, and preshredded mozzarella cheese, don't worry. I give you the option of using purchased pizza dough, which makes these super easy and quick to make.

Regardless of how you make it, serve the pizza fresh out of the oven, when the crust is at its best.

Pizza dough: Homemade versus prepared

In my recipe for Appetizer Pizzas, I give you a recipe for homemade pizza dough. It isn't hard to make, but it does take some time, so you should plan ahead accordingly. The dough is easy to work with, and the result is worth the extra work, but if you really don't care for making your own dough or you simply don't have the time, feel free to use ready-made dough. Most supermarkets give you a few options. You may be able to find frozen pizza dough or pizza dough in a refrigerated section. Almost all supermarkets have the precooked pizza shells in the bread aisle, which you can use in a pinch, but try and find the raw dough. Sometimes it's labeled "bread dough."

In a last-minute situation, you can also use pita bread. Split the bread in half horizontally to produce two flat, round halves and spread your toppings on the cut sides. Bake, cut, and serve!

Take a look at the Pizza Dough recipe, later in this chapter, and then if you want to use premade, just pick up the directions where I describe the rolling-out technique or the step where you add the toppings for pizza shells and pita breads.

Getting the crust crispy

I look for a chewy aspect to my pizza crusts, but I do want the bottoms to be crispy. To get a pizza crust with that combination, you need just the right formula, and the recipe I provide in this chapter is exactly that.

However, your cooking technique has a lot to do with the final outcome. You need a very hot oven, and the type of pizza pan you use to bake the pizza also makes a big difference.

The pizza stones available at kitchenware stores and through catalogs (see Chapter 14) work wonders. If you use a pizza stone, you place it in the oven while the oven is preheating. The stone absorbs the heat and gets really hot. This technique replicates, as well as can be done in a home oven, the stone or brick floors of professional pizzeria ovens. When the dough is then placed on the hot stone, it has a better chance of crisping up well. If you like pizzas and plan to make them even a few times a year, buy a pizza stone. If you have a cast-iron griddle with a flat surface, you can use that, too. But any large, sturdy pan, including a baking sheet, will do.

To transfer the dough from your work surface to the hot stone in the oven, you may want to consider buying a peel, which you've probably seen in your local pizza parlor. A *peel* is a long-handled gadget, usually wooden, that's used to slide a pizza into the oven (see Figure 9-1). You can find them at well-stocked kitchenware stores and through some mail-order sources (see Chapter 14). But if you don't want to invest in another specialty tool, you can use a baking sheet in place of a peel. A rimless baking sheet works great, but if all you have is a rimmed baking sheet, turn it upside down and use the bottom.

If you don't want to buy a peel or don't have an extra baking pan around, you can try another way of making pizzas. Have the dough rolled out and ready to go and have all the topping ingredients ready to go. Preheat the pizza stone or heavy pan in the oven. When it's hot (which takes about 15 minutes), remove it — carefully, because it is hot — and place it on a trivet. Immediately place the dough on the pan, add the toppings, and get it back in the oven as quickly as possible. The dough may even sizzle a little bit when it comes in contact with the pan. This is a good sign and means that the bottom is searing and developing a nice crust. Bake as directed.

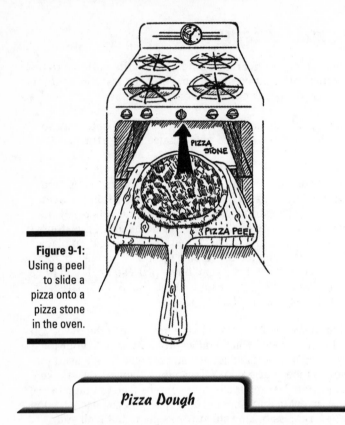

Figure 9-1:
Using a peel
to slide a
pizza onto a
pizza stone
in the oven.

Pizza Dough

This recipe tells you how to make a basic pizza dough. You do need yeast, but the other ingredients are pantry staples. Although you can make this by hand, I prefer to use a stand mixer and suggest that you do the same, if you have one.

Preparation time: *15 minutes active preparation, plus 2¼ hours resting time*

Yield: *About 2 pounds of dough, or 4 long rectangular pizzas, which yield about 50 pieces*

2¼ teaspoons active dry yeast

¼ cup warm (105 to 115 degrees) water

Pinch sugar

2½ to 3½ cups all-purpose flour (or bread flour or combination)

¾ cup plus 2 tablespoons water, at room temperature

½ teaspoon salt

Light olive oil

1 Place the yeast, the ¼ cup warm water, and sugar in a large mixing bowl and stir together well. Place in a draft-free location (such as inside a turned-off oven) for about 5 minutes or until bubbly and foamy.

2 Add 2½ cups of the flour, the ¾ cup plus 2 tablespoons water, and the salt. If using a stand mixer, use a bread hook and mix on low speed until the dough comes together and forms a soft dough. If making by hand, first stir together until you can turn the soft dough out onto a lightly floured board and begin to knead.

3 Add just enough additional flour to make a smooth and elastic dough that doesn't stick to the sides of the bowl or to your hands. When the dough achieves this texture, stop adding flour. Continue to knead to help develop the gluten (the protein that gives the dough its elasticity). Knead until the dough is absolutely smooth — either with the machine or by hand. This process takes about 3 minutes by machine or about 8 minutes by hand.

4 Form into a ball and place in a lightly oiled bowl. Cover with plastic wrap or a clean, damp towel and place in a draft-free location for about 1½ hours or until doubled in bulk. Press down the dough (to expel built-up gas), knead gently, re-form into a ball, cover, and let rise again, about 45 minutes or until doubled in bulk. Press down again, give it a few kneads by hand, and then separate into 4 pieces. Place them on a sheet pan and cover with plastic wrap or a clean, damp towel. You may refrigerate the dough overnight at this point. Or you can double-wrap the balls of dough individually in plastic wrap and freeze for up to 1 week. If using refrigerated dough, allow to come to room temperature for about an hour or until it regains its pliable, elastic texture. If you have frozen the dough, defrost the balls in the refrigerator overnight and then allow them to sit at room temperature until you're ready to roll them out.

5 Prepare all of your toppings at this time so that you'll be set to go when the dough is ready. See the Basic Appetizer Pizza recipe, later in this chapter, for instructions on the rolling out, topping, and baking procedure.

Tip: *Don't leave the salt out of the recipe. Flour, yeast, and water alone make for a very bland dough. The salt really enlivens the taste.*

Per serving: Calories 24 (From Fat 1); Fat 0g (Saturated 0g); Cholesterol 0mg; Sodium 24mg; Carbohydrate 5g (Dietary Fiber 0g); Protein 1g.

Appetizer pizzas: Toppings to make everybody happy

Everybody likes pizza because you can top it with whatever strikes your fancy. Like anchovies? Go for it. Is an all-white pizza up your alley? No problem. If you want to provide your guests with a variety of flavors as pizza toppings, have all the toppings ready to spread or scatter on top. With a bowl of this and a bowl of that at hand, you can mix and match toppings as you go along. Try ingredients from the following lists:

Here are some ideas for fresh and dried herb toppings:

- ✔ **Basil:** Fresh or dried
- ✔ **Oregano:** Fresh or dried
- ✔ **Parsley:** Fresh only, please
- ✔ **Rosemary:** Fresh or dried
- ✔ **Thyme:** Fresh or dried

Consider the following veggie toppings:

- ✔ **Bell peppers:** All colors, thinly sliced, and raw, sautéed, or roasted
- ✔ **Broccoli:** Small florets, lightly cooked
- ✔ **Eggplant:** Thinly sliced and sautéed
- ✔ **Fennel:** Thinly sliced and sautéed
- ✔ **Greens:** Chopped and sautéed spinach, beet greens, broccoli raab, kale, chard, or any greens you like
- ✔ **Mushrooms:** All kinds, thinly sliced, raw or sautéed
- ✔ **Onions:** Thinly sliced and raw or caramelized
- ✔ **Potatoes:** Cooked and thinly sliced
- ✔ **Scallions:** Chopped
- ✔ **Sun-dried tomatoes:** Chopped
- ✔ **Tomatoes:** Thinly sliced
- ✔ **Zucchini:** Thinly sliced and raw or sautéed

Choose from the following meat toppings:

- ✔ **Bacon:** Cooked and crisp
- ✔ **Ham:** Smoked or otherwise, thinly sliced
- ✔ **Pancetta (Italian bacon):** Thinly sliced or chopped
- ✔ **Prosciutto:** Thinly sliced

- ✔ **Sausage (fresh):** Cooked and sliced, either sweet or spicy
- ✔ **Sausage (hard salamis such as pepperoni or Genoa):** Thinly sliced or diced

Here are some cheeses to try. Shred, slice, or crumble them as appropriate.

- ✔ **Blue cheese**
- ✔ **Cheddar**
- ✔ **Chevre (goat cheese)**
- ✔ **Feta**
- ✔ **Fontina**
- ✔ **Mascarpone**
- ✔ **Monterey Jack cheese**
- ✔ **Mozzarella, regular or fresh**
- ✔ **Parmigiano-Reggiano**
- ✔ **Pecorino Romano**
- ✔ **Ricotta**

Top with one of these sauces and spreads:

- ✔ **Crème fraîche (or sour cream)**
- ✔ **Pesto**
- ✔ **Tapenade**
- ✔ **Tomato sauce**

Don't rule out seafood as a topping:

- ✔ **Anchovies:** Whole or chopped
- ✔ **Clams:** Cooked and either whole or chopped
- ✔ **Mussels:** Cooked and either whole or chopped
- ✔ **Shrimp:** Cooked and either sliced in half vertically or chopped
- ✔ **Smoked salmon:** Thinly sliced
- ✔ **Squid:** Cooked and either whole or chopped
- ✔ **Tuna:** Preferably the oil-packed canned variety, drained and crumbled

Miscellaneous toppings include the following:

- **Capers:** A nice tangy kick
- **Garlic:** Sliced, chopped, or minced; sautéed, caramelized, or raw
- **Nuts:** Toasted and chopped
- **Olive oil, extra-virgin:** Drizzled on top of a baked pizza
- **Olives, black or green:** Sliced or chopped

Here's my list of suggested combinations of pizza toppings:

- **Clam pizza:** Mozzarella cheese, Parmesan cheese, garlic, drizzle of extra-virgin olive oil, and clams.
- **Five-cheese pizza:** A blend of mozzarella, Parmesan, pecorino, ricotta, and Gorgonzola cheeses.
- **Margherita:** Tomatoes, fresh mozzarella cheese, and fresh basil leaves. (This pizza got its name because it was served to Queen Margherita in the late 1800s and she loved it.)
- **Pesto pizza:** Pesto topped with mozzarella and Parmesan cheeses. Fresh sliced tomatoes are optional.
- **Provençal pizza:** Tapenade (Chapter 7), capers, fresh basil, sliced tomatoes, and chevre.
- **Smoked salmon pizza:** Thinly sliced smoked salmon, crème fraîche or sour cream, fresh dill, and chopped scallions.
- **Spinach and walnut pizza:** Sautéed spinach, mozzarella cheese, Parmesan cheese, and chopped toasted walnuts.
- **White pizza:** Mozzarella cheese, Parmesan cheese, garlic, drizzle of extra-virgin olive oil.

In many pizzerias, you'll find shakers of Parmesan cheese, hot red pepper flakes, and dried oregano on the tables. As the saying goes, "ain't nothing wrong with that." Any of these common toppings can add a spark to a cooked pizza.

Basic Appetizer Pizza

This pizza recipe includes a basic topping. With an understanding of this recipe under your belt, you can make limitless variations. Check out the suggestions in the section "Appetizer pizzas: Toppings to make everybody happy," earlier in this chapter.

Specialty tools: Sheet pan or peel; a pizza stone or heavy pan, such as a flat cast-iron griddle for baking pizzas

Preparation time: 10 minutes

Cooking time: 7 minutes per batch

Yield: 56 servings

1 recipe Pizza Dough (see the preceding recipe)

Cornmeal

2 cups tomato sauce (homemade or your favorite jarred sauce)

2 cups shredded mozzarella cheese (about 8 ounces)

Parmesan cheese

1 Preheat the oven to 500 degrees. Preheat a pizza stone or other baking surface.

2 Roll out each piece of the dough, one at a time, on a lightly floured board. To maximize the surface area of your baking sheet or stone, make a long, slender rectangle about 16 x 4 inches. (You can, of course, make a traditional round shape. Pizzas that are about 6 inches across will cut into wedges that are a handy size for appetizers.) Sprinkle the cornmeal on the peel, a tool that I describe in the section "Getting the crust crispy," earlier in this chapter. Place the dough on the peel.

3 Spread some sauce over the dough to make a thin, even layer and sprinkle evenly with the mozzarella cheese and a bit of the Parmesan cheese. Transfer the pizza to the hot pan in the oven and bake for about 7 minutes or until the bottom is crisp, the edges are lightly browned, and the toppings are bubbling.

4 To serve, transfer to a cutting board and cut crosswise into small wedges (or cut your round pizza into wedges); you'll get about 14 wedges per long pizza of the suggested size (and 6 to 8 wedges per round). Serve immediately.

Tip: The 4-inch width of the pizza is important in this recipe if you're making the rectangular version. You cut these pizzas crosswise, so this width allows you to cut pieces that are small enough to easily pick up with your fingers. If your pan or pizza stone is 10 or 14 inches long, just adjust the length of your dough, always retaining the 4-inch width. In that case, you may get more than 4 pizzas out of your batch of dough and therefore may need to adjust your topping amounts.

Per serving: Calories 48 (From Fat 16); Fat 2g (Saturated 1g); Cholesterol 4mg; Sodium 114mg; Carbohydrate 6g (Dietary Fiber 0g); Protein 2g.

Super Nachos

How can you go wrong with corn chips, chili, guacamole, salsa, sour cream, and lots of cheese? Check out the corn chip recipes in Chapter 7 if you really want to go all out.

Don't shy away from using the pickled jalapeños, which aren't as spicy as raw hot chiles. Even if you aren't a fan of spicy hot foods, give these a try. Especially with all the cheese and sour cream to temper the flavors, you probably won't mind the extra heat. Just use less if you are faint of palate, however.

Preparation time: *10 minutes*

Cooking time: *12 minutes*

Yield: *4 servings*

8 ounces corn chips

10 ounces (about 2½ cups) shredded sharp cheddar cheese

1 cup prepared chili (meat or veggie/bean)

⅓ cup guacamole (purchased or made using the recipe in Chapter 7)

⅓ cup sour cream

4 pickled jalapeños, drained, stemmed, and minced

2 scallions, thinly sliced, both white and green parts

Salsa (at least 2 cups)

1 Preheat the oven to 450 degrees. Spread half the chips in a 13-x-9-inch or similarly sized ovenproof dish and sprinkle with half the cheese. Top with the remaining chips and cheese. Bake for about 12 minutes or until the cheese is melted.

2 Meanwhile, heat the chili in a small saucepan over medium heat on top of the stove. Some canned chili needs to be thinned out with a little water. It should be thick, but you still should be able to stir it.

3 Remove the nachos from the oven when done and spoon pockets of chili here and there over the mound of chips. Dot the guacamole and sour cream over the chips, scatter the jalapeños and scallions over all, and serve immediately with salsa on the side. Although you can attempt to eat these with your fingers, forks are helpful for the more timid or tidy, as are plates. If you have bibs hanging around, they may not be a bad idea, either.

Tip: *Make sure that your corn chips are fresh. If you've already used some chips in the bag and the bag has been sitting on the shelf, taste some chips before proceeding. They lose their crispness if exposed to air. You can prolong the shelf life of an opened bag of chips by placing them in a resealable plastic bag and removing any excess air.*

Per serving: *Calories 742 (From Fat 390); Fat 43g (Saturated 19g); Cholesterol 94mg; Sodium 1,436mg; Carbohydrate 58g (Dietary Fiber 6g); Protein 28g.*

Chapter 10

International Flare

*T*he cocktail party may be as American as apple pie, but many appetizers served at those cocktail parties originally hail from other countries. With a selection of goat cheeses representing France, herbed and spiced marinated olives reminiscent of Spain, and Asian-inspired tempura, who can resist the temptation of international appetizers?

Although some ingredients may be new to you, most of them are easier to find than ever. Many supermarkets have entire aisles dedicated to worldly cuisines. In my market, the international section is divided into Asian, Mexican, Spanish, Italian, and so on. You may have to go to a specialty food store for some ingredients (like the rice paper wrappers for the spring rolls), but by and large you can find what you need in any large, well-stocked supermarket.

Appetizers are a great way to acquaint yourself with flavors that may be unusual to you. They're easy to make and you start with small amounts, so if you decide that you don't like the taste, you can try something different next time without having wasted too much time, effort, or money.

It's time to dive into the large and varied world of international appetizers — think globally!

Cooking Italian: Bravo!

From pasta to pizza and delicious olive oil, Italian foods have become a permanent part of the American food landscape. With its lusty, hearty flavors and colors, Italian foods rank among the most popular foreign cuisine with Americans. No book on appetizers would be complete without at least a small selection of Italian appetizers and a treatise on antipasti.

Preparing antipasto

Antipasto literally means "before the meal." (Antipasti is the plural form.) Italians love antipasti because there are so many creative ways to combine, often quite simply, foods that make some of the best appetizers around.

An antipasti spread offers something for everyone, including meats, cheeses, vegetables, and breads — all of them fresh, colorful, and enticing. An antipasti spread is a great way to offer appetizers to a large crowd. The word *abbondanza*, which means abundance, is the effect you want to achieve. You know — a little bit of everything. Of course, you can offer just one item, such as prosciutto, but if you want to offer a big spread, here are some tips:

- ✔ **Start with vegetables.** Roast or marinate a variety of vegetables and present them on a platter. Or go to a well-stocked deli and buy both roasted and marinated vegetables and serve those. Roasted peppers and marinated mushrooms are a good place to start and are easy to find in most supermarkets. To make your own, here are some brief directions:

  - **Roasted vegetables:** Here are some of my favorites: Trim the ends of asparagus, coat lightly with olive oil, spread out in a single layer on a jelly-roll pan, and roast at 500 degrees until tender but still crisp, about 4 minutes, shaking the pan once or twice. Or how about peppers? Start with red, green, or yellow peppers and cut into large chunks or 1-inch wide strips. Coat with olive oil and roast in a 450 degree oven until tender but still crisp, shaking the pan once or twice. Half-inch round slices of eggplant can be roasted just like the peppers, as can 1/2-inch wide, long diagonal cuts of zucchini or summer squash.

- **Marinated vegetables:** Start with broccoli and cauliflower florets and 1- to 2-inch chunks of peeled carrots. Steam separately until just tender. Cool and marinate at least overnight in your favorite vinaigrette. Try steaming other veggies too, if you like. Mushrooms can just be cleaned and marinated raw, either whole, quartered, or sliced.

✔ **Accent the presentation with cheeses.** How about a small bowl of the Marinated Mozzarella Balls? (See the recipe later in this chapter.) Or set out some fine Italian cheeses. The harder grating cheeses, such as Parmigiano-Reggiano, pecorino, and Asiago, are not always considered as cheeses to eat out of hand, but they're delicious. Also try Italian fontina, Robiola, ricotta salata (which is a firm cheese), Tallegio, and Gorgonzola. Always serve cheeses at room temperature in order to fully appreciate their taste and texture.

✔ **Get good bread.** Many bakeries and even supermarkets carry focaccia, which is a flat bread with various toppings. Focaccia ingredients can include caramelized onions, tomatoes, garlic, and herbs. Cut the bread into wedges and set them out with the rest of your Italian buffet.

✔ **Add beans.** Buy a can or two of white cannellini beans, drain them, and toss them with extra-virgin olive oil and crushed rosemary or sage. Mound them among the veggies or offer them in a bowl.

✔ **Try a few surprises.** Antipasti can range from seasoned shrimp and tuna to egg-rich frittatas. Those are just some ideas to get you started. Be as adventurous as you want.

✔ **Don't forget the meats.** Italian salami and cured meats all work perfectly here. You may have to go to a specialty food store for these items, but no prep work is necessary once you bring them home, so they're an easy addition. Look for sopressata and Genoa salamis, which are hard salamis. Mortadella, which is like an Italian bologna, is an example of a soft salami. You can have all of these sliced at the store and then serve the slices rolled up for easy finger foods. Or you can buy a hunk of meat, cube it at home, and serve with toothpicks. When you create an antipasti array, think about texture, shape, and color. You want as much variety as possible.

✔ **Serve Prosciutto di Parma.** This meat deserves its own special mention in this list. Not all cured Italian meats are allowed to be imported into this country, but luckily, you can get genuine prosciutto di Parma. This air-dried ham is also salted. Experts say the higher the skill of the producer, the less salt they need, and yet they can still coax a full, complex flavor out of the ham. Unlike in many cured meats, no nitrates are used, nor is sugar needed. What results is a rosy-hued cured ham that almost melts in your mouth. It is served sliced thin and can be enjoyed as is. But if you want to gussy it up, wrap thin slices of prosciutto around thin bread sticks, steamed asparagus spears, slices of ripe cantaloupe, or fresh quartered figs.

Giving squid a chance!

Have you ever had squid? I think the image that a lot of folks have is that of a gigantic squid attacking a submarine, like in *20,000 Leagues Under the Sea.* I suggest smaller, more tender squid for eating. Yes, squid is delicious. It's chewy and satisfying, with the delicate flavor of the sea. You can eat it raw, like Italian fisherman do, right out of the water, but the less adventurous may want to try calamari (the Italian word for squid) marinated, stuffed, or fried. I give you a fried calamari recipe in this section that is super easy to make and uses very few ingredients, so why not try it? Come on, surely you would love to be able to casually mention to your friends, "Of course. I enjoy calamari, particularly my own version."

Finding fresh, cleaned squid should be easy. If the squid is not cleaned, it means that the body still has innards, the eyes and head are intact, and you can see the beak. I know that you're probably wondering what a beak is doing on an animal from the sea, but a squid's mouth is a small, hard beak. On a 60-foot squid, like in the movies, that's one of the things the submarine guys were afraid of. But I digress. If the squid isn't cleaned, ask the fishmonger to do it for you. Trust me, having someone else do the cleaning will make things much easier. And the chances are, the squid in the seafood case is already cleaned anyway. Sometimes, however, the squid are not quite clean enough. Give them a quick once-over. Look for any remnants of the hard beak, which is a hard ball just above the eyes. If the eyes are cleaned away, chances are the beak is too. Just look for a round hard bulge. Also remove the hard quill-shaped part that may be inside the body, and any stray pieces of skin. The head, eyes, and any innards should be removed as well.

Marinated Mozzarella Balls

Nowadays finding fresh mozzarella is easy. It's even available in supermarket deli cases. Try and find the smallest size, which are bite-size — about the size of cherries or large marbles.

Preparation time: *5 minutes*

Yield: *4 servings*

½ pound small fresh mozzarella balls (the size of cherries, called ciliegne)

¼ cup extra-virgin olive oil

½ teaspoon minced garlic

¼ teaspoon red pepper flakes

Coarsely ground black pepper

1½ tablespoons minced fresh basil

1 Drain the mozzarella well and place in a decorative serving bowl; set aside.

2 Place the olive oil in a small saucepan and heat gently over medium heat, about a minute or two. Add the garlic, red pepper flakes, and a few grinds of the black pepper. Remove from heat and let steep while cooling for 5 minutes.

3 Pour the flavored olive oil over the mozzarella, sprinkle with the basil, toss well to coat, and let stand at room temperature for at least 2 hours before serving. Serve with toothpicks. You may pack the mozzarella into an airtight container and refrigerate up to 2 days. Bring to room temperature before serving.

Tip: *Hot red pepper flakes, like the dried chiles they're made from, can vary wildly in terms of "hotness." Use more or less to suit your taste.*

Tip: *When you refrigerate olive oil, it becomes thick and cloudy, but it's still okay to use. It returns to its original state after you bring it back to room temperature.*

Per serving: *Calories 282 (From Fat 231); Fat 26g (Saturated 10g); Cholesterol 45mg; Sodium 81mg; Carbohydrate 2g (Dietary Fiber 0g); Protein 10g.*

Fried Calamari with Fresh Tomato Basil Sauce

You can choose from many ways to prepare fried calamari, including some with heavy batters. This is a light, traditional variation that is not only simple, using few ingredients, but one of the most delicious. Have fresh lemon wedges available, not just bottled lemon juice.

Fried squid has been compared to fried rubber bands by more than one diner. To prevent this extremely chewy texture, which can result all too easily, cook the squid just until done. The squid should just become opaque. Do a test batch, remove a ring or two, cut into them, and assess what your exact cooking time should be. In this case, it's best (and safe) to err on the side of a shorter cooking time. After all, some people eat this raw!

Specialty tool: *Deep-fat fryer equipped with thermostat, or deep, heavy pot with thermometer*

Preparation time: *10 minutes*

Cooking time: *About 1 minute per batch*

Yield: *6 servings*

2 pounds cleaned squid	*Plenty of vegetable oil for deep frying*
1 cup all-purpose flour	*2 lemons, quartered*
1 teaspoon salt	*Fresh Tomato Basil Sauce*
Pepper	

1 Slice the squid body into ½-inch rings. If the tentacles are thicker than ½ inch, slice them lengthwise. Rinse all the squid pieces and pat them dry. The drying step is important for two reasons: The flour will become gummy if the squid are too moist, and the water doesn't mix with the oil in the fryer. Place in a mixing bowl.

2 Sift the flour over the squid, sprinkle the salt and a few grinds of black pepper over them, and toss well to lightly and evenly coat.

3 Meanwhile, fill a fryer or heavy pot with oil to at least a 3-inch depth. Use a thermometer if the unit isn't equipped with one and heat the oil to 350 degrees. Preheat the oven to 200 degrees and place a baking sheet inside. Place a double layer of paper towels near the frying apparatus.

4 When the oil is ready, place a handful of squid in a strainer set over the sink and shake off any extra flour. Gently add squid to the oil, stir around so that no pieces are touching, and cook just until crisp and starting to turn golden brown. This browning will happen fast, perhaps in just 1 minute. Remove with a slotted spoon and transfer to several layers of paper towels to drain briefly. Transfer to the oven on the baking sheet to keep the squid warm while you finish cooking them. Repeat in batches until all the squid are cooked.

5 Serve immediately with wedges of lemon and the Fresh Tomato Basil Sauce. The lemon may seem like a simple garnish, but a squeeze of lemon brings this dish alive, so use the lemons and enjoy!

Per serving: Calories 301 (From Fat 102); Fat 11g (Saturated 1g); Cholesterol 352mg; Sodium 456mg; Carbohydrate 22g (Dietary Fiber 1g); Protein 26g.

Fresh Tomato Basil Sauce

Preparation time: *5 minutes*

Yield: *6 servings*

1 pound (about 3 medium) ripe tomatoes, peeled and seeded (see the sidebar "Peeling tomatoes")	*1 tablespoon extra-virgin olive oil*
	1 teaspoon red wine vinegar
2 tablespoons minced flat-leaf parsley	*½ teaspoon minced garlic*
2 tablespoons minced fresh basil	*Salt and pepper to taste*

Finely dice the tomatoes and combine in a bowl with the parsley, basil, olive oil, vinegar, and garlic. Season with salt and pepper. This sauce is like a fresh salsa, and the acidic flavor of the tomatoes and vinegar and the freshness of the herbs complement the fried calamari wonderfully.

Tip: *If your fishmonger is out of fresh squid, look for frozen squid, which freezes quite well and is often sold this way. Just defrost it in the refrigerator overnight before using.*

Tip: *You can use vegetable oil for frying, but the delicate flavor of the light olive oil really enhances this dish.*

Remember: *Whenever you deep-fry, make sure that the oil is deep and hot enough. Getting the oil just right ensures a light, crispy end product that is not at all heavy or oily.*

Per serving: Calories 37 (From Fat 23); Fat 3g (Saturated 0g); Cholesterol 0mg; Sodium 105mg; Carbohydrate 4g (Dietary Fiber 1g); Protein 1g.

Enjoying the Flavors of France: Ooh La La!

Ah, the foods of France. Paris is one of my favorite places to indulge in food. Although your impression of classic French food may be one of heavy, rich sauces and fancy desserts, there is another side to it. Elaborate preparations do have their place in French cuisine, but the French also have an appreciation for the simplest of presentations — a perfectly ripe piece of cheese, for example.

Goat cheeses come from many countries, including the United States, but the goat cheese recipe in this section features Montrachet, the mellowest and creamiest of the French goat cheeses.

Herbed Goat Cheeses

This recipe doesn't have the exact ingredient amounts that you find in most recipes. You start with cheese and roll it around in herbs and spices until the cheese is evenly coated. Once you start making the recipe, you'll see that you don't need exact amounts. You can easily halve or double this recipe.

Preparation time: 10 minutes

Yield: 15 servings

1 pound Montrachet cheese	Coarsely cracked black pepper
Dried dill	Fresh minced chives
Dried thyme	Fresh minced parsley
Herbes de Provence	

1 Cut the cheese into small logs (Montrachet comes in a log shape) about 3 or 4-inches long. Place the other ingredients in shallow bowls. Roll the cheese logs in the herbs and spices until the cheese logs are evenly coated. If the cheese shows through here and there, that's fine. You simply want to add flavor and color.

2 Place the cheese logs on a cheese board or serving platter and serve with sliced French bread. These are best served within 6 hours of preparing; some of the herbs may get soggy after that. Cover the platter loosely with plastic wrap and let stand at room temperature until serving time.

Vary It! *If you take the time to coat your cheese pieces with many different coatings, you'll have a more impressive presentation. But you may want to consider making blends in which to roll the cheeses. Some of these combinations are far from French in inspiration, but they're still mighty tasty: finely grated lemon peel, coarsely cracked black pepper, and minced parsley; minced sun-dried tomatoes and minced basil; cracked pepper of various colors, including pink, white, green, and black; and finely grated lemon peel and cracked fennel seeds.*

Per serving: *Calories 111 (From Fat 81); Fat 9g (Saturated 6g); Cholesterol 24mg; Sodium 156mg; Carbohydrate 1g (Dietary Fiber 0g); Protein 7g.*

Cast a Net for Spanish Food

If you go into a bar in Spain, you get more than a drink. Those food-loving Spaniards wouldn't think of drinking without eating at least a few snack-type foods with their beverage. These small dishes are collectively referred to as *tapas*. The word *tapas* derives from the verb meaning "to cover"; scholars believe that sometime in the nineteenth century, or possibly even earlier, bargoers covered their drinks with slices of bread to keep out flies. Bread was eventually replaced by small dishes filled with all sorts of nibbles. Tapas keep the patrons in the bar longer, and make the whole experience more satisfying. In addition, the patrons spend more money in the bar.

Tapas are as varied as antipasti (see the section "Preparing antipasto," earlier in this chapter) and include vegetables, meats, and breads. I present two tapas recipes that you can serve in a variety of settings. The olives and the beef pastries showcase the flavors of Spain, but don't let that stop you from serving them with whatever else you're serving, even if it's your Mom's favorite dip.

Empanadas (Beef Turnovers)

In this recipe, a simple pastry encases a highly seasoned meat mixture. The empanadas are small — about three-bite size. If you want tiny empanadas, just use smaller pieces of dough and less filling. When these appetizers are truly bite-size, they're called empanaditas or empanadillas. No matter what size you make them, you can freeze them and bake them right before serving.

Specialty tool: *4-inch round cookie or biscuit cutter*

Preparation time: *15 minutes, plus 2 hours for refrigerating the dough*

Cooking time: *35 minutes*

Yield: *About 20 pastries*

Pastry

3 cups all-purpose flour

1 teaspoon salt

½ teaspoon turmeric (optional)

⅓ cup chilled unsalted butter, cut into pieces

⅓ cup vegetable shortening

1 egg

5 tablespoons to ½ cup ice water

1 Place the flour, salt, and turmeric, if desired, in the bowl of a food processor fitted with the metal blade. Pulse on and off twice to combine. Add the butter and shortening and pulse on and off several times. Turn the machine on briefly, until the dough is the texture of coarse meal. Add the egg and pulse a few times to incorporate. Slowly add 5 tablespoons of water, pulsing on and off until the dough just comes together. Add additional water if necessary. (You may make this pastry dough by hand. Simply place the flour, salt, and turmeric in a bowl and add the butter and shortening. Cut the fats in, using a pastry blender or your fingers, and work the mixture until it resembles a coarse meal. Drizzle in the water a little at a time and mix just until the dough is moistened. Gather into a ball.)

2 Gather the dough together, shape into a flattened disc, and wrap in plastic wrap. Refrigerate for at least 2 hours. This resting time allows the protein in the flour to relax and results in a more tender dough. You may double wrap the dough in plastic wrap and freeze for up to a month, defrosting overnight in the refrigerator. Or keep it refrigerated overnight, in which case it needs to soften slightly before rolling.

Filling

¼ pound lean ground beef

2 teaspoons light olive oil

½ cup minced onion

¼ pound chorizo sausage, removed from casing and crumbled

1 medium russet potato, peeled, cooked, and diced

½ teaspoon cumin

¼ cup dry white wine

1 tablespoon tomato paste

2 tablespoons minced flat-leaf parsley

Salt and pepper

1 egg yolk

2 teaspoons water

1 Crumble the ground beef into a heavy sauté pan and cook over medium heat until browned, stirring frequently. Remove from the pan and set aside, draining any extra fat if necessary. Place the olive oil in the same pan, add the onion, and sauté over medium heat until softened, about 3 minutes.

2 Add the ground beef, chorizo, potato, and cumin and cook for 1 minute, stirring frequently. Turn the heat to high, add the white wine and tomato paste, and stir to combine thoroughly with the meat mixture, cooking for about 2 minutes. Stir in the parsley and season with salt and pepper. (Chorizo is salty, so you may want to taste the filling before you add the salt.) Remove from the heat and cool to room temperature. You may refrigerate the filling overnight in an airtight container.

3 Preheat the oven to 375 degrees. Line a baking sheet with parchment paper and set aside. Whisk together the egg yolk and the water. Roll out the dough on a lightly floured surface to ⅛-inch thickness. Cut as many 4-inch circles as you can. You may have to gather the dough together and reroll it a couple times. If you don't have a cookie cutter, cut the dough into 4-inch squares and proceed as directed. You end up with triangular empanadas rather than half-moon shapes.

4 Place about a tablespoon of filling in the center of each dough circle. Brush all the edges with some of the egg mixture. Fold one half over the other and press the edges with the tines of a fork to seal tightly. Repeat until all the empanadas are filled. You may make these up to this point and freeze them. Place them on a baking sheet and freeze until solid, probably overnight. Place them in a resealable plastic bag and store in the freezer for up to a month. Take them out of the freezer while you're preheating the oven. They may take a bit longer to cook, but they work wonderfully.

5 Place the empanadas on the baking sheet, evenly spaced apart. Brush the remaining egg mixture over the tops of the pastries. Bake for about 25 minutes or until golden brown. Let cool on a rack for 5 minutes and then serve immediately. Alternatively, you can make them up to 6 hours ahead and reheat them in a 300-degree oven for a few minutes before serving.

Tip: *If you love fried food, you can deep-fry these empanadas. Heat a couple inches of vegetable oil in a deep heavy pot. Do not glaze the pastries with the egg mixture. Drop them into 375-degree oil and fry until golden. Drain on paper towels and serve immediately. These are good only if you eat them right away — otherwise, they get soggy.*

Per serving: *Calories 182 (From Fat 94); Fat 11g (Saturated 4g); Cholesterol 38mg; Sodium 223mg; Carbohydrate 17g (Dietary Fiber 1g); Protein 5g.*

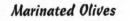

Marinated Olives

This recipe uses sherry, a favorite Spanish drink, to accent salty olives to great effect. Brine-cured green olives are great in this Spanish dish, but feel free to improvise and use a selection of other olives, if you like.

Preparation time: *10 minutes*

Cooking time: *2 minutes*

Yield: *8 servings*

1½ cups brine-cured green olives, drained	*5 black peppercorns*
½ cup Spanish olive oil	*3 medium garlic cloves, quartered lengthwise*
2 teaspoons cumin seeds	*1 bay leaf*
6-inch fresh thyme sprig	*2 tablespoons sherry vinegar*
6-inch fresh rosemary sprig	

1 Place the olives on a work surface and crack the flesh with the broad side of a heavy chef's knife. This step is not absolutely necessary, but it helps the flavors of the marinade sink into the olive's flesh. Place the olives in a storage container, preferably glass.

2 Gently heat the oil in a saucepan over medium heat with the cumin seeds, thyme, rosemary, peppercorns, garlic, and bay leaf just until hot, but not boiling. This process takes only a minute or two.

3 Pour the oil mixture (including the herbs and garlic) over the olives. Add the vinegar, cover the container, and let it sit overnight or up to a week in the refrigerator. To serve, bring to room temperature and scoop the olives out with a slotted spoon and serve in a small dish.

Tip: *When I was developing this recipe, the only Spanish green olives in my market were called "arbequina." They were the size of large peas and worked very well in the recipe. Feel free to use any green olives, preferably Spanish, for some sense of authenticity.*

Per serving: *Calories 156 (From Fat 153); Fat 17g (Saturated 2g); Cholesterol 0mg; Sodium 633mg; Carbohydrate 1g (Dietary Fiber 0g); Protein 1g.*

Assembling Asian Appetizers

In this section, you find just a taste of Indonesian, Chinese, Japanese, and Vietnamese cuisines — all of them a great way to introduce yourself, and your guests, to the worldly flavors of Asia.

Indonesian-Inspired Chicken Saté

You can grill these on a gas or charcoal grill or broil them inside your kitchen oven. Just make sure to leave time for marination so that the spices have a chance to permeate the chicken.

Specialty tools: *Thirty 8-inch bamboo skewers*

Preparation time: *15 minutes, plus 4 hours for marination*

Cooking time: *5 minutes*

Yield: *15 servings*

½ cup coconut milk

½ cup minced onion

¼ cup soy sauce

¼ cup smooth, hydrogenated peanut butter

2 tablespoons lemon juice

2 tablespoons light brown sugar, lightly packed

1 tablespoon minced serrano chiles (about 2 serrano chiles, ribs and seeds removed)

1 tablespoon grated fresh ginger

¼ teaspoon coriander

¼ teaspoon cumin

1½ pounds boneless, skinless chicken breasts

½ cup minced scallion (optional)

1 Whisk together the coconut milk, onions, soy sauce, peanut butter, lemon juice, brown sugar, chiles, ginger, coriander, and cumin in a large bowl. Make sure that the ingredients are well combined and then remove ⅓ cup and set aside for later.

2 Slice the chicken breasts into large finger-sized pieces, about 1 inch across and 4 inches long. (You should be able to get about 30 pieces out of the 1½ pounds of chicken.) Add to the marinade in the bowl and toss well to coat. Refrigerate for at least 4 hours or overnight. Meanwhile, soak the bamboo skewers in water so that they don't burn while you're cooking the chicken.

3 Thread each piece of chicken onto one end of a bamboo skewer.

4 Preheat your grill to a medium-high heat, or turn on the broiler and place the rack at the highest position. Lay the chicken, skewers and all, on a rimmed baking sheet and broil for about 5 minutes or just until it is cooked through. You can cut one open to test for doneness. If you grill them, place the skewers directly on the grill and turn them over once during grilling.

5 Remove from the heat source, brush with the extra marinade that you set aside, and sprinkle with scallion, if desired. Serve immediately.

Per serving: *Calories 101 (From Fat 43); Fat 5g (Saturated 2g); Cholesterol 25mg; Sodium 318mg; Carbohydrate 4g (Dietary Fiber 1g); Protein 11g.*

Chinese Barbecued Spareribs

This recipe calls for baby-back pork ribs, which, not surprisingly, come from the back of the pig. Ask your butcher to cut the ribs lengthwise across the bones to make smaller pieces, sometimes called riblets.

This recipe also calls for a couple ingredients that you may not have used before. Hoisin sauce is a dark, sweet prepared sauce that adds flavor and body to the sauce. You can probably find it in your supermarket's international aisle along with other Asian ingredients. Five-spice powder is a blend (often with more than five spices) that can vary somewhat, depending on the manufacturer; however, it usually includes star anise, cinnamon, fennel, licorice root, pepper, and cloves.

Preparation time: *10 minutes, plus 6 hours for marination*

Cooking time: *35 minutes*

Yield: *8 servings*

¾ cup hoisin sauce	2 teaspoons grated fresh ginger
⅓ cup ketchup	¼ teaspoon cayenne
¼ cup soy sauce	4 pounds pork baby-back ribs (about 2 racks)
¼ cup toasted sesame oil	Chinese mustard for dipping
2 tablespoons minced garlic	Plum sauce for dipping
2 teaspoons five-spice powder	

1 Combine the hoisin, ketchup, soy sauce, sesame oil, garlic, five-spice powder, ginger, and cayenne in a large mixing bowl. Whisk until blended.

2 Cut the ribs between the bones to separate them into individual pieces; add to the bowl of marinade and toss to coat. Cover with foil or plastic wrap and refrigerate for at least 6 hours or overnight.

3 Preheat the oven to 375 degrees. Remove the ribs from the marinade with a pair of tongs and place the ribs on a baking sheet in a single layer. Roast for about 20 minutes or until the ribs start to brown and caramelize. Turn the ribs over and continue roasting for 15 minutes more or until cooked through and glazed. Cut into a rib to make sure that the meat is no longer pink.

4 Place the ribs on a serving platter and serve with Chinese mustard and plum sauce for dipping. These ribs reheat well in the microwave or in the oven; either way, keep them covered while heating so that they stay moist.

Tip: *You put the ribs in a shallow pan so that the small rib pieces roast and don't steam. If they're in a deep roasting pan, the sides of the pan can create a moister environment than you want for this recipe.*

Tip: *You can use this marinade on chicken in other ways. For example, apply it like a bar-becue sauce the next time you grill, or coat chicken pieces with it before roasting them in the oven.*

Per serving: *Calories 451 (From Fat 311); Fat 35g (Saturated 12g); Cholesterol 123mg; Sodium 616mg; Carbohydrate 8g (Dietary Fiber 0g); Protein 26g.*

Tempura: Batter up

Tempura is a Japanese deep-fried dish, but the batter is light and lacy. So if you're thinking tempura is similar heavy fried chicken, stop right there. The coating is very simply made from flour, water, and egg yolks, and the items to be dipped are always vegetables or fish, never chicken or meat. The deep frying does give some substance to the dish, but the Japanese skillfully pair the tempura with a dipping sauce that flavors the food and cuts some of the fattiness.

Tempura must be made right before serving. All fried foods are best served soon after frying, and this dish is no exception. My version of tempura includes shrimp and veggies. If you use shrimp or pieces of fish in your tempura, cook those pieces together (shrimp with shrimp, fish with fish). Similarly, cook like vegetables together so that they cook evenly.

Here are my favorite ingredients to cook as tempura (all ingredients are raw):

- ✔ Broccoli florets
- ✔ Carrots, peeled and cut thinly on the diagonal
- ✔ Daikon radish, cut thinly on the diagonal
- ✔ Green beans
- ✔ Mushrooms, including white button mushrooms and exotic varieties, whole or halved
- ✔ Onion rings, about ½ inch wide
- ✔ Shrimp, left whole, shelled, and deveined
- ✔ Sugar snap beans
- ✔ Sweet potatoes, peeled and cut thinly on the diagonal
- ✔ Whitefish, in hunks of firm varieties, such as monkfish

After washing and peeling your vegetables, make sure that they're dry. The shrimp or fish also need to be completely dry. The drier the items to be fried, the better the batter will stick, and the more effective the hot oil will be at producing a crisp piece of food.

Japanese Shrimp and Veggie Tempura

This lightly battered deep-fried dish is a classic Japanese recipe. The recipe uses 2 pounds of ingredients to be dipped into the batter; you can mix and match whatever you like. Love shrimp? Add more in proportion to the veggies.

The dipping sauce starts with something called *dashi,* which is like a basic Japanese stock. It is classically made with seaweed and bonito, which are fish flakes, but I stream-line the process by using seaweed only. Don't be scared by the seaweed in the sauce. It simply provides a subtle background flavor that, while important, doesn't scream sea-weed at you. You can find the kombu seaweed, as well as the *mirin,* a sweet cooking wine, in specialty food stores or stores featuring Asian ingredients. Check out the online resources in Chapter 14 as well.

Specialty tools: *Deep-fat fryer, electric fryer, or deep, heavy pot; thermometer with range up to 400 degrees*

Preparation time: *20 minutes, plus 10 minutes resting time*

Cooking time: *3 minutes per batch*

Yield: *6 servings*

2 cups water	*Vegetable oil for deep-fat frying*
¼ ounce dried kombu seaweed	*2 egg yolks*
⅓ cup mirin	*2 cups ice water*
⅓ cup soy sauce	*1¾ cups all-purpose flour, sifted*
1½ teaspoons minced fresh ginger	
2 pounds prepared vegetables (uniform in size) and shrimp (see the list of suggestions earlier in this section)	

1 To make the dipping sauce, combine the 2 cups water and seaweed in a small pot and bring just to a boil over high heat. Immediately turn off the heat, cover, and let sit for 10 minutes. The kombu will absorb quite a bit of water for its size. Discard the kombu and measure out 1 cup of the dashi. (That's the word for the now-cooked seaweed water.)

2 Combine the 1 cup dashi with the mirin, soy sauce, and ginger in a small pot and set aside.

3 Have the veggies and shrimp or fish ready to fry. Fill the fryer or heavy pot with oil to at least a 3-inch depth. Use a thermometer if the unit isn't equipped with one and heat the oil to 375 degrees. Preheat the oven to 175 degrees and place a heatproof serving platter on a rack in the oven. (You'll use this platter to keep fried pieces warm while you fry the rest.)

4 While the oil is preheating, make the batter. Place the egg yolks in a large bowl and whisk until smooth. Add the ice water and combine lightly. Swirls of egg will be suspended in the water, which is how it should be. Add the sifted flour all at once and stir it around a few times but leave it lumpy. Do not stir until smooth. The lumpier the batter, the lacier the final effect, which is what you want. Small pockets of flour here and there are okay.

5 Coat the vegetables and shrimp or fish with the batter right before frying. Cook similar ingredients together — for example, shrimp with shrimp and broccoli with broccoli — for the most even cooking. Dip items one by one in the batter, using chopsticks or two forks. Let any excess batter drip back into the bowl. Fry the pieces in small batches until golden brown, turning them frequently with clean chopsticks or a slotted spoon. The pieces should move freely around the pot and have room to be evenly bathed in the fat. This process takes about 3 minutes. The fried pieces should be light golden brown. Remove with a slotted spoon and drain on paper towels. Transfer the fried pieces to the serving platter in the oven to keep them warm while you fry the remaining items. (See Chapter 7 for deep-fat frying tips.) Serve the tempura mounded on a warm platter and accompany with the dipping sauce.

Per serving: *Calories 349 (From Fat 106); Fat 12g (Saturated 1g); Cholesterol 160mg; Sodium 1,035mg; Carbohydrate 41g (Dietary Fiber 3g); Protein 16g.*

Using rice paper wrappers and rice vermicelli

The spring roll recipe in this section is not your average fried egg roll. Some egg rolls and even spring rolls are fried, and many of them are rolled up in a wrapper made with wheat flour. The spring rolls recipe in this chapter, however, uses a rice paper wrapper, which you most likely will find only in a specialty food store. These wrappers are translucent, and the dish is not fried, so the result is a very light, refreshing roll.

The technique for working with rice paper rolls is easy, but you need to get a sense of feel for working with them. You soak the wrappers in water just enough to soften them. But if you soak them too long, they fall apart. If you don't soak them long enough, they don't become tender or pliable enough. You may have to sacrifice a few rolls to get the hang of it, but once you do, making recipes with rice paper wrappers is easier.

The rice vermicelli are very thin noodles made from rice flour. They're thinner than spaghetti and delicate in taste and texture. They come dry and are wrapped in bundles, usually 1 pound per package.

You can find the rice vermicelli at specialty or Asian food stores or through Web sites.

Vietnamese Spring Rolls with Peanut Dipping Sauce

These light, colorful rolls combine the Asian flavors of mint, cilantro, peanut, and hoisin sauce, resulting in a very refreshing appetizer. Making them isn't difficult, but you must have all the ingredients ready ahead of time because you make the rolls in an assembly-line fashion.

Preparation time: *25 minutes*

Cooking time: *3 minutes*

Yield: *8 servings*

Peanut Dipping Sauce:

¼ cup smooth, hydrogenated peanut butter

¼ cup hoisin sauce

⅓ cup water

2 tablespoons tomato paste

1 tablespoon peanut oil (or vegetable oil)

2 teaspoons minced garlic

1 teaspoon sugar

½ teaspoon cayenne

Spring Rolls:

3 ounces rice vermicelli

10 rice paper wrappers (about 8½ inches in diameter; 8 wrappers for the recipe and 2 for experimenting)

4 large leaves Boston lettuce, any large, hard center stems removed and halved

1 large cucumber, peeled, seeded, and cut into ¼-inch-wide strips

2 large carrots, peeled and finely grated

½ cup firmly packed fresh mint leaves

8 medium shrimp, peeled, deveined, and cooked (see Chapter 6) and sliced in half lengthwise (so that each half still looks like a "whole" shrimp)

½ cup firmly packed fresh cilantro leaves

1 For the sauce, combine all the ingredients and whisk together until smooth. The mixture should be thick but fluid. Add more water if necessary. You may make the sauce up to 3 days ahead and refrigerate in an airtight container. Bring back to room temperature before serving. You can adjust the cayenne to your taste.

2 Bring a large pot of water to a boil. Add the rice vermicelli, which will immediately soften. Stir around with a chopstick or spoon to loosen the strands. Boil for about 3 minutes or until tender but al dente (which means they still retain their shape and haven't turned mushy). Drain and rinse well with cold water; set aside.

3 Fill a shallow bowl with very warm water and have a double layer of paper towels nearby. One by one, dip a rice paper wrapper in the warm water and submerge it for about 10 seconds. Remove from the water and lay out on paper towels. Do not let the wrapper soak. The wrapper becomes pliable, but it still will feel a little too stiff to roll. It softens more after you lay it out on the paper towels. You have 2 extra wrappers to experiment with.

4 Place half a lettuce leaf on the bottom half of the wrapper. Top with noodles. (The correct amount is about the thickness of a hot dog and the width of the lettuce.) Cover this with the strips of cucumber, grated carrot, and mint leaves. Fold the bottom end of the wrapper up and over the filling, completely encasing it, about halfway up the wrapper, and fold both sides in towards the center. Place two shrimp halves, cut side up, side by side on the wrapper and put a few leaves of cilantro around the shrimp. Finish rolling the wrapper into a cylinder, pressing the edges of the wrapper to seal itself. Place on a platter and cover with a clean, damp cloth. Repeat with the remaining rolls. The finished rolls will stay fresh under the damp cloth for 2 hours. Figure 10-1 illustrates how to roll spring rolls.

5 To serve, slice the rolls in half (between the shrimp) to expose the colorful filling. Place on a serving platter and accompany with a bowl of the dipping sauce. Dip the rolls into the sauce before eating.

Tip: For a shellfish-free and vegetarian version, eliminate the shrimp.

Per serving: *Calories 189 (From Fat 59); Fat 7g (Saturated 1g); Cholesterol 9mg; Sodium 193mg; Carbohydrate 27g (Dietary Fiber 3g); Protein 7g.*

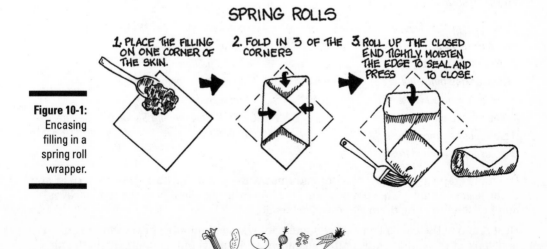

SPRING ROLLS

1. PLACE THE FILLING ON ONE CORNER OF THE SKIN.

2. FOLD IN 3 OF THE CORNERS

3. ROLL UP THE CLOSED END TIGHTLY. MOISTEN THE EDGE TO SEAL AND PRESS TO CLOSE.

Figure 10-1: Encasing filling in a spring roll wrapper.

Getting a Taste of Greece

The flavors of Greece are all their own. Ouzo, the national drink, has an unmistakable anise flavor that will make you forget all your problems! Retsina, the local wine, often accompanies *mezethes,* the small plates of appetizers that you find in the tavernas of Greece. Fish is popular and fresh from the sea, the olive oil is heady and fragrant, and lamb is a favorite food. Small pastries, both sweet and savory, are wrapped in the traditional Greek phyllo pastry.

Greek cuisine is a topic I could write an entire book about, but unfortunately, I don't have the space to go into it at length in this chapter. So I'll simply let you know that one of my very favorite dishes is dolmathes, or stuffed grape leaves. Sometimes they're filled with meat, but I prefer the vegetarian version, which is stuffed with rice, currants, and pine nuts.

Stuffed Grape Leaves

This classic Greek appetizer, known as dolmathes, is comprised of grape leaves stuffed with seasoned rice. Many traditional recipes for dolmathes suggest stuffing the grape leaves with raw rice and then simmering the packages until tender. But this approach has never worked for me, and I always end up with a crunchy final product (which proves that bad things do happen to good cooks). This recipe solves that problem by using cooked rice. The grape leaves are easy to eat with the fingers and make a great addition to any party. Serve with the Garlic-Yogurt Dipping Sauce in Chapter 8, if desired.

Preparation time: *30 minutes*

Cooking time: *1 hour and 15 minutes*

Yield: *30 stuffed grape leaves*

16-ounce jar grape leaves	*¼ cup currants*
⅔ cup extra-virgin olive oil	*1½ cups water*
1 cup minced onion	*Salt and pepper*
⅓ cup toasted pine nuts	*2 tablespoons lemon juice*
1 cup long-grained white rice	*1 cup water*
¼ cup minced parsley	*Garlic-Yogurt Dipping Sauce (see Chapter 8) (optional)*
3 tablespoons minced fresh dill	
3 tablespoons minced fresh mint	

1 Drain the grape leaves in a colander and rinse with cool water. Take care not to tear any of the leaves. Bring a large pot of water to a boil over high heat, add the grape leaves, and boil for 1 minute; drain again and set aside.

2 Heat ⅓ cup of the olive oil in a large sauté pan over medium-high heat. Add the onions and cook, stirring frequently, until translucent and soft, about 4 minutes. Add the pine nuts and rice and stir to coat the rice well. Continue cooking, stirring frequently, for about 3 minutes. Add the parsley, dill, mint, currants, and 1½ cups water. Cover, bring to a boil, reduce the heat, and simmer until the liquid is absorbed, about 15 minutes. Let stand, covered, off the heat for 10 more minutes. Taste the rice mixture and season with salt and pepper.

3 One leaf at a time, spread out the grape leaves on a work surface. The broad stem side should be near you, and the veins should be facing up. Cut out any large or hard stems near the bottom, if necessary. Place a generous teaspoon of filling near the broad edge of the leaf and fold that bottom end up and over the filling, completely encasing it. Use your fingers to form the filling into a little log shape sitting horizontally across the leaf. Now fold both sides in toward the center and finish rolling the log up toward the top. This process is shown in Figure 10-2. Repeat with remaining leaves and filling; you should have some leaves left over. Or, if you tear one badly, you can use one of the extra leaves.

4 Line a large, deep, heavy, straight-sided pan with some of the extra leaves; these keep the stuffed ones from sticking to the bottom of the pan. Place the stuffed grape leaves in the pan, tightly nestled together, seam side down. Drizzle with half of the remaining ⅓ cup oil and 1 tablespoon of the lemon juice. Lay a few more of the extra leaves over the first layer of stuffed leaves, and make another layer of stuffed grape leaves. Drizzle the rest of the ⅓ cup oil and the remaining 1 tablespoon lemon juice over all the stuffed leaves. Add the 1 cup water and place a dinner plate on top to weight the grape leaves down. Cover the pot and bring the water to a boil over medium-high heat. Reduce the heat to low-medium and simmer for at least 1 hour or until the water is almost completely absorbed. Turn off the heat and let the grape leaves sit and steam, cover still on, until all the liquid is absorbed.

5 Serve slightly warm or at room temperature with or without the Garlic-Yogurt Dipping Sauce. You may make these up to 3 days ahead. Store in an airtight container in the refrigerator and bring back to room temperature before serving.

Tip: Look for the grape leaves in the international section of your supermarket. You may have to buy two 8-ounce jars. You just need a total of 16 ounces.

Per serving: *Calories 85 (From Fat 52); Fat 6g (Saturated 1g); Cholesterol 0mg; Sodium 90mg; Carbohydrate 8g (Dietary Fiber 0g); Protein 1g.*

Wrapping Stuffed Grape Leaves

Figure 10-2: Stuffing a grape leaf.

Place the leaves on a board.

and drop about 1 teaspoon of the filling on each leaf.

Wrap the leaves around the mixture,

rolling and folding the ends.

DON'T WRAP TOO TIGHTLY!

I'm stuffed!

Garlic Potato Dip (Skordalia)

This garlicky potato dip is creamy and thick without the usual high-fat dairy products of many dips. You do have to start the day before to dry out the bread and soak the almonds. These steps aren't difficult, but they do require planning ahead. I have heard of versions that use bread only and others that use potato only. My version has both, so you get the thick creaminess of the potatoes with the lightness provided by the bread. Some Greek cooks never use lemon juice in this recipe, only vinegar. Both work well for me (and I have seen both used by Grecian cuisine experts), so you have a choice.

Preparation time: *15 minutes, plus overnight sitting time*

Yield: *about 2⅔ cups*

6 slices firm-textured white sandwich bread, crusts removed and cubed

¾ cup whole natural (skin-on) almonds

5 medium-sized garlic cloves

⅓ cup extra-virgin olive oil

2 tablespoons lemon juice or white wine vinegar

2 medium russet potatoes, peeled, boiled until tender, drained, and liquid reserved

Salt to taste

Pepper (preferably white) to taste

1 Place the cubes of bread on a baking sheet and let them sit at room temperature overnight to dry out. Place the almonds in a saucepan with water to cover. Bring to a boil over medium heat and boil for 1 minute. Remove from the heat, cool, and let them sit at room temperature overnight.

2 The next day, soak the bread in a bowl with water to cover, and then squeeze dry with your hands. (You may think the bread is going to dissolve and disappear, but this technique really works.) Place the bread in the bowl of a food processor fitted with the metal blade. Add the garlic cloves. Slip the almonds out of their peels, add to the processor, pulse on and off, and then process continuously until the mixture is smooth. With the processor running, slowly add the oil and then pulse in the lemon juice.

3 Meanwhile, place the potatoes in a mixing bowl and mash well. Scrape the bread mixture over the potatoes. Fold together well and season to taste with salt and pepper. Add potato water if needed to achieve a consistency of smooth, thick dip. Serve immediately, or cover with plastic wrap and hold at room temperature for up to 4 hours.

Tip: Almonds come in many variations. The term "natural" refers to almonds that still have their skin on. If you can find the skinless variety, which will be called "blanched," feel free to use them. They're more difficult to find, however, and more expensive. But it's your choice.

Per serving: *Calories 48 (From Fat 28); Fat 3g (Saturated 0g); Cholesterol 0mg; Sodium 37mg; Carbohydrate 4g (Dietary Fiber 1g); Protein 1g.*

Making Mexican and Latin American Fare

Guacamole (see Chapter 7) and tamales and quesadillas (both in Chapter 8) are some Mexican foods you may be familiar with. In this chapter, I present miniature tostadas. My version uses round corn chips layered with various fillings, and I include a variation that tells you how to fry your own chips from fresh tortillas.

Latin flavors, such as chiles, bananas, coconut, cumin, saffron, and cilantro, aren't so unusual anymore. They flavor many of your favorite foods, both in traditional preparations as well as in fusion dishes, which combine those Latin flavors with essences of other cuisines. Here I present my version of ceviche, a delicious, fresh-tasting seafood appetizer. It may appear raw, but it's "cooked" enzymatically by the citrus juices. The acid from the citrus "cooks" the protein in the fish to some degree just as heat does. Some of the seafood is blanched first.

Mixed Seafood Ceviche

Seafood lovers, rejoice! This appetizer is easy to put together and amazingly delicious. It's low in fat, too! The word "ceviche," sometimes spelled "seviche," indicates a dish made with seafood that is treated with citrus juices, which effectively cook (enzymatically) the seafood. Serve this at the end of a hot summer day for maximum refreshment. The flavor of the citrus juices play an important role in this dish, so please use freshly squeezed juices.

Preparation time: *15 minutes*

Cooking time: *30 seconds*

Yield: *6 servings*

½ pound small shucked raw clams

½ pound extra-large raw shrimp, peeled, deveined, and chopped into ½-inch pieces

½ pound squid, cleaned and chopped into ½-inch pieces

½ pound large sea scallops, quartered

½ pound fresh, raw tuna, skin removed and chopped into ½-inch pieces

½ cup freshly squeezed lime juice

½ cup minced onion

½ cup minced red onion

½ cup diced, roasted red bell pepper

⅓ cup freshly squeezed orange juice

¼ cup freshly squeezed lemon juice

2 serrano chiles, stemmed, seeded, and minced

1 teaspoon minced garlic

1 cup seeded, diced tomato (unpeeled)

⅓ cup minced fresh cilantro

¼ cup minced flat-leaf parsley

¼ cup extra-virgin olive oil

Salt and pepper

2 ripe Haas avocados, diced

1 Bring a large pot of water to a boil over high heat. Add the clams, shrimp, and squid and cook for 30 seconds. (The water probably won't return to a boil, but that's okay.) Drain and run cold water over the seafood to stop the cooking. Place the seafood in a large mixing bowl made of a nonreactive material, such as Pyrex or stainless steel.

2 Add the scallops, tuna, lime juice, onion, red onion, red pepper, orange juice, lemon juice, chiles, garlic, tomato, cilantro, parsley, and olive oil. Stir together well, taste, and season well with salt and pepper. Refrigerate at least 1 hour to allow the flavors to blend. Taste again and adjust the seasoning. You may make this up to 6 hours ahead, but keep it refrigerated because seafood is perishable.

3 Add the avocado right before serving. To serve, scoop out into bowls or plates, maybe on some lettuce leaves, if you like.

Remember: *As with any dish using fresh chiles, adjust the amount to the level of heat that you like.*

Vary It! *Check out the Tortilla Cups (Chapter 7). These little crispy cups are made out of corn tortillas and are perfect for filling with a bit of ceviche. If you want to turn this seafood appetizer into finger food, this is the way to go.*

Vary It! *Serve the ceviche in martini glasses for an impressive presentation. Set each martini glass on a small plate and serve immediately, maybe with some good bread on the side.*

Per serving: *Calories 402 (From Fat 178); Fat 20g (Saturated 3g); Cholesterol 197mg; Sodium 302mg; Carbohydrate 17g (Dietary Fiber 6g); Protein 39g. (not low-fat)*

Miniature Shrimp and Avocado Tostadas

Tostadas are crispy corn chips or fried tortillas topped with flavorful ingredients. The tostadas in this recipe are miniature in size so that you can easily pick them up with your fingers at a cocktail party. The topping is a classic Mexican combination of avocado and shrimp. Although the recipe is easy, you can make it even simpler by buying shrimp that's already cooked.

Shop several days ahead for the avocado because you'll most likely have to let it ripen. To ripen, place the avocado in a paper bag with a ripe apple and seal the bag tightly. The gases thrown off by the ripe apple hasten the ripening of the avocado. (For more information about avocados, turn to Chapter 7.)

Preparation time: *15 minutes*

Yield: *80 tiny tostadas*

1 pound shrimp, shelled, cooked, deveined, and cut into ¼-inch dice

1 ripe avocado, preferably Haas variety, cut into small dice

1 large tomato, seeded and cut into small dice

½ cup minced red onion

2 tablespoons lime juice

2 tablespoons minced fresh cilantro

½ teaspoon cumin

Salt and pepper to taste

Tabasco to taste (optional)

80 miniature round corn chips (about 1¾ inches in diameter)

Cilantro sprigs (optional)

1 Combine the shrimp, avocado, tomato, onion, lime juice, cilantro, and cumin in a bowl and toss to coat. Season with salt and pepper to taste; add the Tabasco to taste, if desired. (I do like it with a few drops.) You may use this immediately or store in an airtight container up to 6 hours. The flavor improves if it's allowed to sit for 30 minutes.

2 To serve, spread the corn chips on a serving tray and top with a mounded spoonful of the shrimp mixture. Top with fresh sprigs of cilantro, if desired, as a garnish. Serve immediately.

Tip: *My guess is that you don't have a tray that holds 80 tostadas. So just fill up your tray with as many tostadas as you can and reserve the extra filling in a covered bowl and keep the extra chips tightly closed in the bag they came in. Just make more as you go along for a second or third round; you can put together a tray full in a minute or two.*

Per serving: *Calories 16 (From Fat 7); Fat 1g (Saturated 0g); Cholesterol 11mg; Sodium 25mg; Carbohydrate 1g (Dietary Fiber 0g); Protein 1g.*

Savoring Scandinavian Specialties

Thank the Scandinavians for giving us their version of the Italian antipasti spread — drum roll please — the smorgasbord. This array of foods often includes open-faced sandwiches; sliced meats (tongue is a popular item); cheeses; egg dishes, such as omelets or hard-cooked eggs in a mustard sauce; marinated fish, such as the herring described in the sidebar "The herring platter"; vegetable dishes; and more. Add some beer, aquavit (a traditional Scandinavian drink made from rye and caraway), or a wine glogg and you can make a meal out of these little dishes.

I give you two Scandinavian dishes. First is my version of Swedish meatballs. These are a great make-ahead hot dish, so get out the toothpicks! Then read on for a simple homemade gravlax, a home-cured salmon.

Swedish Meatballs

If you have a stand mixer with a flat paddle, use it to beat the meat mixture. If not, give your upper arms a workout and be prepared to thoroughly beat the mixture with a wooden spoon. This extended mixing lightens the mixture.

This recipe calls for allspice, which is not a blend of spices (as in "all the spices") but an actual spice unto itself. It looks like a large black peppercorn and comes whole or ground. The ¼ teaspoon suggested in the recipe is for the ground version.

Preparation time: *20 minutes*

Cooking time: *10 minutes per batch, plus another 8 minutes total*

Yield: *About 36 meatballs*

2 tablespoons unsalted butter, plus additional as necessary for cooking the sauce

½ cup minced onion

1 teaspoon minced garlic

¾ pound ground beef

¼ pound ground pork

¼ pound ground veal

3 tablespoons milk

2 slices white bread, crusts removed

1 egg

2 tablespoons minced fresh dill

¼ teaspoon allspice

¼ teaspoon nutmeg

Salt and pepper

¼ cup all-purpose flour

2 cups beef stock (canned is fine)

½ cup heavy cream

1 Line a rimmed baking sheet with parchment paper; set aside. Place 1 tablespoon of the butter in a heavy skillet (such as cast-iron), add the onion, and sauté over medium heat, stirring frequently, until soft, about 3 minutes. Add the garlic and cook for 1 minute more.

2 Meanwhile, combine the beef, pork, and veal in a mixing bowl; beat the meat with the flat paddle attachment to your mixer until light and fluffy, about 2 minutes. If you don't have a stand mixer, beat the meat vigorously with a wooden spoon until light and fluffy. Place the milk in a small bowl and soak the bread slices, one at a time, squeezing each one dry as you go; discard any excess milk and add the bread to the meat. Add the onion mixture, egg, 1 tablespoon of the dill, allspice, and nutmeg to the meat mixture and mix in well. Season with salt and pepper.

3 Moisten your hands with water and form the mixture into meatballs about 1¼ inches in diameter. (You don't have to pull out a ruler; just remember to make them bite-sized.) Place them in a single layer on the parchment-lined baking pan as you go along, until all the meat is rolled. The mixture may be soft, but that's okay. Just keep cleaning your hands of any sticking meat and keep them moist, which will facilitate rolling the meatballs.

4 Heat the remaining 1 tablespoon butter in a heavy skillet, such as a cast-iron pan, and fry the meatballs over medium-high heat, several at a time, for about 10 minutes per batch, turning to cook all sides. Drain on paper towels and repeat until all the meatballs are cooked. The meatballs will produce some fat, so you shouldn't need to add any more butter. Make sure that the meatballs are cooked all the way through, with no pink in the center. (You can cut one open to check for doneness.)

5 You should have about ¼ cup fat in the skillet. If not, add enough butter to give you that amount. Add the flour and whisk to blend. Cook over medium heat, stirring frequently, for about 2 minutes, to remove the flour's raw taste. Add the broth gradually, whisking well, and cook until it comes to a boil and thickens; whisk until smooth. Add the cream and cook for 1 minute more, stirring well. Strain the sauce into a chafing dish; season with the remaining 1 tablespoon dill and salt and pepper.

6 Combine the meatballs and sauce in a chafing dish or combine in a heatproof dish and place on a warming tray. Serve immediately with toothpicks and napkins, and plates if you like. You may also combine the meatballs and sauce and refrigerate in an airtight container for up to 3 days. Gently reheat on the stovetop or in the microwave before serving.

Tip: This recipe makes a lot of sauce. Foods that sit in a chafing dish need a lot of sauce because they dry out easily. With this amount of sauce, they'll stay moist and be better suited to plates and forks. If you want to serve them with toothpicks, make them a bit drier. Start with 2 tablespoons fat in pan, add 2 tablespoons flour, and use 1 cup beef broth and ¼ cup cream (basically half of the sauce-making ingredients). Proceed as directed.

Tip: You can turn this dish into dinner. Make the recipe as is, with the large amount of sauce, and serve over cooked egg noodles. Add a salad and your meal is complete.

Per serving: *Calories 56 (From Fat 34); Fat 4g (Saturated 2g); Cholesterol 23mg; Sodium 93mg; Carbohydrate 2g (Dietary Fiber 0g); Protein 4g.*

Easy Homemade Gravlax

If you like smoked salmon and salmon sushi, you'll like gravlax. You simply cure raw salmon for a few days in the refrigerator with sugar and salt — that's it.

Preparation time: *10 minutes, plus 3 days of curing in the refrigerator*

Yield: *20 servings*

4 pounds salmon fillet

8 juniper berries (optional)

2 teaspoons black peppercorns

¼ cup kosher salt

¼ cup sugar

1 cup plus 2 tablespoons chopped fresh dill

¼ cup gin

10 slices dark pumpernickel bread

¼ cup (½ stick) unsalted butter

1 Using your fingers, locate any small white bones, called pin bones, embedded in the salmon flesh; they'll feel like splinters. Grab the end of the bones with needle-nose pliers and pull them out, working in the same direction as the bone's insertion angle. The bones are embedded in single file, so find one and work your way down the fillet.

2 Line a large glass or other nonreactive baking dish with enough plastic wrap to cover the bottom completely and hang over the edges. Place the salmon, skin side down, in the dish.

3 Crush the juniper berries (if you're using them) and peppercorns with a mortar and pestle, or place them on a work surface and crush with the broad side of a heavy chef's knife. Combine them with salt and sugar and sprinkle the mixture evenly over the salmon. Spread the 1 cup of dill over the fish. Drizzle the gin over the fish as evenly as possible.

4 Wrap the plastic up and over the fish. Over the fish, place a pan or plate that fits inside the baking dish. Weigh down the fish by placing heavy canned goods on top of the pan or plate.

5 Place in the refrigerator for 3 days. The fish should lose its translucence. Unwrap and scrape off the dill, salt, and sugar. Slice the salmon thinly on the bias, leaving the skin behind.

6 Stack 3 slices of the bread and slice crosswise into 5 pieces, creating small rectangles. Repeat with the remaining bread. Place the gravlax on a serving platter, surrounded by a crock of sweet butter and the sliced dark bread. Garnish with the remaining 2 tablespoons fresh dill and serve.

Tip: *You can find juniper berries in natural food stores or other stores that have bulk herbs. Buying herbs in bulk, by the way, is the most cost-effective way. Although the juniper berries are optional, use them if you can find them, as they add an elusive flavor. Some say it is a pine-y taste, but that doesn't sound so great and their flavor really is! Just trust me and try them in the dish if you can find them.*

Per serving: *Calories 169 (From Fat 53); Fat 6g (Saturated 2g); Cholesterol 53mg; Sodium 846mg; Carbohydrate 7g (Dietary Fiber 1g); Protein 19g.*

Discovering Indian Food

Indian food is possibly my favorite exotic cuisine. The complex seasonings and accompanying aromas are intoxicating, whether you're dining in an Indian restaurant or whipping up a recipe yourself. If your only familiarity with Indian food is with curries, then you're missing out on all the interesting appetizers — including pakoras (chickpea flour vegetable fritters), fried semolina wafers, and spiced nuts. Calling these "little dishes" as opposed to appetizers is probably more appropriate. In a traditional Indian meal, many foods, including appetizer-like "little dishes," are set out at the same time as the main dishes. My absolute favorite appetizers are samosas, which are savory pastries enclosed in a tender dough. They're sometimes filled with meat, but I prefer a vegetarian version that's filled with potatoes and peas and served with a cilantro chutney.

Potato and Pea Samosas with Cilantro Chutney

The pastry is very easy to make, and the whole-milk yogurt makes it exceedingly tender. You can use lowfat yogurt, but the pastry will be a tad less tender. Make sure that all your spices are fresh to get the maximum aromatic effect of the recipe.

The Cilantro Chutney calls for garam masala, which is a blend of Indian spices. You can often find it in the spice section of a store that carries bulk spices.

Preparation time: *30 minutes*

Cooking time: *10 minutes, plus 3 minutes per batch*

Yield: *About 30 samosas*

Pastry:

2¼ cups all-purpose flour

1 teaspoon salt

Pinch baking soda

⅓ cup melted unsalted butter or ghee (clarified butter)

⅓ cup whole-milk yogurt

1 to 2 tablespoons water, if needed

Filling:

3 tablespoons unsalted butter or ghee (see the sidebar "Ghee: Clarified butter" in this chapter)

¾ cup minced onion

1 garlic clove, minced

1 teaspoon cumin

½ teaspoon grated fresh ginger

½ teaspoon coriander

½ teaspoon yellow mustard seed

¼ teaspoon cayenne

1 pound russet or Yukon Gold potatoes, peeled, cooked, and finely diced (about 1⅓ cups)

½ cup thawed, frozen peas

1 teaspoon lemon juice

Salt and pepper to taste

Vegetable oil

Cilantro Chutney (see following recipe)

1 To make the pastry, place the flour, salt, and baking soda in a mixing bowl and whisk them around to combine and aerate. (Aerating is kind of like sifting and makes the dry mixture light.) Stir in the ⅓ cup melted butter and the yogurt, stirring gently until combined. If the dough is dry, add a little bit of water until the dough comes together. Form the dough into a flat ball, wrap in plastic wrap, and let sit at room temperature for at least 30 minutes. (You may refrigerate the dough overnight, if desired. Just bring it back to room temperature before proceeding with the recipe.)

2 Meanwhile, make the filling: Heat the 3 tablespoons butter in a heavy skillet, such as a cast-iron pan. Add the onion and sauté over medium heat, stirring frequently, until soft, about 3 minutes. Add the garlic, cumin, ginger, coriander, mustard seed, and cayenne and cook for 2 minutes more over medium heat, stirring frequently. Remove from the heat and add the potatoes, peas, and lemon juice. Season with salt and pepper. (Take care not to crush the peas when mixing.) Let cool to room temperature. (You may make this filling 1 day ahead and refrigerate it in an airtight container. Bring it back to room temperature before proceeding with the recipe.)

3 Fill a glass with water and have nearby. Pinch off a piece of dough and roll into a 1-inch ball. Roll out the ball on a lightly floured surface to a 6-inch round, about ⅛-inch thick. Cut the circle in half; moisten all the edges with water, using a pastry brush dipped in water. Fold the half-moon in half crosswise, bringing each point together, and pinch this straight edge to seal well. You will have a cone; add a heaping tablespoon of filling and seal the remaining edge. Repeat with the remaining samosas. Figure 10-3 shows the procedure.

4 Meanwhile, fill a deep fryer or heavy pot with oil to at least a 3-inch depth. Use a thermometer if the unit isn't equipped with one and heat the oil to 375 degrees. Place a double thickness of paper towels nearby. Preheat the oven to 200 degrees and place a baking sheet inside.

5 Fry the samosas in small batches until golden brown, turning them frequently with a slotted spoon. The pastries should move freely around the pot and have room to be evenly bathed in the fat. This process takes about 3 minutes. Remove with a slotted spoon and drain on paper towels; place the samosas on the baking sheet to keep them warm in the oven as you fry subsequent batches. Serve immediately for best results. You may hold them at room temperature for a few hours if necessary and reheat them in the oven, but they will lose some of their crispness. Serve with the Cilantro Chutney. For a change of pace, serve it with the Cranberry Chutney in Chapter 8.

Per serving: *Calories 179 (From Fat 132); Fat 15g (Saturated 3g); Cholesterol 9mg; Sodium 105mg; Carbohydrate 11g (Dietary Fiber 1g); Protein 2g.*

Cilantro Chutney

1 cup firmly packed fresh cilantro leaves	2 teaspoons sugar
3 scallions, root end and half the green removed	1 teaspoon garam masala
1 clove garlic	½ teaspoon salt
½ large jalapeño chile, stemmed and seeded	3 tablespoons lemon juice
	¼ medium onion

Place all the ingredients in the bowl of a food processor fitted with the metal blade. Pulse on and off and then leave on until the mixture is uniform and has formed a fluid paste. Add water if necessary to create a dippable texture. You can also make the chutney in a blender.

Remember: *If you buy your spices in bulk, you can buy just what you need, ensuring that it will be fresh when you use it. Natural food stores are a good place to look for them. The mustard seeds may seem unusual, but you can often find them where bulk spices are sold.*

Simplify: *If you don't have a pastry brush, don't fret. Just use your finger to moisten the dough. Dip your finger in the water and swipe it over all the edges of the dough.*

Remember: *Review the deep-fat frying instructions in Chapter 7 to help you when frying your samosas.*

Per serving: *Calories 3 (From Fat 0); Fat 0g (Saturated 0g); Cholesterol 0mg; Sodium 40mg; Carbohydrate 1g (Dietary Fiber 0g); Protein 0g.*

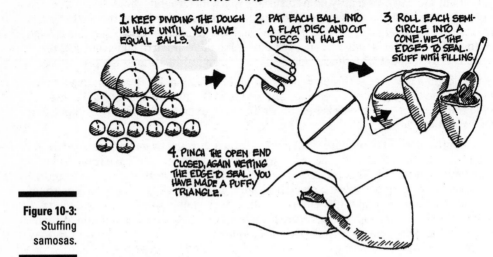

Figure 10-3:
Stuffing
samosas.

Part IV
Formal and Fabulous: Starters for Sit-Down Dinners and Special Occasions

In this part . . .

Are you looking for something a little fancy to impress the boss or the in-laws? Or are you simply tired of making the same old standbys? If so, you've come to the right part of the book. Here's where you can find recipes for formal plated appetizers, such as goat cheese salad or salmon mousse. In addition, I give you ideas for serving such indulgent foods as smoked salmon, caviar, and foie gras.

Chapter 11

At the Table: Formal Plated Appetizers

In This Chapter

▶ Arranging salad greens with artistry

▶ Stirring up a chilled soup

▶ Sharing a salmon mousse

▶ Using artichokes and roasted peppers in your appetizers

▶ Cooking with wasabi and miso

*Y*ou may not have heard of the term "plated appetizer," but you definitely would know one if you saw it. When you order an appetizer in a restaurant, it's very often a plated appetizer, which for the purposes of this book is defined as an appetizer that's artfully arranged on the plate in the kitchen and served to one individual. So when you are presented with a white plate topped with slices of colorful red, orange, yellow, and green tomatoes, all drizzled with a vivid and zesty mustard vinaigrette, that, my friends, is a plated appetizer. (You can read more about this tomato idea later in the chapter.) Chopping up the tomatoes and tossing them with a vinaigrette may be easier, but you don't get the same impact upon presentation. As you can see, you can turn a recipe into a plated appetizer simply by using the same ingredients but a different approach.

Plated Salads: Getting Fancy with Greens

Salads readily lend themselves to a plated arrangement and are a good place to start. The first recipe, a warm goat cheese salad, is by no means original, but it's a must in any appetizer repertoire. It's also very easy.

Warmed Goat Cheese Salad

Fresh baby lettuces and goat cheese combine to make a quick, light, elegant starter.

Preparation time: *10 minutes*

Cooking time: *7 minutes*

Yield: *6 servings*

9 cups mesclun, lightly packed

½ cup dry bread crumbs (homemade or Progresso makes good ones)

½ teaspoon herbes de Provence

Salt and pepper

3 to 4 tablespoons extra-virgin olive oil

7½ ounces Montrachet or other mild, rindless, log-shaped goat cheese that is approximately 1¾ inches across (see the sidebar "Selecting goat cheese")

Sherry Vinaigrette (see the following recipe)

1 Wash and dry the mesclun mix and place in a mixing bowl; set aside. Place the bread crumbs in a small bowl; add the herbs de Provence and season with salt and pepper; set aside. Place the olive oil in a small bowl.

2 Preheat the oven to 400 degrees. Slice the goat cheese into six ¾-inch-thick rounds. Dip the cheese rounds into the olive oil and then into the bread crumbs. Make sure to coat the cheese completely. Place the cheese rounds in a roasting pan, evenly spaced apart. Bake for about 7 minutes, or until the bread crumbs are golden and the cheese is soft.

3 Meanwhile, gently toss the salad with a couple tablespoons of vinaigrette; you may need additional dressing. The salad should just be lightly coated. Divide among 6 plates. As soon as the cheese is ready, place a round on each plate on top of the greens and serve immediately.

Sherry Vinaigrette

2 tablespoons sherry vinegar

1 teaspoon Dijon mustard

7 tablespoons light olive oil

Salt and pepper

Whisk together the vinegar and mustard in a small bowl until combined. Very slowly drizzle the olive oil into the mixture, whisking constantly until creamy. Season with salt and pepper, and it's ready to use.

Per serving: *Calories 379 (From Fat 304); Fat 34g (Saturated 11g); Cholesterol 28mg; Sodium 496mg; Carbohydrate 10g (Dietary Fiber 2g); Protein 10g.*

Roasted Beets, Blue Cheese, and Walnut Salad

Don't like beets? You haven't tried this salad. If you give it a go, you may be converted. Beets are actually very sweet, and the pungency of the blue cheese and the nuttiness of the walnuts accent them perfectly.

Preparation time: *10 minutes*

Cooking time: *1 hour and 15 minutes*

Yield: *4 servings*

1 large beet, unpeeled, scrubbed, all but 1 inch of top removed

5 cups mesclun, lightly packed

⅓ cup walnut halves, toasted and roughly chopped

3 ounces blue cheese (such as Maytag Blue), coarsely crumbled (about ⅔ cup)

Sherry Vinaigrette (see the recipe earlier in this chapter)

1 Preheat the oven to 400 degrees. Tightly wrap the beet in aluminum foil and place directly on an oven rack. Roast until tender when pierced with a knife, about 1 hour and 15 minutes. Remove from the oven and let cool to room temperature. You may roast the beet a day ahead and refrigerate until needed; allow to come to room temperature before using.

2 Meanwhile, wash and dry the mesclun mix, if desired, and place in a mixing bowl; set aside.

3 Peel and cut the beet into ½-inch cubes (about ¾ cup) and add to the bowl of mesclun. Add the walnuts and cheese.

4 Gently toss the salad with a couple tablespoons of the Sherry Vinaigrette; you may need additional dressing. The salad should just be lightly coated. Divide among 4 plates and serve immediately.

***Tip:** The beets color the cheese with a tinge of pink. If you want the cheese to remain white, just toss everything except the cheese together, divide the tossed salad among the serving plates, and sprinkle the cheese on top right before serving.*

***Warning:** This information may not be what you expect from a cookbook, but I feel compelled to warn you about a side effect of eating beets. I'll just say that your toilet water may turn pink the next morning. The natural coloring of the beets is very strong and stays with you for a day or two. I know too many inexperienced beet eaters who panic and immediately call their doctors. My suggestion is to wait a day and see what happens.*

Per serving: Calories 365 (From Fat 319); Fat 36g (Saturated 8g); Cholesterol 16mg; Sodium 515mg; Carbohydrate 7g (Dietary Fiber 3g); Protein 8g.

Caesar Salad with Garlic Croutons

This recipe isn't for the garlic timid! Make the croutons first and then make the salad right before serving for best results.

Preparation time: *15 minutes*

Cooking time: *12 minutes*

Yield: *6 servings*

2 large heads romaine lettuce	*4 anchovy fillets, minced*
2 eggs	*⅓ cup extra-virgin olive oil*
3 tablespoons freshly squeezed lemon juice	*½ cup freshly grated Parmigiano-Reggiano cheese*
1 teaspoon minced garlic	*Croutons (see the following recipe)*
¼ teaspoon Dijon mustard	*Salt (optional)*
¼ teaspoon black pepper	

1 Remove any tough or wilted outer leaves of lettuce. Trim the heads of lettuce by removing several inches of the dark green tops and the very bottom, including any hard core. Tear into large bite-size pieces. (You should have 12 cups.) Place the lettuce in a large mixing bowl.

2 Bring a small pot of water to a boil and carefully submerge the eggs in the water and time for exactly 1 minute. Remove from the boiling water and allow to cool slightly.

3 Meanwhile, make the vinaigrette by whisking together the lemon juice, garlic, mustard, black pepper, and anchovies. Slowly drizzle in the olive oil, whisking all the while to make a smooth vinaigrette.

4 Crack the eggs directly over the lettuce, using a teaspoon to help release any of the white that sticks to the inside of the shell. Toss well to coat the leaves. Slowly pour the vinaigrette over the salad, tossing as you go; add the cheese and croutons and keep tossing until the salad and croutons are evenly coated with the dressing. Taste to see whether you need any salt and season as desired. Serve immediately.

Tip: The salt is optional in this recipe because the anchovies and Parmesan cheese already have a lot of sodium, and the saltiness of those ingredients varies from brand to brand. Taste your salad and season with salt only if it still needs it.

Per serving: *Calories 353 (From Fat 264); Fat 29g (Saturated 6g); Cholesterol 80mg; Sodium 583mg; Carbohydrate 15g (Dietary Fiber 2g); Protein 10g.*

Croutons

4 cups ½-inch cubes of French bread or sourdough French bread

⅓ cup extra-virgin olive oil

1 tablespoon minced garlic

½ teaspoon salt

Preheat the oven to 350 degrees. Toss the bread cubes, olive oil, garlic, and salt together in a bowl until the cubes are evenly coated. Spread out in a single layer on a rimmed baking sheet and bake for 6 minutes. Stir around to rotate the cubes and bake for 6 more minutes, or just until they begin to brown. They should be crusty along the edges but remain chewy. Cool to room temperature.

Tip: This recipe makes a lot of croutons. I find that people always want more, so I doubled the typical amount. Use as many or as few as you like. The croutons will keep for a few days in an airtight container stored at room temperature. Toss any extra croutons on top of other salads or a bowl of soup.

Fennel and Orange Salad

This salad is refreshing, and the citrus makes it a great addition to a rich meal. If you've never used fennel, see the sidebar "Looking for fennel" in this chapter for information about this ingredient. The vinaigrette recipe makes more than enough; save the extra for other salads.

Preparation time: *15 minutes*

Yield: *4 servings*

1 fennel bulb

2 navel oranges

1 head Bibb or Boston lettuce, leaves separated, washed, and dried, or 2 cups mesclun, lightly packed

Sherry Vinaigrette (see the recipe earlier in this chapter)

1 Trim the fennel bulb by slicing off the stem end and discarding. Trim off the leafy greens on top and any stalks, leaving the round bulb; reserve the greens. Quarter the bulb and very thinly slice; place the slices in a bowl. Chop the reserved leafy greens from the top, measure out ¼ cup of them, and add to the bowl of fennel slices.

2 Peel the oranges and remove the white pith. Use a sharp paring knife to cut between the membranes and release the segments. Remove any seeds and place the segments in the bowl with the fennel. You may make the salad several hours ahead up to this point. Cover loosely with plastic wrap and refrigerate.

3 When ready to serve, add a couple tablespoons of the vinaigrette and toss gently; you may need additional dressing. The salad should just be lightly coated. Divide the salad among 4 plates and serve.

Simplify: *Instead of removing the oranges from their membranes, simply peel, remove the white pith and any seeds, and section them. Toss in with the fennel. The orange sections are a bit less tender with their membranes still attached, but if you're in a rush, go fo it.*

Per serving: *Calories 255 (From Fat 216); Fat 24g (Saturated 3g); Cholesterol 0mg; Sodium 190mg; Carbohydrate 11g (Dietary Fiber 3g); Protein 2g.*

Cooling Off with Chilled Soup

Not all soups are served hot and regulated to the cold winter months. Spring and summer are perfect times to present cold soup as a starter. They make very flavorful, light appetizers, and, in the case of my avocado soup below, are creamy as well and easy to make.

Place your soup bowls in the refrigerator at least 1 hour ahead of time; they will keep your soup at a nice chilly temperature even after you bring it to the table.

Chilled Avocado Soup with Coriander Cream

Serve this avocado soup before a summer meal. It's as cool and soothing as it is delicious and creamy. Buy a fresh caramelized onion or olive focaccia (a flat Italian bread) from the bakery and serve thick slices of it with the soup.

Preparation time: 15 minutes

Yield: 4 servings

3 ripe Haas avocados	Salt
2 tablespoons lime juice	White pepper
2½ cups low-sodium vegetable stock	Coriander Cream (see the following recipe)
1½ cups buttermilk	Fresh cilantro

1 Peel and pit the avocados and place all the flesh in a blender. Add the lime juice, 1¼ cups of the vegetable broth, and the buttermilk. Blend until creamy, adding the remaining 1¼ cups vegetable stock as needed to make a thick but fluid texture. Season with the salt and white pepper. The soup may be prepared up to 1 hour ahead. Keep refrigerated, in the blender, until needed.

2 To serve, give the soup a last-minute buzz in the blender and adjust the texture, if necessary, by adding a little more stock or water. (It can thicken upon standing.) Divide the soup among the serving bowls. Drizzle a swirl of Coriander Cream in each bowl. Top with a sprig of fresh cilantro and serve immediately.

Tip: The easiest way to get to the avocado flesh is to run your knife around the avocado lengthwise, pressing your knife all the way to the pit. Then twist the two halves apart; the large pit will be attached to one side. Remove the pit with your fingers and use a teaspoon to scoop out the flesh right into the blender.

Tip: I suggest white pepper for the soup because black pepper leaves black flecks and mars the solid green creaminess of the soup. If you don't mind that and you don't want to buy white pepper just for this dish, go ahead and use black pepper. The dish is very mild, though, and does need the heat of a little pepper, whether it's black or white.

Coriander Cream

½ cup sour cream

¼ cup heavy cream or buttermilk

½ teaspoon coriander

Tabasco to taste

Gently stir together the sour cream and heavy cream in a small bowl. Stir in the coriander and Tabasco.

Tip: *I prefer using the heavy cream because it and the sour cream provide a nice contrast to the tangy buttermilk flavor in the soup. But because you'll already have the buttermilk on hand to make the soup, feel free to use it instead of buying extra heavy cream if you like.*

Per serving: *Calories 366 (From Fat 283); Fat 32g (Saturated 13g); Cholesterol 36mg; Sodium 417mg; Carbohydrate 19g (Dietary Fiber 12g); Protein 8g.*

The Romance of Sharing: Salmon Mousse for Two

Sharing a plate of food can be a very intimate romantic endeavor. The Smoked Salmon Mousse recipe uses 6-ounce custard cups for the mousse. This amount is perfect for a couple to share. Because the recipe makes enough to fill 4 custard cups, my suggestion is to invite over three other couples, seat them together, and serve the unmolded mousses on plates for the couples to share.

If you don't want to make individual mousses, you can make it in any 3-cup mold or bowl. Either way, the mousse needs to refrigerate for at least 5 hours, so plan ahead.

Individual Smoked Salmon Mousse

This impressive-looking and -tasting appetizer is actually very easy to make.

Specialty tools: *Four 6-ounce custard cups*

Preparation time: *20 minutes, plus 5 hours for refrigeration*

Yield: *8 servings*

Vegetable oil

½ cup water

2½ teaspoons unflavored gelatin

5 ounces thinly sliced smoked salmon

7¼-ounce can salmon, drained and skin or large bones removed

1 tablespoon fresh lemon juice

¼ cup finely chopped scallion

1 tablespoon minced fresh dill

1½ cups sour cream

Tabasco to taste

Flat-leaf parsley for garnish

⅓ cup salmon roe (optional)

French bread

Hothouse cucumber slices, skin on

1 Lightly oil the inside surfaces of the custard cups, using a pastry brush. Place ¼ cup of the water in a small bowl, sprinkle the gelatin over it, and stir. Let sit 5 minutes to soften the gelatin. Bring the remaining ¼ cup water to a boil, pour over the softened gelatin, and stir until dissolved.

2 Place the smoked salmon, canned salmon, lemon juice, scallion, and dill in a food processor fitted with a metal blade. Pulse on and off and then run the processor for several seconds, until the mixture is smooth and creamy. Pour the dissolved gelatin over the mousse and pulse once or twice to combine. Add the sour cream and pulse once or twice just until smooth. Season with Tabasco.

3 Scrape the mousse into the 4 custard cups, dividing evenly. Refrigerate for at least 5 hours or overnight.

4 Unmold the cups right before serving. To unmold, dip a small, sharp knife in hot water and run the tip around the edges of the mousse cups, along the inside of the cup's lip. Fill a bowl with warm water and briefly dip the molds into the water, submerging as far as you can go without allowing any water to run up and over the top. Remove the cups from the bowl and wiggle them to loosen the seal. Place a serving plate over the mousse cups and invert them; they should release. If they don't unmold, turn everything back, right side up. Once again, wiggle the custard cups back and forth to loosen. Try again. Still no luck? Dip them in the warm water again.

5 Garnish each mousse with a sprig of parsley on top. I like to press a few leaves flat against the mousse. Scatter some salmon roe around each mousse, if desired. Serve with sliced French bread and slices of cucumbers. Because each serving serves two, present with two spreading knives and place between the guests who will share the plate.

Per serving: Calories 159 (From Fat 112); Fat 12g (Saturated 6g); Cholesterol 39mg; Sodium 490mg; Carbohydrate 2g (Dietary Fiber 0g); Protein 10g. (bread and cucumber not included)

Getting a Raw Deal: Beef Carpaccio

You may have eaten raw fish in sashimi and sushi, but raw beef may not be something that you've tried before. Steak tartare, which is raw ground beef, often with a bit of egg, is a classic dish, as is carpaccio, the thinly sliced raw beef dish invented at Harry's Bar in Venice. Legend has it that the dish was devised for a demanding customer with special dietary needs. It became a popular dish and was added to the menu for any and all customers.

You can make it at home quite easily. Just as with sushi, the freshness of the ingredients is paramount. Tell your butcher how you'll be using the beef and use the highest grade of meat you can find.

Beef Carpaccio

Buy the best beef fillet you can find for this classic Italian dish. The meat will be very cold when served, as it should be. The chilled beef adds to the textural experience of the dish.

Preparation time: *15 minutes, plus 30 minutes freezing time*

Yield: *6 servings*

1 pound lean beef fillet	*Salt and pepper*
¼ cup freshly squeezed lemon juice	*2 tablespoon capers, drained*
1 tablespoon red wine vinegar	*4-ounce solid piece of Parmigiano-Reggiano cheese*
1 teaspoon Dijon mustard	
½ cup extra-virgin olive oil	

1 Begin the preparations about 40 minutes before serving time. Wrap the beef fillet in plastic wrap and freeze for about 30 minutes. Place individual serving dishes in the refrigerator to chill. Meanwhile, prepare the rest of the recipe.

2 Whisk together the lemon juice, vinegar, and mustard in a small bowl. Slowly add the olive oil, whisking all the while. Season with salt and pepper.

3 After the meat has been freezing for 30 minutes, unwrap and slice on the diagonal as thinly as possible and place on plates, overlapping the pieces. Drizzle with the dressing, top with some freshly cracked black pepper, and scatter the capers over all. Using a cheese plane (as described in Chapter 3), make curls of Parmesan and scatter on top of the meat and serve immediately.

Tip: *Try to get your meat cut from the thicker end of the fillet and trim it of any visible fat.*

Tip: *Briefly freezing the meat at the start of the recipe allows you to slice it very thinly. Take care not to freeze it solid, however, or the meat will develop an unpleasant texture.*

Per serving: *Calories 451 (From Fat 363); Fat 40g (Saturated 13g); Cholesterol 67mg; Sodium 562mg; Carbohydrate 2g (Dietary Fiber 0g); Protein 20g.*

Eating Your Vegetables

Hollywood movies of decades past used to treat vegetables as something to fear. If a kid had to eat his veggies, it was understood to be the worst situation possible! Nowadays we have such incredibly fresh and delicious vegetables at our disposal, they are some of the yummiest ingredients around. In this section, I present to you a slightly complicated roasted vegetable terrine that must be prepared the day ahead.

Roasted Vegetable Terrine

This dish features a combination of roasted red peppers, eggplant, zucchini, and goat cheese in an easy-to-slice loaf shape. Plan ahead because the terrine must sit overnight. Pass the French bread, and you have a colorful plated appetizer, which can be made up to 2 days ahead.

Preparation time: *30 minutes, plus overnight refrigeration*

Cooking time: *15 minutes*

Yield: *6 servings*

1 large purple eggplant (about 1¼ pounds), ends trimmed, cut lengthwise into ⅜-inch slices

3 medium zucchini, ends trimmed, cut lengthwise into ¼-inch slices

3 medium yellow summer squash, ends trimmed, cut lengthwise into ¼-inch slices

Light or extra-virgin olive oil

Salt and pepper

8 ounces soft, fresh goat cheese, such as Montrachet

½ teaspoon thyme or herbes de Provence

¼ cup black or green olive paste

½ red bell pepper, roasted; stem, seeds, and ribs removed; cut into ½-inch squares

1 Preheat the broiler. Brush both sides of the eggplant slices with the olive oil. Place in a single layer on a baking sheet and broil until cooked through and golden, about 8 minutes. Flip the slices over and cook on the other side until golden, about 5 minutes. Remove from the oven and the pan and place on paper towels to absorb the excess oil. You may have to broil the eggplant in two batches. Repeat the process with the zucchini and yellow squash, arranging the vegetables in a single layer and cooking for about 6 minutes, then flipping over and cooking further until golden, about 3 minutes. Remove from the pan and drain on paper towels. You'll probably have to cook the zucchini and squash in batches, too. Lightly season all the vegetables with salt and pepper.

2 Place the goat cheese in a food processor fitted with a metal blade and pulse on and off to break up the cheese. Add 2 teaspoons of olive oil and process just until it reaches the consistency of a smooth paste. Pulse in the thyme and a few grinds of pepper.

3 Line an 8-x-4-inch loaf pan with plastic wrap, leaving a 4-inch overhang on every side. You may need to use a few pieces of plastic wrap. Line the bottom of the pan with a double layer of zucchini strips, cut to fit the bottom. Arrange a double layer of yellow squash, cut to fit, on top. Spread evenly with a third of the goat cheese mixture. Add a layer of eggplant, cut to fit, and top with another third of the cheese. Make a single layer of red pepper squares and dollop the olive paste over the pepper layer, spreading as smoothly as possible. Repeat the layers of green and yellow squash and the remaining cheese. Finish with a layer of eggplant. Bring the edges of the plastic wrap over the top to cover completely. Press down gently and refrigerate overnight. You can place a couple canned goods on their sides on top of the terrine to provide weight, which will compress the vegetables, thereby compacting them, which will make the terrine easier to slice.

4 To serve, remove the terrine from the refrigerator at least 30 minutes before serving to allow it to come to room temperature. Peel back the plastic wrap, place a large serving plate on top of the terrine, and invert. Lift the loaf pan off and peel the plastic off the terrine. Use a very sharp knife to cut into slices. Place the slices on individual serving plates with several slices of freshly cut French bread.

Tip: Look for the olive paste, which is available in black or green, in specialty food markets.

Tip: Don't try to cook the eggplant with the squashes. The ingredients must be cooked separately because they cook at different rates. You can, however, cook the two squashes (the zucchini and the yellow squash) together.

Per serving: Calories 227 (From Fat 138); Fat 15g (Saturated 7g); Cholesterol 17mg; Sodium 328mg; Carbohydrate 14g (Dietary Fiber 6g); Protein 10g.

Adding Wasabi and Miso to Your Ingredient List

Wasabi is Japanese horseradish and is a root in its natural state, but in the United States, you probably will find it only in its dried form. Although anything fresh is usually better than dried, there are exceptions, and this is one of those times. Wasabi is perfectly good in its dried form. In fact, when you find a small mound of spicy, green paste on your dish at a sushi restaurant, that's wasabi, and it most likely was reconstituted from dried.

Miso is a fermented soybean paste that's available in natural food stores in the refrigerated section. It is made by combining a base of soybeans with a grain such as brown rice or barley. The miso is labeled according to the grain that is used, such as "brown rice miso." Miso ranges from a dark reddish brown to a very light beige, and usually the darker variety is more fermented and saltier. The miso in the Wasabi-Ginger Dressing in the following recipe is a small amount, but it does add a complex flavor. If you don't want to buy the miso just for this sauce, adjust the seasonings of the sauce with an extra dash or two of soy sauce and maybe a pinch of sugar.

Seared Tuna with Wasabi-Ginger Dressing

Buy the freshest tuna fillet you can find for this appetizer. The wasabi and miso, which are specialty items, have flavors that can't be duplicated. You'll probably have to go to a specialty store to find them, but they're worth it. Have the Wasabi-Ginger dressing ready before you begin with the Tuna Steaks.

Preparation time: *10 minutes*

Cooking time: *4 minutes*

Yield: *6 servings*

¼ cup toasted sesame seeds (see the tip after Step 3 in the recipe)

Salt and pepper

16 ounces fresh tuna steak, preferably at least 1½ inches thick (you may have more than one steak)

Light olive oil

⅔ cup pea sprouts

⅔ cup sunflower sprouts

Wasabi Ginger Dressing (see the following recipe)

1 Place the sesame seeds in a shallow, wide bowl and season with salt and pepper; stir around so that the seeds and seasonings combine. Press the tuna into the sesame seeds on both sides to cover as completely as possible, top and bottom only.

2 Coat a heavy-bottomed pan, such as a cast-iron pan, with a thin film of oil and heat until very hot over high heat. Add the tuna and sear the bottom, about 2 minutes. Flip over and sear the other side, about 2 minutes more. Only the outer ¼ inch should be cooked. Remove from the heat and transfer to a cutting board.

3 Slice the tuna on the diagonal into broad slices about ½ inch thick and divide slices among the 6 plates. (You probably will have enough for 2 to 3 slices per plate.) Arrange small mounds of the sprouts on top of the tuna slices. Give the dressing a last-minute whisking and drizzle over the sprouts and tuna; serve immediately.

Tip: To toast sesame seeds, you have two options. Preheat the oven to 350 degrees, spread the seeds on a rimmed baking sheet, and bake for about 4 minutes or just until the seeds begin to turn light brown. Alternatively, spread the seeds in a heavy pan, such as a cast-iron pan, and toast over medium-high heat, stirring constantly, until lightly toasted. This method takes only a couple minutes.

Wasabi-Ginger Dressing

3 tablespoons rice vinegar

2 tablespoons orange juice

1 tablespoon soy sauce

2 teaspoons wasabi powder

1 teaspoon white or yellow miso

½ teaspoon minced fresh ginger

3 tablespoons light olive oil

Place all the ingredients in a blender to combine. Alternatively, you can whisk together all the ingredients except the olive oil and then slowly drizzle in the oil, whisking constantly to combine. Dressing may be stored in an airtight jar or container at room temperature for 1 day, after which the flavors will dull.

Per serving: Calories 215 (From Fat 112); Fat 12g (Saturated 2g); Cholesterol 33mg; Sodium 343mg; Carbohydrate 7g (Dietary Fiber 2g); Protein 20g.

Chapter 12

Puttin' on the Dog: Extravagant Appetizers

Sometimes a platter of crudités or chicken wings just doesn't cut it. Don't get me wrong. I love a good finger-lickin' chicken wing, but not if I'm in formal dress. There is definitely a time to pull out all the stops and serve the most elegant food you can get your hands on. If you want to bring the ultimate luxury foods to your table, read on.

Anytime you want to present ultra-elegant appetizers, this is the chapter to refer to. This chapter is meant to be a primer on my favorite extra-special foods, including caviar and foie gras (pronounced *fwah-grah*), which is a creamy goose or duck liver. Smoked salmon, while more readily available and accessible, is no less scrumptious. If you're planning an event for an important occasion, such as an engagement party or significant anniversary, why not go for broke? Now, I don't want you to literally go broke in order to put food on your party table. Caviar and foie gras are pricey, and smoked salmon less so. I give you the lowdown on them all in this chapter so that you can decide which way to go. There is a time and place for everything, including these fancy foods.

The Joys of Smoked Salmon

I love salmon in all of its incarnations. Whether it is raw (as in sashimi), roasted, or smoked, I'll take it all. Smoked salmon itself has a few variations, including cold-smoked and hot-smoked. I focus here on the cold-smoked variety, which is the silkiest and most versatile type of smoked salmon when it comes to the appetizer table. Hot-smoked salmon is more similar to a cooked fillet. Confusing? It can be, but I try and clarify the situation so that you can buy your smoked salmon with confidence.

The first thing you need to know is that if the only smoked salmon you ever eat is with your bagel and cream cheese from the deli, then you may not be enjoying smoked salmon to it fullest, as your deli might offer but one kind. To understand smoked salmon, you need to know something about the various origins of the salmon itself and the techniques used to smoke it.

Atlantic salmon, which is fattier than most Pacific salmon, makes a better smoked salmon. The extra richness of the raw Atlantic salmon translates to a smoother, silkier end product. Nova is from Nova Scotia and is made from Atlantic salmon and is usually a good product. You will very often find "Nova Scotia" salmon served at your local bagel deli. But if you want the best for your appetizers, try European-style smoked salmon, which is a cold-smoked salmon. It is literally smoked with a colder smoke, which allows the smoke to permeate the flesh somewhat, but retain the delicate inherent properties of the raw fish. The Scots are known for their smoked salmon, and you can find some pretty good Norwegian smoked salmon on the market, too, and both kinds will be labeled with their origin. Also keep an eye out for domestic salmon smoked in the European style. You may be wondering how to recognize a good smoked salmon flavor. Well, you do want to taste the smokiness a little bit, but not to the extent that it overpowers the salmon's natural essence. The texture should be silky, moist, and resilient. How do you know whether you're eating good smoked salmon? Do you like it? Do you want another slice? Then it's good! I refuse to be a dictator in the kitchen. I can tell you what I like and what is considered the best by the pros in the field, but the most important thing is that you like eating it! Use my notes as background information for pointing you in the right direction.

Shopping for smoked salmon

You can find smoked salmon in supermarket delis, freestanding delis, and specialty food stores. Some stores even specialize in smoked fish products. The salmon will most likely be sold by the pound and be available sliced or whole. Although the salmon loses some moisture if you buy it presliced, the presliced option is probably worth it, unless you happen to have a special slicing knife and a lot of experience. Slicing salmon isn't that easy if you want slices so thin you can practically see through them, which is preferable. Salmon slicing is an art best left to the experts. If someone is going to slice your salmon to order, you can specify that you want large, broad slices cut as thin as possible. This type of slicing shows off the delicate striations of fat within the flesh that offer visual and textural interest to the salmon.

Keep your smoked salmon wrapped well in plastic wrap and use as soon as possible, especially if it is sliced already. If you find smoked salmon that is vacuum-packed, it will have a longer shelf life.

Serving smoked salmon

Smoked salmon is so delicious that you don't have to do much to it to enjoy it at its fullest. Some connoisseurs insist that it should be placed on a plate and eaten as is, to experience it in all its glory. But by adding a few ingredients, you can enhance the flavor of smoked salmon. Consider these ideas:

- Add a wedge of lemon and a scattering of capers.
- A few grinds of black pepper provide an interesting counterpoint.
- Try a smear of sweet, unsalted butter on pumpernickel bread with your salmon.
- Add a dollop of caviar and crème fraîche. Before you serve it this way, at least try it au naturel first. You may find that caviar and crème fraîche are gilding the lily. But if you want to go that route, roll up a slice of salmon into a cornet shape and secure with a toothpick. Fill the center, which should have a bit of a hollow, with a dollop of crème fraîche and caviar and serve.

Take the smoked salmon out of the refrigerator about a half-hour before you serve it. If you serve it ice-cold, the fat in the fish will be very firm, prohibiting maximum enjoyment. Permitting it to warm slightly allows the silky texture to come through to its best advantage. If you wonder what I mean by "silky," you'll understand when you take your first bite.

Caviar: Eggs-traordinaire

Classic caviar is fish eggs, or roe, of sturgeon. Sturgeon swim in various parts of the world, but the best caviar comes from the largest and best fish, which are found in the Caspian Sea, bordered by Russia and Iran.

The Hudson River flowing parallel to Manhattan was once so full of sturgeon that it was said that you could walk from Manhattan to New Jersey on the backs of the large fish! That's an exaggeration of course, but it's a sad state of affairs that the fish are no longer in these waters.

The fresh sturgeon eggs are harvested and lightly salted, and that's it! Caviar is sold pretty much the way it comes out of the fish. That may not sound very palatable, and in fact, caviar is an acquired taste. But if you're a salty-food lover, this may be up your alley. If you like seafood and can appreciate the briny flavor it brings to your taste buds, then caviar may be worth a try.

Getting to know caviar

There are three main types of caviar:

- **Beluga:** Beluga caviar has the most delicate flavor of the three types and is often the most expensive. The beluga sturgeon are the scarcest and the largest, some reaching up to 20 feet! Their eggs are the largest, too, and coveted by many connoisseurs. The eggs can range from light gray to very dark gray, with the lighter hues being preferred.

    Although beluga is the rarest and most expensive caviar, that doesn't necessarily mean that it's the best. Whichever you like is what is the best for you.

- **Osetra:** Osetra eggs are favored by some caviar aficionados because they're more assertively flavored, often with a nutty accent. The color can range from yellowish gray to the darkest brown/black. Osetra caviar is often considered a best buy — more flavor for less money than beluga. Osetra sturgeon do not usually grow beyond 7 feet long, and their eggs are correspondingly smaller. These fish swim in deeper, colder water than the beluga and have a different diet, which affects the flavor of the eggs.

- **Sevruga:** These eggs have the briniest flavor and are therefore usually experienced as the most intensely flavored. Sevruga is usually the least expensive caviar and comes from the smallest sturgeon, and as I'm sure you can figure out by now, the eggs are the smallest, too. The eggs range from medium gray to black.

The term "caviar" is used to describe other fish eggs, too. Salmon roe, also called salmon caviar, is a deep sunset orange color with large eggs. It is very popular in sushi bars. Whitefish caviar is pale yellow and referred to as golden caviar. The very inexpensive caviar that you can find in supermarkets in small jars is from lumpfish. It is made of salted eggs, but it doesn't taste a thing like high-quality sturgeon caviar. It is also dyed deep black or vivid red. Personally, I would rather pass over this type of "caviar."

Buying caviar

The supermarket is not the place to buy caviar. You can find caviar in jars somewhere near the canned tuna, but leave it there! You need to go to a specialty store, either a gourmet food store that carries caviar or a caviar specialty store. You can also find great caviar through some Web sites I list in Chapter 14.

When you buy caviar, look for the term "malossol," which means "lightly salted" and is considered the preferred type. If you can taste before you buy, all the better, but doing so may not be possible. If you can find a reputable dealer who handles a lot of caviar and is very informed, then put yourself in his hands.

Good caviar doesn't come cheap. If you're going to serve it, make sure that your wallet can handle it. In terms of quantity, one ounce per person is about the least you should offer.

Sometimes caviar is discounted, albeit not a lot, around the winter holidays, so look for specials.

Serving caviar

If you buy good beluga, osetra, or sevruga caviar, then serve it to its best advantage. Most caviar comes in lined tins or glass containers, which you can set directly on crushed ice. Caviar is very perishable, so although this presentation is a bit fancy, it also serves a purpose.

You also need to consider what kind of spoon to use to scoop up your caviar. You most likely can find caviar spoons wherever caviar is sold. These spoons are made from mother-of-pearl, horn, or, occasionally, ivory. Caviar experts explain that metal spoons, particularly silver ones, affect the taste of the delicate eggs by imparting a metallic flavor that ruins your enjoyment of this indulgent appetizer. Not only is it kind of fun to have the proper accouterments, but they won't set you back very much. Most of these proper spoons are under $20, with some of them just a few bucks.

So now that you have set your caviar on ice and have the correct spoons, how do you serve it? Straight up! There's nothing better than lifting a spoon of pure caviar to your mouth. If you want to add some thin sliced toast points, be my guests, but you can concentrate on the bread, and I'll work on the caviar.

Toast points are nothing more than thinly sliced bread that has been trimmed of the crusts, toasted, and cut, usually into triangles, hence the "points." Use white bread or, if you can find it, a buttery brioche.

If your caviar isn't the finest and can use a little help, here are a few items to offer with the toast points:

- Finely chopped and separated egg yolks and egg whites
- Crème fraîche or sour cream (Crème fraîche is a cultured cream product, like sour cream. You can find it in some cheese departments or near the sour cream in upscale supermarkets and specialty stores.)
- Finely minced flat-leaf parsley

Although some folks serve champagne with caviar, some experts prefer ice-cold vodka. Try both and see which one rings your bells. The neutrality of the vodka (unflavored, please) cuts the richness of the caviar without detracting from it.

Foie Gras: The Liver of Luxury

"Foie gras" means fattened liver in French. Livers are already fatty enough, but goose or ducks raised for foie gras are fed in such a way as to add extra fat to their livers. Most goose foie gras that you find in the United States is imported. Domestic duck foie gras, which can be quite good, is also available.

Foie gras must usually be special ordered from specialty stores or mail-order sources and comes whole, that is, in two lobes. Sometimes it is sealed in vacuum packaging, which means that the foie gras will last longer than if it's packaged by another method. Ask the supplier about the shelf life of the product you're buying because it is hard to make a general statement about this. No matter how it is packaged, foie gras is quite perishable and should be used soon after you receive it and immediately after opening any kind of package.

Handling foie gras

Foie gras is mostly fat and crumbles easily when very cold, so always handle it carefully, but particularly right after taking it out of the refrigerator.

To clean it, gently separate the two lobes and remove any visible veins and connective tissue that you see.

Preparing foie gras

You can prepare foie gras in one of two ways — by slicing and sautéing it or making it into a *terrine,* which is a type of pâté. (The term "terrine," by the way, is also used to describe the traditional vessel in which you pack a pâté like terrine.) Slicing and sautéing is simple, so that is what I discuss here. There are myriad ways to serve sautéed foie gras, very often with some sort of sweet accompaniment, such as sautéed apples, quinces, or peaches. But there is nothing wrong with searing the foie gras and serving it with toast points.

Seared Foie Gras

This dish is a very basic foie gras preparation, but the result is rich, buttery, and delicious. Save this recipe for an important occasion.

Preparation time: *10 minutes*

Cooking time: *30 seconds per batch*

Yield: *8 servings*

1 whole duck foie gras (about 12 ounces), cleaned and deveined

Salt and pepper

Vegetable oil

Toast points, preferably made from brioche

1 Allow the foie gras to sit at room temperature for an hour. Carefully cut it into ½-inch-thick slices and season both sides well with salt and pepper.

2 Heat a skillet over high heat and add a thin film of vegetable oil. When the oil is hot, arrange several slices of foie gras in the pan so that they aren't touching. Sauté only until the bottoms are seared, about 20 seconds. The bottoms will be dry and lightly browned. Carefully flip over and sear the other side. Remove the slices to a plate and cook the remaining slices.

3 Serve immediately with toast points on individual plates.

Tip: *To make the neatest, cleanest slice of foie gras, use a very thin, sharp blade and rinse with hot water between slices.*

Per serving: *Calories 73 (From Fat 33); Fat 4g (Saturated 1g); Cholesterol 219mg; Sodium 132mg; Carbohydrate 2g (Dietary Fiber 0g); Protein 8g.*

Trying Pâté: A Delicious Alternative to Foie Gras

Foie gras is expensive and a little intimidating for some cooks, but that doesn't mean that you have to give up the experience of dining on a rich and creamy appetizer. Pâtés of all kinds —including liver, duck, veal, and pork — come ready to eat and make a great appetizer. They're a cinch to serve because all the work has been done for you.

You can, of course, find recipes for homemade pâtés, and in fact, the technique is similar to making a meat loaf, but I want to introduce you to the world of prepared pâtés.

Finding pâté

Most specialty stores that carry fine cheeses also have a selection of pâtés. Some are smooth in texture and enriched with cream and occasionally eggs, while others are rougher and chunkier. The latter are sometimes referred to as pâté de campagne (country pâté) or pâté maison (pâté of the house). They are usually in some kind of loaf shape and can be sliced. Very soft pâtés are occasionally packed into a crock or terrine.

The term *terrine* can be used to describe a recipe (such as my Roasted Vegetable Terrine in Chapter 11) or the dish in which you might serve such a recipe.

Serving pâté

You don't need much in the way of accompaniments to serve your pâté in style, but do purchase them if you want to do it up right. Cornichon are tiny, very tart pickles that are the traditional French accompaniment to pâté. Pâté, by its very nature, is rich, and the sourness and crunch of the cornichon cut through the pâté's lushness like nothing else. Some pâté admirers like a smear of Dijon mustard, which has a similar effect as the pickles. Add some French bread, and you have a fast, delicious appetizer.

Whether your pâté is smooth or chunky, simply arrange slices or a small crock (terrine) of it on a platter. Surround by small dishes filled with cornichon and mustard and have slices of French bread at hand.

Part V
The Part of Tens

In this part . . .

*E*very *Dummies* book ends with top-ten lists, and so does mine. I give you my top ten party planning tips. In addition, you can find the best mail-order and online sources for cooking ingredients and kitchen tools.

Chapter 13

Ten Tips for Planning an Appetizer Party

The process of making appetizers should be fun and the results delicious. Sometimes you need to whip up appetizers in a hurry, and at other times, you've planned your appetizer party so far ahead that you made your food days before the event and froze it till you needed it. Either way, you can take specific steps to ensure a positive outcome.

Stock the pantry

If you keep a well-stocked pantry and refrigerator, you can pull off impromptu appetizer cooking with flair and minimal stress. As I detail in Chapter 3, you can accomplish a lot in very little time if you always have basics such as olive oil, cans of beans, herbs, spices, and a loaf of bread or two on hand.

Plan, plan, plan

Any kind of party you throw benefits from planning and organization. Plan ahead as far as possible. Announce dibs on Valentine's Day or a friend's birthday. Or decide to throw a party just because you want to gather your friends together.

Make those lists

If you've read any of the preceding chapters in this book, you've probably figured out by now that I'm very fond of lists. I like to make lists, cross items off as I complete a task or buy an item, and otherwise use lists in any way I can to help me get — and stay — organized.

Read and follow the recipes

For best results, read a recipe — every recipe — all the way through and follow it step by step. This way, you won't leave anything out on your shopping lists, and you'll become acquainted with what the recipe is supposed to taste like and look like. After making it once, you can tailor it to your liking, adding more garlic here, less salt there, and so on.

Make recipes ahead if possible

Take advantage of any opportunity to make part of or the entire recipe ahead of your party. I can't stress this advice enough. Many home cooks approach a recipe in the same way every time. They think they have to start at the beginning and work through to the end, timing it so that the recipe is done when they're ready to serve it.

Rely on favorites

If you have a favorite recipe, it can become your signature dish — and there's nothing wrong with that! You'll become known for your delicious dish, and it will be easy for you to put together because you're so familiar with it. In addition, having one sure-fire hit ensures the success of your party in general.

Ask for help

Allow yourself to ask for assistance. Maybe a guest can shop for the wine or bring the crudités; make it easy on your guests by asking them to bring things that don't require any preparation.

Be prepared for anything

Even with all your planning, you'll encounter glitches. One dish may take longer to cook than you expect, or the first half of your guests through the buffet line may wipe out your entire cheese platter. But you know what? It's okay. Parties are not about being perfect. Be prepared for surprises and take them in stride.

Relax, breathe, and enjoy the process

Throwing a party should be fun! Take the time to enjoy the shopping, prepping, and cooking. You'll enjoy the process more if you're organized, so use those lists I mention earlier.

Relax, breathe, and enjoy your party

The best parties are those where the hosts are relaxed and enjoying themselves. Guests, consciously or not, look to the host for social cues. Are you playing a classical music or jazz? Are you making the rounds and participating in animated conversation? You can set the mood, but whatever your mood, be it romantic, funky, restrained, or high energy, relax and enjoy your own party.

Chapter 14

Ten-Plus Great Mail-Order and Internet Sources

Shopping locally is a way of supporting your local economy. But you may not be able to find the kitchen tools or recipe ingredients you need at a nearby store. If that's the case, don't fret. Specialty ingredients and tools are as near as the phone or the Web.

Mail-Order Sources

Bridge Kitchenware
214 East 52nd Street (between 2nd and 3rd Avenues)
New York, NY 10022
800-274-3435
212-688-4220
Fax: 212-758-4387
www.bridgekitchenware.com

This New York institution has almost everything you need to outfit your kitchen, including pots, pans, knives, spatulas, tart pans, and more. A catalog is available.

Caviarteria
502 Park Avenue (at 59th Street)
New York, NY 10022
800-422-8427
800-4-CAVIAR
In California: 800-287-9773
www.caviarteria.com

This is your one-stop shopping spot for caviar, caviar serving pieces, smoked salmon, and foie gras.

Citarella
2135 Broadway
New York, NY 10023
212-874-0383
Fax: 212-595-3738
www.citarella.com

This store, which has several outposts in the New York City area, has become an institution. The stores have all sorts of specialty ingredients, such as sun-dried tomatoes, spices, and caviar. Perishable products are sent FedEx Priority Overnight within the continental United States.

Crate and Barrel
1860 West Jefferson
Naperville, IL 60540
800-323-5461
www.crateandbarrel.com

This all-purpose housewares company puts out a catalog with gorgeous linens, candles, candleholders, bowls, serving pieces, dinner plates, and more. If you need inexpensive but well-made wine glasses or platters for serving appetizers, you can find them here.

D'Artagnan
280 Wilson Avenue
Newark, NJ 07105
800-327-8246
Fax: 973-465-1870
www.dartagnan.com

This is a great source for foie gras. A catalog is available.

Dean & Deluca
Catalog Center
8200 East 34th Street Circle North
Building 2000
Wichita, KS 67226
800-221-7714
Catalog@deandeluca.com
www.deandeluca.com

This New York City institution has a catalog and Web site for those who can't make it to the Soho store. This way, from the comfort of your own home, you can order fine cheeses and pâtés, olives, olive oils, balsamic vinegar, linen cocktail napkins, herbs, and spices. Definitely order the catalog or peruse the Web site.

King Arthur Flour Baker's Catalog
P.O. Box 876
Norwich, VT 05055
800-827-6836
Fax: 802-649-5359
www.kingarthurflour.com

This constantly updated catalog has scales, flavored oils, all-purpose and bread flours, all kinds of thermometers, high quality measuring cups and spoons, pizza stones, peels, and more.

Penzey's Spices
P.O. Box 933
Muskego, WI 53150
800-741-7787
www.penzeys.com

This is possibly the best single source for high-quality herbs and spices. Supermarket spices don't hold a candle to these. A catalog is available.

Sur La Table
Pike Place Farmers Market
84 Pine Street
Seattle, WA 98101
206-448-2244
800-243-0852
www.surlatable.com

This source has a catalog that offers pans, rolling pins, sheet pans, and more. It also offers cooking classes through some of its stores.

Williams-Sonoma
P.O. Box 7456
San Francisco, CA 94120
415-421-4242
800-541-2233
Fax: 415-421-5253

Famous for its mail-order catalog, Williams-Sonoma also has stores nationwide. You can find great pots, pans, cookie sheets, measuring tools, and other equipment. A catalog is available.

Web-Based Sources

If you have Internet access, take advantage of the following sources of cooking ingredients or information:

- ✔ www.ethnicgrocer.com: Visit this site for all kinds of exotic ingredients and other ingredients not usually stocked in your basic supermarket.

- ✔ www.epicurious.com: Here's where to turn for basic information on just about any food.

- ✔ www.shamra.com: This site specializes in Mediterranean and Arabic groceries, such as pita bread, chickpeas, grape leaves, and nuts.

- ✔ www.orientalpantry.com: This site specializes in Asian ingredients, including duck sauce, hoisin sauce, and soy sauce.

- ✔ www.asiafoods.com: Come here for soy sauce and wasabi powder.

- ✔ www.fromages.com: Need a cheese? Search no further. This site is a great resource for general information on cheese as well.

- ✔ www.wine-searcher.com: This site scans hundreds of on-line merchants to help you find the perfect wine.

- ✔ www.wineenthusiast.com: Here you will find everything to go with wine: wine racks, glassware, corkscrews — even wine cellars and caves!

Index

Fried Calamari with Fresh Tomato Basil
Sauce recipe, 170–171
Fried Corn Chips recipe, 109
Fried Flour Tortilla Chips recipe, 110
frozen puff pastry, 130–133
fruit, canapé topping, 117

• *G* •

garbanzo beans, 26
garlic, 26, 162
Garlic Mussels on the Half Shell recipe, 151
Garlic Potato Dip (Skordalia) recipe,
186–187
Garlic-Yogurt Dipping Sauce recipe, 137
garnishes, appetizer presentation, 36
Genoa salami, 161, 167
gin, mixed-drink bar item, 17
ginger ale, mixed-drink bar item, 20
Ginger-Orange Walnuts recipe, 55
glass pie plate, 30
Glazed Chicken Wings recipe, 153
goat cheese, canapé topping, 117
goat's milk based cheeses, 51
golden caviar, 218
Gorgonzola cheese, antipasto accent, 167
Gouda cheese, 50
Grand Marnier, 18
grape leaves, wrapping, 185
grape tomatoes, 66
grapefruit juice, mixed-drinks bar item, 20
grated cheese, freezer considerations, 29
grated parmesan cheese, 28
Greek hors d'oeuvres, 184–187
green beans, tempura ingredient, 179
green olives, 117, 162
greens, pizza topping, 160
Gruyère cheese, 50
Guacamole recipe, 93
guacamole, canapé topping, 117

• *H* •

ham, 117, 160
hard-cooked egg slice, canapé topping, 117
heavy cream, 29
height, presentation item, 35

Herbed Goat Cheeses recipe, 172–173
Herbed Popcorn recipe, 59
Herbes de Provence, 28
herbs, 117, 160
hoisin sauce, 27
Homemade Potato Chips recipe, 104
hors d'oeuvres. *See also* appetizers
antipasto, 166–168
Asian, 176–183
Brie cheese, 154–155
calamari, 168
chicken wings, 152–153
French, 172–173
Greece, 184–187
Indian, 193–196
Italian, 166–171
Japanese tempura, 179–181
kid-friendly, 53
Latin American, 187–189
Mexican, 187–189
mussels, 152
nachos, 164
nut combinations, 53
pizza, 156–163
potato skins, 147–149
scallops, 149–150
Scandinavian, 190–193
Spanish, 173–176
squid, 168
horseradish, Japanese wasabi, 211–213
Horseradish Sour Cream and Chive Dip
recipe, 149
Hot Crab Dip recipe, 102
hot dogs, pigs in a blanket, 74
Hot 'n' Spicy Pecans recipe, 56
hot sauce, 28
hummus, canapé topping, 117
Hummus recipe, 96

• *I* •

ice
caviar presentation, 219
freezer item, 29
raw bar item, 87–88
ice bucket, appetizer presentation, 35
icing spatula, 30, 31